# The 'Easternization' of Development

## Praise for this book

'The idea of "Easternization" is very much needed in the development community where North/South dimensions have been dominant for too long. This book challenges our basic assumptions and opens up new avenues for productive conversations about the future of aid and development.'

*Jin Sato, Professor of Development Studies, the University of Tokyo and the President of the Japan Society for International Development*

'This is a timely and important book, written with evident regional and global expertise. It examines the 'Easternization' of development in China, Japan and Korea with nuance and insight. The leadership of these countries for many global development trends – and the possibilities and challenges of these trends – are expertly dissected.'

*Professor Emma Mawdsley, Geography Department, University of Cambridge*

'A refreshing account of aid practices of Japan, South Korea, China that is grounded in these countries' own theories and policy strategies about 'development', this edited volume provides unique insights into the politics shaping East Asian developmentalist cooperation.'

*Sakiko Fukuda-Parr, Professor of International Affairs, The New School*

# The 'Easternization' of Development

## The Politics of East Asia's Developmentalist Cooperation

Edited by
Sanae Ito

Practical
ACTION
PUBLISHING

Practical Action Publishing Ltd
25 Albert Street, Rugby,
Warwickshire, CV21 2SD, UK
www.practicalactionpublishing.com

A catalogue record for this book is available from the British Library.
A catalogue record for this book has been requested from the Library of Congress.

ISBN 978-1-78853-229-7 Paperback
ISBN 978-1-78853-228-0 Hardback
ISBN 978-1-78853-230-3 Electronic book

Citation: Ito, S. (2023) The *'Easternization' of Development: The Politics of East Asia's Developmentalist Cooperation*, Rugby, UK: Practical Action Publishing <http://dx.doi.org/10.3362/9781788532303>.

Since 1974, Practical Action Publishing has published and disseminated books and information in support of international development work throughout the world. Practical Action Publishing is a trading name of Practical Action Publishing Ltd (Company Reg. No. 1159018), the wholly owned publishing company of Practical Action. Practical Action Publishing trades only in support of its parent charity objectives and any profits are covenanted back to Practical Action (Charity Reg. No. 247257, Group VAT Registration No. 880 9924 76).

Cover design by Katarzyna Markowska, Practical Action Publishing
Typeset by vPrompt eServices, India

# Contents

# Acknowledgements

This edited book has come out of a research project funded by the Japan Society for the Promotion of Science (JSPS) for the period between 2016 and 2021. While not all the authors of this book were original members of the project, the funding covered the costs for compiling the individual work into an edited volume. Some of the book's chapters were originally discussed at a two-day workshop held at Nagoya University in September 2017, and later at the University of Freiburg in July 2019. The editor would like to thank Jürgen Rüland for organizing the latter, Joe Devine for suggesting the Practical Action Publishing for the book's publication, Andreas Heller for editing and proofreading the manuscript, Stuart Rutherford for extending advice and moral support, anonymous reviewers for providing constructive feedback, as well as Chloe Callan-Foster, Jutta Mackwell, Rosanna Denning, Jenny Peebles, and Clare Tawney from the Practical Action Publishing for their continuous support throughout the entire process of publication. It goes without saying that the views expressed in the book's chapters are those of their authors and not of any organizations that they work for.

# About the editor and contributors

## Editor

**Sanae Ito** is Professor of Development Studies at the Graduate School of International Development, Nagoya University, Japan. She has been teaching and researching on a wide range of issues including development discourses, global production systems, rural institutions, and financial services in Asia. Her current research interests include the politics of development cooperation for infrastructure, and social protection in Asia. Outside academia, she has worked for Japan's Ministry of Foreign Affairs, Japan International Cooperation Agency, and ILO in Asia and the Pacific on short-term assignments.

## Contributors

**Christian von Lübke** is Professor of Southeast Asian Studies at HTWG Konstanz, Germany. He has researched and published on Asian perspectives on development, investment climates, civil society, and good governance.

**Marieline Bader** is Responsible Programs and Project Manager of 'Refugees Go Solar+' at the Solafrica in Switzerland. She received her MA in International Cooperation at the Graduate School of International Studies, Seoul National University.

**Taekyoon Kim** is Professor of International Development at the Graduate School of International Studies, Seoul National University, South Korea. He has worked extensively on aid accountability, global governance, and South–South Cooperation.

**Meibo Huang** is Professor and the Director of the International Development Cooperation Academy at Shanghai University of International Business and Economics, China. Her current research focuses on world economy, Chinese foreign aid, and development finance.

**Zhaoli Shen** is a research assistant at the International Development Cooperation Academy at Shanghai University of International Business and Economics, China. Her current research focuses on Chinese foreign aid and development finance.

**Kiyoshi Fujikawa** is Professor at the Faculty of Economics, Aichi Gakuin University and Professor Emeritus at Nagoya University, Japan. His speciality is environmental economics with a focus on East Asia.

**Kyungyon Moon** is Assistant Professor of the School of International Studies at Jeonbuk National University, South Korea. He specializes in international development cooperation, humanitarian assistance, and North Korea's development.

**Isamu Okada** is Professor at the Graduate School of International Development, Nagoya University, Japan. He works on resource politics and social movements in developing countries.

**Zhao Wang** is Assistant Professor at Shanghai University of International Business and Economics, China. Her research focuses on international political economy and China's South–South Cooperation.

# CHAPTER 1
# Introduction*

*Sanae Ito***

It has been just over a decade since the global community started talking about the paradigm shift in development cooperation. The paradigm shift is largely attributed to the changing power dynamics caused by emerging economies, some of whom the United Nations once classified as low-income countries. This new paradigm, in contrast to the conventional type of development assistance by which the Global North vertically supports the Global South, is built upon horizontal relationships between equal partners seeking mutual benefits from development cooperation. As this paradigm shift continues to evolve, East Asian aid donors are receiving renewed attention. For their practices contain some important features that are integral parts of the new paradigm.

This book looks at these features of East Asia's development cooperation and examines how they can be understood in relation to the developmental state tradition, both imagined and real. Scholars in the area of international development studies have long pointed out similarities between East Asian donors. Shimomura and Wang (2013), for example, have discussed the evolution of 'the East Asian Aid Model', focusing on China's and Japan's attempt to synthesize aid, investment, and trade. Stallings and Kim (2017) have argued that East Asian countries formed a distinct sub-group of foreign aid donors enthusiastic about transferring their developmental state model to Asian aid recipients. Many of these authors assume that because Japan, South Korea, and China share a uniquely East Asian development experience, it is only natural that a similar pattern of development cooperation based upon this shared experience would emerge (Sato and Shimomura, 2013). Such development experience is presumed to demonstrate the effectiveness of the developmental state, prioritizing economic development by selectively investing in key strategic industries while dispensing administrative guidance to business corporations. Japan, South Korea, and China are therefore viewed as supporting developing countries to follow the same developmental strategy.

## Developmental state policy and foreign aid

This book takes a closer look at this perspective to argue that the relationship between the developmental state tradition and the observed patterns of East Asia's development cooperation is more complex than is often assumed. For one thing, it is unconventional to expand discussions about the developmental state beyond a country's economic policy domain to include foreign policies where official development assistance is mobilized as an industrial policy tool to support aid donors' own not-so-strategic, and at times even stagnant, industries. Arase (1995) was one of the authors to unequivocally argue that Japan's foreign aid policy was the outcome of a developmental state policy. At that time, Japanese Official Development Assistance (ODA) was commonly differentiated from the Western donors' within the Organisation for Economic Co-operation and Development (OECD)'s Development Assistance Committee (DAC) and was criticized for its mercantilist tendencies (see Chapter 2 of this book). Arase (1995: 249) described how the Japanese bureaucracy, coordinated mainly by the then Ministry of International Trade and Industry, used its foreign aid policy to steer the private sector towards shifting its 'manufacturing with declining competitiveness to lower-cost production sites in Asia'. Here Japanese foreign aid policy was clearly viewed as being part of its developmentalist policy packages.

While it may be true that Japan's foreign aid policy has always been embedded in a broader developmentalist policy framework, the primary role of developmental states' industrial policy, at least in the mainstream developmental state literature, has been to identify and selectively invest in key strategic industries to create international competitiveness (Johnson, 1982). The idea of developmental states using foreign aid as an industrial policy tool to rescue their declining domestic industries may have been implied in the aid literature[1] but has only occasionally been discussed in the developmental state literature.[2] The more recent literature focusing on East Asian donors tends to analyse the countries' development cooperation in terms of their unique 'development experience' without referring to the developmental state per se (see Sato and Shimomura, 2013; Feasel, 2015).[3]

This may be due to the authors' reservations about using the contested notion of 'developmental states' to explain the East Asian development experience. It may also be related to the fact that significant changes have occurred in Japan's foreign aid landscape since Arase made his argument. In fact, the once-powerful Japanese bureaucracy involved in foreign aid policy-making in the 1980s would later be subjected to closer scrutiny as the influence of civil society began to increase in Japan (Hirata, 2002). Throughout the 1990s, there was increased pressure from the international community and non-governmental organizations (NGOs), both domestic and transnational, demanding that Japan reform its ODA structures (Arase, 1995). A new breed of Japanese development professionals, trained at US and European universities, returned home to join the efforts to normalize Japanese aid practices to meet the expectations of Western donors (Ito, 2017). As a result of these changes, some of the features of the earlier Japanese ODA, which Arase had described as 'developmental', have been abandoned, at least in a clearly visible form.[4] In the meantime, the Japanese government came to embrace the notion of 'human security' as one of its key ODA principles, as can be seen in the revised ODA Charter from 2003 (MOFA, 2015; Kamidohzono et al., 2015). The notion of human security subsequently became the ideological backbone of the Japan International Cooperation Agency (JICA) while Sadako Ogata, the former United Nations High Commissioner for Refugees (UNHCR), headed the organization. Japan's example points to the ambiguity in our knowledge about the relationship between a country's developmentalist leanings and its more recent practices of development cooperation. It should therefore come as little surprise if the three East Asian countries we are focusing on in this book, each having experienced a unique post-war history, should come to demonstrate different patterns of this relationship. It would indeed be misleading to assume that the kind of development experience, based solely on East Asia's regional characteristics, should dictate how East Asian countries practise their development cooperation.

## The global context

In addition to the regional factors, we should also take the dramatic changes in the global context in which these countries operate into consideration. In the new global development context associated with the UN's Sustainable Development Goals (SDGs), a variety of partnerships have been forged, for example between traditional donors and emerging powers as well as between the international development community and the private sector. The concept of development cooperation has been significantly broadened within this new context to include market flows, as long as they benefit developing countries and are not exclusively profit-driven (Alonso and Glennie, 2015). This conceptualization of development cooperation reflects a shift in the focus of the international community away from the issue of increasing the effectiveness of foreign aid to improving development outcomes regardless of whether they are publicly funded or market-driven (Pichon, 2020).

The Fourth High Level Forum on Aid Effectiveness held in Busan, South Korea, in 2011 was not only a major turning point in foreign aid practices, but also marked 'a paradigm shift in dominant constructions of "foreign aid" and a substantive shift of power within the architecture of global development governance' (Mawdsley et al., 2014: 27). Simultaneously, the influence of emerging powers as providers of South–South Cooperation has greatly increased since then, triggering what may be called the 'Southernization' of development[5] (Mawdsley, 2018) within the traditional donor community. Against this backdrop, each of the three East Asian countries seeks to reposition itself within the global context by evoking its historical experiences to varying degrees. This is not the same as their fulfilling the regionally embedded patterns of developmentalism. Rather, the countries' attempt to reconfigure the new relationships between what may be seen as developmental state characteristics and their development cooperation practices is to be understood as a process of reinventing the narrative around their 'unique Asian development experience'.

This book thus explores these relationships not only from a regional perspective but in view of the changing discourse on global development, specifically in reference to the SDGs. In particular, it looks at the mechanisms by which the countries' unique development experiences and the global development agenda intersect to produce, and in some cases, reproduce *developmentalist* cooperation policies. The developmentalist cooperation policies discussed here are characterized by their reliance on the strategic use of official development assistance in alignment with a donor country's industrial policy, while its partner countries are encouraged to formulate their own interventionist industrial policy in line with the donor country's policy. The book also revisits the concept of development itself to understand to what extent the paradigm shift in global development that seems increasingly conducive to East Asia's developmentalist cooperation hinges on the conventional understanding of development as we know it.

## The developmental state concept

The concept of the developmental state was popularized by Chalmers Johnson (1982), who analysed the historic role of Japan's Ministry of International Trade and Industry in steering its economy "through" industrial policy. Johnson characterized the developmental state as having developed later than other countries, then driving domestic industrialization by "selectively" supporting certain industries in order to create international competitiveness and thus catch up with other industrialized states. The concept has since been expanded into a general analysis of East Asian capitalist economies where governments were viewed as 'governing' the market (Wade, 1990). More recently, China, which, under Deng Xiaoping, gradually shifted from central planning to a partially market-oriented economy, can arguably be included as one of East Asia's developmental states.

As the external environment surrounding the East Asian economies has undergone a significant transformation, the debate about developmental states has also shifted. Stubbs (2009), for example, argues that the state's relationship to both business and civil society changes as successful economic growth increases the power of companies and citizens. Simultaneously, the increasing pace of globalization weakens the ability of each state to exert developmental influence on the market through industrial policy alone. Some even argue that the whole concept of the developmental state has become obsolete (see Pirie, 2013). Others, such as Nem Singh and Ovadia (2019) and Hayashi (2010), see the current relevance of the concept as a means for analysing the state's role in leading development initiatives in the Global South.

The appropriateness of these views depends in part on how we understand the concept. The developmental state has often been defined in terms of the government's ability to choose the right mix of policy measures that have positive developmental effects on the domestic economy and, at the same time, is viewed as a challenge to free-market economic orthodoxy. The definition is arguably elusive since almost any state that has seen rapid economic development is likely to possess some set of policy measures that may be considered, ex-post facto, right and developmental. It is quite possible, on the other hand, that the same set of policy measures would fail in other countries (Fine et al., 2013). The range of policy measures that enables states to drive economic growth has, in any case, become significantly constrained due to the changing economic environment caused by globalization.

The developmental state has also been defined in terms of the state's political intent as well as the institutional arrangements it has created to govern the market (Fine et al., 2013; Haggard, 2018; Horikane, 2004). Such characteristics may also be viewed as self-selecting in that any state that has achieved rapid economic growth may subsequently be associated with having a strong growth-oriented intent as well as the institutional capacity to achieve it, while the state that has failed to do so may be seen as lacking these factors. As mentioned above, the state's relationship with business and society in the domestic context changes as its economy grows, which may reduce the state's ability to make developmental interventions. Yet, the developmental intent as well as the institutional mechanisms that have developed over the years may be more durable and 'sticky' compared to a set of economic policies, as state corporatist and neo-mercantilist ideas and practices become embedded in government bureaucracies as well as large firms and quasi-governmental organizations that have generated strong 'connectedness' to pursue developmental objectives (Evans, 1995; Stubbs, 2009). Thus, the developmental ideas and practices entrenched in powerful organizational culture may, at least partially, outlast the increasing levels of globalization and the louder voices emanating from the private sector and civil society.

## The developmental donor state and its development model

The concept's continuing relevance may thus be explained by its focus on the political and institutional aspect of the developmental state rather than by the government's ability to choose the right mix of economic policies. Here, the state's developmental intent as well as its institutional ability to intervene in the economy are associated with its political and administrative skills in planning and implementing effective development strategies. These are then analysed in terms of its 'transferability' to the Global South (see, for example, Nem Singh and Ovadia, 2019). Japan and South Korea thus formulate their aid policies based on their countries' own development experiences which they see as having been shaped by their developmental state intent and institutional capacity. China, though not a foreign aid donor to the Global South in the traditional sense, also attempts to transfer its own development strategies through South–South Cooperation. Here the developmental state becomes the developmental donor state; it views development cooperation as an opportunity to pursue state corporatist ideas and practices for its own needs as well as for its developmental partners of the Global South.

The fact that China, South Korea, and Japan like to highlight their own unique development paths when they engage in developmentalist cooperation reflects their belief that their particular form of 'development' offers an alternative to the dominant discourse of development espoused by the Western aid community. Their own 'development' paths do not fit neatly into classical theories of development, such as modernization and dependency theories. They did not consistently pursue neoliberal economic policies, either. Nor did they focus specifically on social development goals such as gender equality or empowering the poor. Rather, they prioritized investing in infrastructure and human resource development to support industrial policies for strategic productive sectors which helped create jobs in urban industrial centres that then attracted abundant labour from rural areas. This *did* lead to a significant reduction in poverty, although some of the social development goals, such as gender equality, remained unfulfilled. The model of development epitomized by such experience is built upon the general belief that citizen's social, and to some extent, political conditions will improve once their economic needs have been met, without the need for targeted interventions to change those conditions.

## The historical context

Japan, South Korea, and China's experience with developmentalist cooperation has taken place along their own unique historical paths, and "the levels of" their exposure to the international norms and principles associated with foreign aid differs accordingly. What all three countries have in common is that they were once recipients of foreign aid, and that they started delivering aid while still receiving aid themselves. Japan received foreign aid in the aftermath of the Second World War (WWII), principally from the United States and the World Bank, to help the country recover from the destruction caused by the war. By the 1950s, its economy had recovered sufficiently to enable it to start paying post-war reparations to the victims of its wartime aggressions. Japan's foreign aid programme officially began in 1954 when it joined the Colombo Plan to initiate 'economic cooperation' with developing country governments (MOFA, 1994). In the same year, Japan signed a peace treaty with Burma (now called Myanmar) and started paying war reparations and extending 'economic cooperation' there and later also to other Asian countries. The phrase 'economic cooperation' was preferable to 'development assistance' presumably because Japan was itself a recipient of foreign aid at the time (Kitano, 2011). 'Economic cooperation' in this context implied a broader framework than development assistance and was intended to encourage private-sector investment in Asia's developing countries through a combination of ODA, export credit, and investment insurance (Kato, 1998). Japan joined the Development Assistance Group in 1960, the predecessor to the Development Assistance Committee of the OECD. Over time, Japan's continued focus on economic cooperation emphasizing economic infrastructure, the preferential use of loans rather than grants, and the close ties between the aid provided and Japan's business community came to distinguish the country from the other DAC member countries, making it something of 'an odd man out' in the group (Söderberg, 2010).

Domestically, these traits also became the subject of intense debate during the 1980s, drawing strong criticism from Japan's nascent civil society. Yet, Japan subsequently began to emulate other DAC member countries and made steady progress in realigning its aid with partner countries' domestic priorities. Untying its aid loans to increase open competition for aid-funded procurement in the mid-1990s was a step in that direction. Though Japan's approach was still different from other member countries', it did not present a major challenge to mainstream DAC norms and principles in the way emerging powers' actions have in more recent years. Japan's position within the club of rich donors started to shift subtly, however, as the influence of China's South–South Cooperation began to grow and was reflected in the discourse of global development. Thus, some of the old practices that Japan had earlier discarded started to re-emerge. For example, in 2012, the Japanese government decided to resume its ODA loans for supporting Japanese companies' investments overseas, a practice which had been discontinued in 2001 amidst a strong public outcry over the purpose of such loans. In 2015, Japan adopted the new Development Cooperation Charter (MOFA, 2015), abandoning the term ODA in the title to recognize the growing role of the private sector, local governments, and NGOs in mobilizing resources. It also, for the first time, explicitly referred to the need to secure its own national interests when providing development cooperation. While such changes were not unique to Japan, the changes happening in Japan were arguably linked to the revival of its developmental state policies and the practice of developmentalist cooperation.

South Korea, one of the poorest countries in the world at the end of WWII, subsequently suffered the devastating effects of the Korean War (1950–1953). While it was heavily dependent on foreign aid to rebuild its economy, the country simultaneously started providing technical cooperation overseas in the 1970s (Marx and Soares, 2013). As its economy continued to grow steadily over the next decades, the amount of foreign aid it provided grew significantly, and by 2010 it reached the level of traditional DAC donors. South Korea joined the OECD in 1996 and the DAC in 2010. As a new ODA donor, South Korea has struggled to adjust its aid practices to the international norms endorsed by the OECD-DAC. The international community has thus been pressuring South Korea to fall in line with other DAC members.

Bader and Kim (Chapter 3 of this book) argue that South Korea's aid industry remains enmeshed with its developmental state politics, suffering from fragmentation between its planning and implementation agencies, weak engagement with civil society, a low ODA/gross national income ratio, and a comparatively high proportion of concessional loans and tied aid, as well as regional allocation preference over actual need-based geographical allocation. Most of these features were once pointed out in reference to Japan's foreign aid. In the meantime, China has emerged as a dominant development cooperation partner in East Asia. Given Japan's recent shift back to its seemingly old ways of using foreign aid as an industrial policy instrument amidst the growing influence of China, it remains to be seen whether South Korea likewise decides to stick to its current aid practices to follow this pattern of developmentalist cooperation.

China's path as a development cooperation provider has been significantly different from South Korea and Japan's. China became a recipient of foreign aid after the founding of the People's Republic of China in 1949, with the Soviet Union as its main donor. In the 1960s and much of the 1970s, China pursued a self-reliant strategy, limiting the use of foreign capital. It had begun offering foreign assistance to other communist countries during the 1950s, while the Afro-Asian Conference in Bandung in April 1955 marked a significant turning point in China's foreign aid policy. During the conference, China announced that it would assist all countries, communist or non-communist, fighting for self-determination and independence (Watanabe, 2013). China's assistance to developing countries in Asia and Africa continued throughout the 1960s and into the mid-1970s when the country eventually started facing its own financial challenges. In 1978, Japan offered bilateral aid to China, with other Western donors following suit. Foreign aid to China thus grew significantly between 1979 and 1995. In the meantime, China's open-door policy, initiated in 1978, set in motion an economic transformation under Communist rule, which gradually reduced its reliance on foreign aid. China's own foreign assistance programmes to other countries were then restarted in the late 1990s. This has continued up to the present time, evolving into China's current practice of South–South Cooperation. Here the connection between China's developmental state-like policy-making and South–South Cooperation appears to be more obvious than in the case of Japan and South Korea. China's South–South Cooperation is explicitly linked to its 'Belt and Road Initiative' where the government supports Chinese enterprises in expanding trade and investment along the land and sea routes through Central Asia (UNDP, 2021). As a communist state not aligned with the DAC and an advocate of alternative forms of international cooperation, China is therefore under no pressure to abide by the rules set by the international aid regime. Given its history as a champion of the Non-Aligned Movement and its official status as a developing country, China can more easily set its own standards than Japan or South Korea.

## Chapter overviews

The chapters in this book first provide a general overview of the region's developmentalist cooperation, followed by discussions about each country's specific pattern of the developmentalist cooperation. In the chapter following this Introduction, Christian von Lübke provides a historical overview of the politics and practices of East Asia's developmentalist cooperation. Von Lübke analyses the prevalent policies and programmes in China, Japan, and South Korea today and captures the growing current momentum for developmentalist approaches as can be seen in the reinforced emphasis on state guidance and private-sector engagement in development cooperation. This trend, he argues, coupled with a weakening of trans-Pacific cooperation and shifting power balances, reawakens the old paradigm of East Asian developmentalism guided more by state-corporatist overtones – and less by humanitarian considerations.

This is followed by Marieline Bader and Taekyoon Kim's analysis of South Korea's aid industry in terms of the historical trajectories of its developmental politics. Specifically, they argue that the symbiotic relationship between the state and businesses in the period of the Korean developmental state parallels the country's policy as a new ODA donor and its developmental politics. As a relatively new ODA donor, South Korea faces increasing pressure to adhere to the DAC standards by untying aid. This is in contrast to Japan, which, as a long-term DAC member country, appears to be reviving its historical experience of using the ODA as an instrument for its developmental state policies. In both cases, the renewed rhetoric about public–private partnerships in the age of the SDGs is helping to strengthen the conventional ties between the state and businesses in implementing developmentalist cooperation.

Meibo Huang and Zhaoli Shen's chapter looks at China's 'Belt and Road Initiative' (BRI) against the backdrop of its state-sponsored development experience. Citing Lin Yifu (Lin et al., 2011), they argue that economic development is achieved by governments that actively promote industrial upgrading, technological innovation, infrastructure development, and changes in the economic structure. At the same time, they regard the BRI as essentially China's globalization initiatives driven by its commercial enterprises, with the Chinese government providing policy guidance and financial support to assist them. Whether we view the role of the Chinese state as governing the market or merely assisting it by providing 'hard' and 'soft'[6] infrastructure (Lin et al., 2011) may be a matter of interpretation and debate. The Chinese government publicly declares that the market-driven BRI is providing a major platform for China's development cooperation (State Council Information Office of the People's Republic of China, 2021), with the government simply creating 'space and opportunities' (UNDP, 2021: 2) for the market. Here the language used in the official Chinese description of the relationship between the state and the market appears to be different from the one offered in the standard developmentalist literature. What does seem clear, however, is that the Chinese idea of development cooperation is broadly synonymous with regional economic cooperation and is much more openly mercantilist than either Japan's or South Korea's. As a developing country, China has fewer qualms about reaping mutually beneficial commercial benefits through the combined forces of the state and the market, or what we might call its 'developmentalist' cooperation.

The discussion on China is followed by three chapters on Japan, which, compared to China, does display certain qualms about the developmentalist nature of its cooperation. These chapters explore Japan's developmentalist cooperation in connection with infrastructure, the environment, and natural resources. The qualms Japan displays can be explained in terms of its trajectory as one of the first OECD-DAC member states, which has led the country to vacillate between Western and East Asian discourses of development. Sanae Ito examines Japan's 'Partnership for Quality Infrastructure', the governmental programme set up to promote Japan's infrastructure investment overseas. Ito explores the changing political economy of Japan's developmentalist cooperation through the promotion of 'connectivity', and argues that *quality infrastructure*, far from being a universalistic, technical initiative as presented in the context of the SDGs, is actually the centre piece in Japan's revived developmentalism and developmentalist cooperation across Asia. The chapter also draws attention to the underlying notion of development that the developmentalist partnership is based upon. Ito argues that this notion is characterized by an emphasis on state-led economic processes to selectively address the SDGs and by an understanding of poverty reduction that is intrinsically tied to a donor country's own industrial revival.

The second chapter on Japan is Kiyoshi Fujikawa and Sanae Ito's exploration of the country's developmentalist cooperation through the Joint Crediting Mechanism (JCM), a bilateral environmental scheme by which the Japanese government covers part of developing countries' initial investment costs for installing low-carbon and zero emission technologies in partnership with Japanese businesses. Here Japan's ODA is mobilized to encourage private sector participation in achieving threefold targets: for Japan, its developing country partners, and the environment. Domestically, three Japanese ministries benefit from this approach: the Ministry of Economy, Trade and Industry, which promotes the export of quality infrastructure associated with clean air technologies; the Ministry of Environment, which seeks to achieve Japan's emission reduction targets; and the Ministry of Foreign Affairs, which pursues its mission of extending financial and technical assistance to developing countries. The authors argue that the global context of the SDGs serves to depoliticize the developmentalist policy framework for the JCM, leading to the view that using the ODA to catalyse Japanese business investment in developing countries constitutes an important contribution towards sustainable development.

This is followed by Isamu Okada's chapter which focuses on oil as a strategic commodity, the acquisition of which should serve as a strong incentive for developmental states to direct their developmentalist cooperation to oil-rich countries in the Global South. Okada argues that the responses of the three East Asian countries in this regard are conditioned by the historical trajectories that have shaped each country, leading to different relationships between oil interests and foreign aid allocations. In particular, he compares the historical contexts in which the oil industries in Japan and China evolved and contends that Japan has never managed to exert strong state support to develop its oil industry. Hence, as much as Japan was dependent on oil imports for its economic growth, the Japanese state lacked the domestic structure by which it could influence foreign aid allocation to secure oil. Okada argues therefore that the countries' developmental profile does not always result in the same patterns of developmentalist cooperation despite the common strategic importance of the resource–aid nexus.

Kyungyon Moon's chapter on South Korea's development cooperation practices are focused on its Knowledge Sharing Program (KSP), a policy consultancy programme strongly anchored in the mission of imparting South Korea's development experience to the developing world. With its more recent experience as an impoverished country compared to Japan, there seems to be a stronger passion in South Korea for sharing its development model with other countries. The KSP does not propagate a particular set of developmental state policies, such as the symbiotic alliance-making between the state and *chaebol* (a family-owned industrial conglomerate), which have historically been ascribed to the South Korean government. However, it is strongly couched in the language of 'the Korean development model', one that prioritizes economic infrastructure and human resource development over social development and is built upon the assumption of a strong government and weaker civil society.

Zhao Wang's chapter on China's social organizations – the equivalent of civil society organizations in other countries – illuminates the new dimension of China's developmentalist cooperation, one that contradicts the stereotypical image of China single-mindedly pursuing neo-mercantilist approaches. Wang reminds us that China provides significant amounts of grants and interest-free loans to social sectors in developing countries. According to Wang, the Chinese government increasingly recognizes the importance of joining transnational networks to help tackle global challenges such as climate change, food security, and health, and is keen to nurture Chinese social organizations that can play a greater role in addressing them. Wang argues that the social organizations lie somewhere between government-organized NGOs and genuine grassroots organizations with no government backing and that they are generally more efficient and better placed to secure official support in fulfilling such a role. Wang's argument suggests that China's developmentalist cooperation is more flexible than we are accustomed to thinking, allowing for greater space to be filled by social organizations as long as they are willing to work in partnership with the Chinese state and its enterprises. Since civil society organizations in South Korea and Japan have relatively more space in which to play a positive role, China's flexibility may indicate the fact that the three East Asian countries are edging closer towards one another in terms of shaping the new alignment of state, market, and society even in the context of developmentalist cooperation. How such a new alignment fares with the conventional developmentalist framework and can accommodate non-economic development objectives remains to be seen in the coming years.

Taken together, these chapters elucidate the politics of East Asia's developmentalist cooperation in its different forms. While many of the traditional Western donors are also showing signs of 'Southernization' (Mawdsley, 2018), increasingly bringing national interest ahead of altruism, many of the features ascribed to China as the champion of the South–South Cooperation can also be found in Japan and South Korea, and what we are witnessing here might be more appropriately described as the 'Easternization' of development. To understand this phenomenon is becoming increasingly important in the current global context in which the impacts of the Covid-19 pandemic and the climate change crisis are calling for an urgent re-examination of priorities in development cooperation.

## Notes

\*     This book project was funded by the JSPS KAKENHI Grant Number 16KT0088.
\*\*    Professor at the Graduate School of International Development, Nagoya University, Japan. ito@gsid.nagoya-u.ac.jp
1.    See, for example, Fukuda-Parr and Shiga (2016) for a discussion about a specific form of industrial policy involving aid, trade, and investment as a package.
2.    Robert Wade's (1996) extensive description of Japan's struggle with the World Bank from the late 1980s to the early 1990s showed how this was primarily over its role as a developmental state prescribing more interventionist policies to the recipients of its concessional loans.
3.    Stallings and Kim (2017) is one of the small number of recent foreign aid studies that make explicit mention of the developmental state.
4.    In protest over a *Financial Times* article appearing on 19 June 2000, Yutaka Imamura (n.d.), writing on behalf of Japan's Foreign Ministry, noted that Japan's ODA loans became fully untied on a commitment basis for fiscal year 1996 and that nearly half of the products and services used for its grant aid for general projects were locally procured for the same year.
5.    Mawdsley (2018) points to the three aspects of the Northern donors' movement towards the South: 1) a claim to 'win-win' development ethics and outcomes; 2) an emphasis on economic growth rather than poverty reduction; and 3) the explicit blending of development finances with trade and investment.
6.    According to Lin et al. (2011: 201), soft infrastructure includes 'institutions, regulations, social capital, value systems, and other social, economic arrangements'.

## References

Alonso, J.A. and Glennie, J. (2015) 'What is development cooperation?' *2016 Development Cooperation Forum Policy Briefs*, February 2015, no. 1. Available from: https://www.un.org/en/ecosoc/newfunct/pdf15/2016_dcf_policy_brief_no.1.pdf [accessed 26 July 2021].

Arase, D. (1995) *Buying Power: The Political Economy of Japan's Foreign Aid,* Lynne Rienner Publishers, Inc., Boulder, CO.

Evans, P. (1995) *Embedded Autonomy: States & Industrial Transformation*, Princeton University Press, Princeton, NJ.

Feasel, E.M. (2015) *Japan's Aid: Lessons for Economic Growth, Development and Political Economy*, Routledge, London.

Fine, B., Saraswati, J. and Tavasci, D. (2013) *Beyond the Developmental State: Industrial Policy into the Twenty-First Century*, Pluto Press, London.

Fukuda-Parr, S. and Shiga, H. (2016) *Normative Framing of Development Cooperation: Japanese Bilateral Aid between the DAC and Southern Donors*, No. 130, JICA-RI Working Paper 130. Available from: https://www.jica.go.jp/jica-ri/ja/publication/workingpaper/jrft3q0000005y6n-att/JICA-RI_WP_No.130.pdf [accessed 11 November 2022].

Haggard, S. (2018) *Developmental States*, Cambridge University Press, Cambridge.

Hayashi, S. (2010) 'The developmental state in the era of globalization: beyond the Northeast Asian model of political economy', *The Pacific Review* 23(1): 45–69 <https://doi.org/10.1080/09512740903398330>.

Hirata, K. (2002) *Civil Society in Japan: The Growing Role of NGOs in Tokyo's Aid and Development Policy*, Palgrave Macmillan, New York.

Horikane, Y. (2004) 'Kaihatsu shugi no keifu: Kaihatsu dokusai, developmental state and kaihatsu shugi' [Genealogy of developmentalism: Developmental autocracy, developmental state and developmentalism], *Seikei Ronso* 73(1–2): 141–71. Available from: https://m-repo.lib.meiji.ac.jp/dspace/bitstream/10291/1856/1/seikeironso_73_1-2_141.pdf [accessed 1 August 2021].

Imamura, Y. (n.d.) 'Japan's position on untied aid' [website], Ministry of Foreign Affairs of Japan <https://www.mofa.go.jp/j_info/japan/opinion/iimura.html> [accessed 26 July 2021].

Ito, S. (2017) 'Teaching development studies in Japan: navigating between Eastern and Western discourses of development', *Journal of International Development* 29(7): 981–92 <https://doi.org/10.1002/jid.3043>.

*Johnson, C.A. (1982)* MITI and the Japanese Miracle: *The Growth of Industrial Policy, 1925–1975, Stanford University Press, Stanford, CA.*

*Kamidohzono, S.G., Gómez, O.A. and Mine, Y.* (2015) *Embracing Human Security: New Directions of Japan's ODA for the 21ˢᵗ Century*, JICA-RI Working Paper 94, JICA Research Institute. Available from: https://www.jica.go.jp/jica-ri/publication/workingpaper/jrft3q00000026bz-att/JICA-RI_WP_No_94.pdf [accessed 26 July 2021].

Kato, K. (1998) *Tsusho Kokka no Kaihatsu Kyoryoku Seisaku: Nichi Doku no Kokusaiteki Ichi to Kokunai Seido tono Renkan* [Development Cooperation Policy of Trading Nations: The Relationship between International Positions and Domestic Institutions in Japan and Germany], Bokutakusha, Tokyo.

Kitano, S. (2011) *Kokusai Kyoryoku no Tanjo: Kaihatsu no Datsuseijika wo Koete* [The Birth of International Cooperation: Beyond the De-politicization of Development], Soseisha, Tokyo.

Lin, J.Y., Krueger, A. and Rodrik, D. (2011) 'New structural economics: a framework for rethinking development [with comments]', *The World Bank Research Observer* 26(2): 193–229 <https://doi.org/10.1093/wbro/lkr007>.

Marx, A. and Soares, J. (2013) 'South Korea's transition from recipient to DAC donor: assessing Korea's development cooperation policy', *International Development Policy* 4.2: 107–42 <https://doi.org/10.4000/poldev.1535>.

Mawdsley, E. (2018) 'The "Southernisation" of development?', *Asia Pacific Viewpoint* 59(2): 173–85 <https://doi.org/10.1111/apv.12192>.

Mawdsley, E., Savage, L. and Kim, S.M. (2014) 'A "post-aid world"? Paradigm shift in foreign aid and development cooperation at the 2011 Busan High Level Forum', *The Geographical Journal* 180(1): 27–38 <https://doi.org/10.1111/j.1475-4959.2012.00490.x>.

Ministry of Foreign Affairs of Japan (MOFA) (1994) 'History of official development assistance', *Japan's ODA Annual Report (Summary) 1994*. Available from: http://www.mofa.go.jp/policy/oda/summary/1994/1.html [accessed 10 August 2021].

MOFA (2015) 'Development cooperation charter' [website] <https://www.mofa.go.jp/policy/oda/page_000138.html> [accessed 10 August 2021].

Nem Singh, J.T. and Ovadia, J.S. (2019) *Developmental States beyond East Asia*, Routledge, London.

Pichon, E. (2020) *Understanding Development Effectiveness: Concepts, Players and Tools*, European Parliamentary Research Service Briefing. Available from: https://www.europarl.europa.eu/RegData/etudes/BRIE/2017/599401/EPRS_BRI(2017)599401_EN.pdf [accessed 26 July 2021].

Pirie, I. (2003) 'Globalisation and the decline of the developmental state', in B. Fine, Saraswati, J. and Tavasci, D. (eds), *Beyond the Developmental State: Industrial Policy into the Twenty-First Century*, pp. 146–68, Pluto Press, London.

Sato, J. and Shimomura, Y. (eds) (2013) *The Rise of Asian Donors: Japan's Impact on the Evolution of Emerging Donors*. Routledge, Oxford.

Shimomura, Y. and Wang, P. (2013) 'The evolution of "aid, investment, trade synthesis" in China and Japan', in J. Sato and Y. Shimomura (eds), *The Rise of Asian Donors: Japan's Impact on the Evolution of Emerging Donors*, pp. 114–32, Routledge, Oxford.

Söderberg, M. (2010) 'Challenges or complements for the West: Is there an "Asian" model of aid emerging?', in J.S. Sörensen (ed.), *Challenging the Aid Paradigm: Western Currents and Asian Alternatives*, pp. 101–37, Palgrave Macmillan, New York.

Stallings, B. and Kim, E.M. (2017) *Promoting Development: The Political Economy of East Asian Foreign Aid*, Palgrave Macmillan, Singapore.

State Council Information Office of the People's Republic of China (January 2021) *China's International Development Cooperation in the New Era*. Available from: http://www.xinhuanet.com/english/2021-01/10/c_139655400.htm [accessed 10 August 2021].

Stubbs, R. (2009) 'What ever happened to the East Asian developmental state? The unfolding debate', *The Pacific Review* 22(1): 1–22 [accessed 10 August 2021] <https://doi.org/10.1080/09512740802650971>.

United Nations Development Programme (UNDP) (2021) *Brief on White Paper on China's International Development Cooperation in the New Era,* Issue Brief 7, Jan 2021. Available from: https://www.undp.org/china/publications/issue-brief-brief-white-paper-chinas-international-development-cooperation-new-era [accessed 8 November 2022].

Wade, R. (1990) *Governing the Market: Economic Theory and the Role of Government in East Asian Industrialization,* Princeton University Press, Princeton, NJ.

Wade, R. (1996) 'Japan, the World Bank, and the art of paradigm maintenance: The East Asian miracle in political perspective', *New Left Review* 217: 3–36 <https://www.proquest.com/scholarly-journals/japan-world-bank-art-paradigm-maintenance-east/docview/1301907186/se-2?accountid=12653>.

Watanabe, S. (2013) 'Donors' impact on China: How have major donors affected China's economic development and foreign aid policy?', in J. Sato and Y. Shimomura (eds), *The Rise of Asian Donors: Japan's Impact on the Evolution of Emerging Donors,* pp. 87–113, Routledge, Oxford.

# CHAPTER 2

# The politics of East Asian developmentalism: paradigms, practices, and prospects of foreign development assistance

*Christian von Lübke**

## Introduction

The 21st century is witnessing a remarkable shift of global powers and discourses. In this increasingly polycentric world order, the key ideas and norms that define international relations – including the concepts and policies of 'development' and 'development cooperation' – are being renegotiated. The emergence of non-Western (and in particular Asian) actors is exerting a growing influence on global trade and development. In view of China's stellar rise and the region's track record of successive economic miracles (including Japan, Korea, and Southeast Asia), it therefore does not come as a surprise that the centre of economic gravity is steadily shifting eastwards.

Does Asia's ascendency undermine the neoliberal minimal-state consensus that has been a keystone of the development industry since the Reagan-Thatcher era? Or, to put it differently, will the first half of the 21st century see a revival of the development state? Is there a consensual development theme in East Asia, or is it more accurate to distinguish between competing models? To what extent will a developmentalist consensus, if it exists, move beyond the boundaries of East Asia? Finding answers to these guiding questions will require us to take a closer look at the historical and institutional trajectories that have shaped development policies in contemporary East Asia. The experiences in Japan and China are particularly relevant in this assessment. For one thing, these two countries continue to be the largest donors in the region and, hence, have a profound influence on recipient countries in and outside Asia. For another, as the world's second and third largest economies, China's and Japan's policy regimes are bound to gain international traction.

The discussion in this chapter is divided into five sections. Following this introduction, the second section takes a detailed look at the developmental state model and the notion of a recent re-emergence of developmental ideas and interests in East Asia. The third section traces Japan's post-war development experience, its sequential stages of foreign assistance, and the gradual emergence of an increasingly sophisticated official development assistance (ODA) system. The fourth section takes a closer institutional look at China's emerging role as an international donor country. It also explores to what extent the Chinese model evinces similarities with developmentalist structures and interests elsewhere in the region. The fifth section offers some synthesizing and concluding thoughts. It considers converging and diverging trends in regional ODA practices, sheds light on how large-scale infrastructure programmes (e.g. Belt and Road Initiative (*BRI*) and *Quality Infrastructure*) have been received, and discusses the institutional, economic, and (geo)political prospects of a wider developmentalist consensus.

## Renaissance of the developmental state

Whether and to what extent states can intervene in markets in the pursuit of economic development has long been a contested question. Not only did the 20th century witness changing perceptions in Europe and the US regarding state intervention – ranging from neoclassical via Keynesian to neoliberal paradigms – the Cold War also gave rise to ideological debates that placed diverging emphases on free-market and statist development models.

### Counter-narrative to Washington's development consensus

Since the late 1970s, Western development policies have strongly endorsed market-oriented development approaches. This includes the liberalization of trade regimes, the privatization of state-owned enterprises, the deregulation of bureaucratic rules, and the winding back of state power. The notion of 'less state, more market' continues to be a keystone in Washington's development consensus. Numerous economists (Bates, 2008; Krueger, 1974; Krugman, 1995; Srinivasan, 1985) have pointed to state failure as the fundamental detriment to development, indicating that the invisible hand of unfettered market forces would generate higher levels of investment and growth. The orthodox consensus, which emerged in the 1980s, was that large state administrations had become breeding grounds for public corruption, bureaucratic inefficiency, and dismal public services.

Case studies from Latin America, Africa, and South Asia (Krueger, 1978; Shleifer and Vishny, 1998; Wunsch and Olowu, 1990) indicated that corrupt and bloated bureaucracies, political clientelism, and state protectionism undermined the development prospects in the Global South.

The Washington Consensus received additional political support when election outcomes in Western countries took a conservative shift. As Stephan Haggard summarizes it:

> The new orthodoxy about liberalization provided the key empirical referent for what economist John Williamson in 1989 called 'the Washington Consensus': a condensed checklist of ten policy reforms that gained currency as a result of the conservative turn in the major advanced industrial states marked by the elections of Margaret Thatcher (1979), Ronald Reagan (1980) and Helmut Kohl (1982). Given the larger political climate, neoclassical prescriptions moved quickly and seamlessly from academia into the development policy community and the international financial institutions (Haggard, 2018: 14).

The rapid rise of East Asian economies, however, presented a powerful counter-narrative to the Washington Consensus and the orthodoxy of minimal state and maximal market liberalization. Undoubtedly, Japan's rise to become the world's second largest economy in the late 1960s, Korea's breath-taking industrialization and technological catch-up since the 1970s, Southeast Asia's fast growing dirigiste economies since the 1980s (e.g. Singapore, Malaysia, Indonesia, and Vietnam), and China's economic ascendency since the late 1990s clearly marked a departure from the neoliberal playbook.

Much of the East Asian experience arguably lends itself to a different framing of development thinking and policy, which Chalmers Johnson (1982) famously described as the 'developmental state' model. This heterodox development pathway did not deny the appeal of unimpeded market forces (particularly in stages of advanced industrialization), but it certainly placed more emphasis on industrial policy and state guidance particularly in the early phases of industrialization. Proponents of the developmental state model highlight the role of strong and decisive executive power, meritocratic bureaucracies that operate in a Weberian ideal-typical manner,[1] strong private-sector investment under state-guidance, and a subordination of labour (Haggard, 2018: 4).

Developmentalists remain sceptical towards (neoliberal) structural adjustment policies, in which rapid privatization and deregulation have undermined the capacities of state institutions in the Global

South. The theoretical underpinning for this scepticism is basically twofold. On the one hand, we find notions that economic growth can be undermined by market failures and information imperfections and, hence, may benefit from complementary state-led development policies (Rodrik, 1996; Haggard, 2015). On the other hand, there is a consensus among developmental state analysts – including Amsden (1989), Rodrik (1994), Evans (1995), and Leftwich (1995) – that laissez-faire policies are often insufficient to jump-start latecomer economies; not least because adequate levels of nationally embedded industrialization, investment, and human capital are pivotal for attaining success in global competitive markets. Accordingly, governments and executive policy coordination can play an integral role in promoting investment and economic growth.

East Asia's economic development is a case in point. Here, a set of state interventions and industrial policies – including low-interest policy loans, conditional state subsidies and tax breaks, infrastructure investments, R&D and technology transfers, vocational training – have paved the ground for domestic growth and international competitiveness. By providing strong financial and infrastructural support and, at the same time, setting clear institutional conditions (timelines and exit strategies for state subsidies), East Asian governments created a conducive environment for infant industries to succeed domestically before entering international markets.

Development state policies in East Asia have displayed a rather fluid approach that changed over time and space according to economic and political contexts. For example, during the early post-war period, the Japanese government fostered industrial catch-up by sustaining 'import substitution' that had already been a fixture of Japan's pre-war policies. During this time, protectionist and preferential measures provided a targeted stimulus to national steel, textile, and chemical industries (Johnson, 1982; Mass and Miyajima, 1993). In the 1960s and 1970s, Japan's developmentalist guidance shifted to promoting export-oriented industries – with a special emphasis on advanced electronics and consumer products. Eventually, in the 1980s, the Ministry of International Trade and Industry (MITI) began focusing on high-tech industries and promoting regional value chains. This included a combination of public–private sector collaboration, preferential subsidies, and tax incentives for Japanese investments in Southeast Asia, and expanding development aid and infrastructure funding in the region (Arase, 2005; Coates, 2000).

A similarly fluid policy progression is evident in the case of South Korea. While the first five-year development plans in the 1960s focused on establishing a self-sustaining and stable national economy, the emphasis in the 1970s changed considerably. According to Lie (1998: 52), the Korean government shifted its focus to the 'dynamic development of the rural economy, a dramatic and sustained increase in exports and the establishment of heavy and chemical industries'. Meanwhile, government agencies also promoted corporate growth and supported the formation of powerful family-owned conglomerates (*chaebols*) that were to become the backbone of the Korean economy. Eventually, in the 1980s and 1990s, state policies shifted towards fostering export-oriented high-tech industries (similar to Japanese benchmarks) and regional outsourcing. Samsung and LG's large-scale investments in countries like Vietnam, Indonesia, and India are recent manifestations of these policy shifts.

### What are the key features of the developmental state model?

The fluid industrial policies that can be observed in the post-war experiences in Japan and Korea – and to some extent in the development of post-Mao China – highlight some common features that seem to have accelerated structural transformation and economic growth. Although preferential policies and government interventions are not historically restricted to East Asia (industrial policies in Europe, Latin America, and North America were also coloured by considerable protectionist and state-led measures during early industrialization periods), Asia's heterodox development path has certainly attracted much attention; and will continue to do so as the centre of economic gravity moves in easterly directions. In view of the experiences outlined here, the developmental state model seems to entail the following three keystones.

First, the developmental state model is predicated on a strong state with meritocratic bureaucracies. Far-sighted state leadership and public administration have played an important role in East Asia's success story. Governments have achieved development objectives by flexibly utilizing preferential policy instruments such as tax breaks, subsidized loans, infrastructure support, market entry barriers, protectionist tariffs and quotas, trade guarantees and insurances, as well as synchronizing development aid with private-sector interests (Haggard, 2018; Arase, 2005). For the planning and implementation of these policies a developmental state requires meritocratic and highly skilled bureaucracies. Japan's Ministry of International Trade and Industry, China's National Development and Reform Commission (NDRC), and Korea's Economic Planning Board (EPB) have played a critical role in this regard. By identifying promising industries based on long-term analyses and strategic planning, bureaucratic agencies accelerated growth trajectories and economic prospects. The political regime in each country protected these lead agencies from civil society and labour interference and, in doing so, provided sufficient discretion and freedom for technocrats to plan, review, and implement industrial policies (Haggard, 1990; Johnson, 1982).

Second, developmental state policies seem to be characterized by a high degree of fluidity and pragmatism. Rather than following fixed blueprints, Japan, Korea, and post-Mao China applied (as outlined in the discussion below) a fluid amalgamation of industrial, fiscal, trade, and development cooperation policies. The policy mix was continuously adjusted to changing domestic and international markets, life cycles in key industries, and to international pressure and global institutional frameworks.

Third, the developmental state model calls for state–market synergies. Undoubtedly, state agencies and bureaucrats are predominantly in the driver's seat when it comes to making strategic choices and setting industrial policy directions. But they do not act in isolation, nor should the influence of private sector interests be underestimated. Japan's domestic 'economic cooperation' system (*keizai kyoryoku*) is a case in point. Although MITI and other line ministries were instrumental in crafting industrial policies, they also relied on collaborations with industry representatives and Japanese firms to refine their priorities and practices. Public–private sector cooperation has been a key feature of the developmental state model – and this holds true for the Japanese, Korean, and Chinese development trajectory (Mao et al., 2017; Evans, 1995; Arase, 2005).

How developmental statism evolved in leading East Asian economies – such as Japan and China – and how this affected their respective development cooperation practices will be discussed in the following sections.

## Japan: disseminating East Asian developmentalism

The Japanese development path in the 19th and 20th centuries exhibits many of the key features that were outlined in the developmental state discussion above. The roots of developmentalist inclinations are arguably intricately intertwined with Japan's contemporary history. In the late 19th century – shortly after the Meiji Restoration – Japan was strongly influenced by Continental European and US theories of 'late industrialization'. Protectionist arguments were put forth by German economist Franz List (1841) as well as the US statesman Alexander Hamilton,[2] who, in the 18th century, criticized that trade between Britain and the former North American colonies was heavily skewed in favour of British merchants during the Industrial Revolution. Such arguments resonated well with Japanese policy-makers during the Meiji period. Thus, notions of state-led measures to cope with late development, protect infant industries (i.e. through import quotas and tariffs), and foster sectoral development (i.e. with targeted loans, infrastructural support, tax breaks, subsidies, and exchange rate controls) find their roots in Japan's early industrial catch-up period (Sheridan, 1998).

Developmentalist inclinations gained further traction in the 20th century. These experiences, I argue, are closely interlinked with the formation of Japan's ODA system. The national economic and political challenges that arose during Japan's periods of industrial recovery, catch-up, and maturation, predetermined the country's industrial policies – but also the direction of its accompanying ODA policies. The confluence of these interlinked developments can be roughly divided into three phases.

### Phase 1 (1950s): post-war recovery, ODA reparations, and increasing state influence

The first developmental phase in the 1950s was characterized by Japan's post-war recovery and the stabilization of Asia-Pacific relations. With the signing of the San Francisco Peace Treaty in 1951, Japan rejoined the international community and was called upon to compensate Asian countries for war atrocities. During these early post-war years, ODA policies also became an effective and subtle means to make initial reconciliatory efforts. Although the repercussions from World War II prevented Japan from taking an active political stance in the region, Japanese government agencies utilized the ODA system to pursue national interests of political and economic normalization (Buckley, 1998; Yasutomo, 1986).

After regaining sovereignty, Japan was chiefly concerned with attenuating strained relations with East and Southeast Asian neighbours by initiating the disbursement of reparation payments. Between 1954 and 1967, these reparation contracts, which were officially categorized as ODA commitments, accounted for more than 50 per cent of Japan's development aid during this period (Burnell, 1997: 147).[3] The lion's share of reparation payments were provided in the form of tangible Japanese goods and services to neighbouring Asian countries. US-led allied forces 'allowed Japan to repay its reparations through product provision and services such as machinery and power plants. Japanese engineers would therefore be dispatched for construction and instal-lations. ... [This] had a major impact on the character of Japan's foreign assistance. ... [ODA was increasingly considered] as a tool for its economic growth' (Ogawa, 2019: 9). This provided a much-needed stimulus to Japanese firms and helped them to secure natural resources and expand commercial interests in Southeast Asian markets. By joining the Colombo Plan in 1954, Japan also initiated measures of technical cooperation in the Asia-Pacific (Shimomura et al., 2016), generating new policy spaces for aid-supported private sector opportunities in the region.

Meanwhile, the Japanese government and key state ministries gained considerable autonomy and policy powers vis-à-vis the private sector. On the one hand, the dissolution of pre-war economic power concentrations (including the *zaibatsu* structures of large business conglomerates) by Allied Forces weakened the influence of the established corporate elites. Meanwhile, during the Korean War and China's communist transition, East Asian markets had become virtually inaccessible. Japanese companies therefore became increasingly dependent on state support and public measures in their pursuit of expanding regional exports and business operations.

### Phase 2 (1960–1970s): export promotion and expansion of ODA bureaucracies

In the 1960s, Japan's economic and development policies became increasingly intertwined with the objective of promoting exports. To this end, the government advocated the so-called 'income doubling policy' which officially connected the objectives of increasing exports and expanding ODA flows (Koppel and Orr, 1993). New export opportunities emerged in the context of large infrastructure projects in South-East and South Asia. Some of these projects were initiated as part of reparation contracts and finalized or expanded through ODA loans. Many of these ODA projects were assigned to Japanese contractors and, hence, paved the way for what Burnell (1997: 147) calls 'export drive through tied aid'. According to Ensign (1992), Japan's increasing ODA disbursements correlate closely with a rising flow of export revenues from Asian recipient countries.

Strong criticism from abroad led Japan to officially reduce its emphasis on tied aid over time. But even without officially tied contracts, many recipient countries continued to assign projects to Japanese firms. As Arase (1995: 98) summarizes it:

> In practice Japan's project loans favored Japanese contractors even if they were formally untied. For example, in the mid-1980s

the [Japanese government] made it a practice to recommend Japanese consultants to Thailand for design work. As a result design specifications for loan projects were written to Japanese standards. These specifications, along with short bidding periods (sometimes less than two months), did not allow others to bid on an equal footing with Japanese firms.

These ODA practices arguably provided a welcome stimulus for the export of Japanese services and goods to Asian markets. While official statistics indicated that tied aid was similarly low compared to other OECD Development Assistance Committee (DAC) member countries, Japan's actual ODA practices entailed a strong bias towards Japanese contractors. Although recipient countries were autonomous in their decision-making, complex ODA procedures informally tied loan agreements to Japanese content (Kevenhörster, 1993). This also applies to international projects financed through ODA grants and technical cooperation, as these were almost exclusively executed by Japanese contract partners (Ehrke, 1996).

Even today, the acquisition of ODA-based assignments is strongly skewed towards Japanese contractors. Over the past two decades, Japanese firms and institutions have carried out a considerable share of ODA loan projects (in most years ranging between 30 and 40 per cent). In recent years, these figures have increased considerably. Since 2016, the lion's share of loan-funded ODA projects – roughly 60 to 70 per cent – were assigned to Japanese contractors (see Figure 2.1).

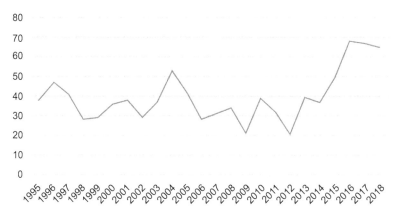

**Figure 2.1** Share of ODA loan contracts (in percentage points) awarded to Japanese firms/institutions
*Source:* Author's estimates based on JICA Annual Reports from 1998 to 2019.
Note: Estimates are based on foreign currency contracts and exclude commodity loans.

*Phase 3 (1980s onwards): promotion of Japanese foreign*
*direct investment and regional industrialization*

In the 1980s, development cooperation strategies adapted, once again, to the profound changes in Japan's economic transformation. As the country moved from middle-income to high-income status, Japanese industries faced rising pressures to relocate or outsource labour-intensive production. In view of industrial change and increasing wage structures, Japan's powerful Ministry of International Trade and Industry (MITI) forged a new regional strategy that combined industrial and development policies. In 1987, MITI's New Asian Industries Development Plan (New AID Plan) envisaged integrating East and Southeast Asian countries into a regional production network. The key idea was to generate valuable development impulses for Asian developing countries and, at the same time, make Japan's global manufacturing more cost efficient. To this end, MITI advocated the joint promotion of ODA, foreign direct investment (FDI), and trade.

The Association of Southeast Asian Nations (ASEAN) region provided the ideal conditions for such an integrated production and development network. Emerging Southeast Asian economies – such as Indonesia, Thailand, Malaysia, and the Philippines – were particularly attractive partners in the New AID Plan; not least because they offered low labour costs and rich resource endowments. Increasingly, Japan shifted labour- and resource-intensive production segments to Southeast Asia and, in doing so, sharpened its competitive edge in international trade.

Conceptually, the New AID Plan resonates with Akamatsu's (1962) 'Flying Geese' paradigm and the notion of sequential regional industrialization.[4] The overarching argument is that Japan, as the lead goose, has been providing valuable impulses to a second tier of industrializing Asian economies (i.e. South Korea, Singapore, and Taiwan). The fact that two of East Asia's miracle economies – namely South Korea and Taiwan – experienced colonial Japanese rule,[5] has further strengthened the 'regional incubator' narrative, highlighting that Japan (apart from its imperial atrocities) has facilitated administrative and technological advancement in East Asia's industrialization.

The next step in the model envisions that these second-tier miracle economies (together with Japan) generate additional industrial and technological impulses for the development of third-tier ASEAN economies (Malaysia, Indonesia, Thailand, and the Philippines). In return, emerging ASEAN economies provide affordable resources, inexpensive labour, and low-cost components to higher-tier economies.

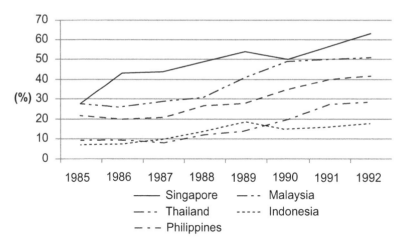

**Figure 2.2** Share of manufactured goods in Japan's imports from Southeast Asia
*Source*: Author's calculations based on Foerster (1994: 5).

Consistent with this understanding, the third generation of Southeast Asian economies hence followed the flow (or flock) of regional industrialization in the late 1980s, relying heavily on Japanese FDI and accompanying ODA programmes. While this hierarchical explanation of regional industrialization remains controversial, there are indications that the combination of ODA, FDI, and trade has coincided with the profound industrial upgrading in the ASEAN region – exemplified, for instance, by the rising percentage of manufactured goods in Japanese imports (see Figure 2.2).

According to Stallings and Kim (2017), the flying geese logic and related ODA-cum-FDI strategies can also be observed in sequential development stages in the 1990s and beyond:

> A similar process took place in China, which became the largest recipient of Japanese aid in the 1980s and 1990s. Now, with a fourth generation of East Asian nations in Indochina beginning to open up to the world economy, these poorer neighbors are again being helped by packages of resources from Japan where ODA complements trade and FDI. Beyond bilateral ODA to this new group, Japan is heavily involved in a set of Mekong Delta projects, which involve several Chinese provinces as well as the CLMV nations (Cambodia, Laos, Myanmar, and Vietnam). The aim is to further the integration of the new set of nations into East Asian economic networks (Stallings and Kim, 2017: 38).

**Table 2.1** Japan's domestic and foreign development orientations over time

|  | Domestic development objectives | Foreign development assistance objectives |
|---|---|---|
| 1950s | Post-war recovery | Reparations, grants/loans, and resource access |
| 1960s and 1970s | Import substitution and export promotion | Grants/loans and (tied) trade |
| 1980s onwards | Regional outsourcing | Grants/loans, (tied) trade, and FDI support |
| 1990s and early 2000s | ODA Charters (1992/2003) | Grants/loans, (tied) trade, and FDI support; formal emphasis on human development |

*Source*: Author's timeline drawing on Arase (1995), Ogawa (2019), and von Lübke (1999).

The stages of domestic and foreign development objectives outlined above are briefly summarized in Table 2.1. The discussion highlighted several examples that indicated overlapping interests in ministries concerned with national and international economic affairs. In other words, there is a clear indication that ODA policies generated valuable synergies and economic impulses for Japan's national economy during the different phases of economic transformation. These benefits included supporting infant or declining industries (e.g. by introducing preferential trade policies and tied aid), laying infrastructural foundations to tap foreign resources, and providing FDI support schemes for regional production networks and business offshoring.

Admittedly, Japan's developmentalist approach has not been without controversies – both internationally and in Japan. Both OECD-DAC members and Japanese NGO observers have repeatedly criticized the Japanese government for its strong focus on ODA loans (rather than grants), its preoccupation with physical infrastructure (rather than human development), and its 'tied aid' practices that benefit Japanese business interests. In response to external and internal scrutiny, the Japanese government adopted an ODA Charter in 1992 (and a further revision in 2003) that emphasized the importance of human resource development, poverty reduction, institution building, and South–South Cooperation. Yet, as many critical observers have noted (Ogawa, 2019; Arase, 2005; Foerster, 1994), these adjustments have only scratched the surface of Japan's ODA practices, while many line ministries and private sector partners remained deeply embedded in the developmentalist mindset.

In sum, Japan's sequential policy stages were characterized by distinct economic challenges that paved the ground for a strong development bureaucracy and an increasingly sophisticated ODA system. The early post-war years (1950s) were defined by economic recovery and war compensations, which prompted reparation agreements across Asia that were primarily paid 'in kind' with Japanese ODA projects and services. The US occupation forces strengthened selected public bureaucracies – while weakening established economic and political elites (Johnson 1982: 132) – to ensure a steady economic recovery and reduce the risk of reactionary backsliding. This provided stability but did not bode well for democratization and public accountability. Indeed, this reshuffled constellation of policy power served to elevate Japan's bureaucracies and technocratic ODA system. Key bureaucratic actors in post-war Japan – such as MITI, the Ministry of Finance (MOF), and the Ministry of Foreign Affairs, and implementing agencies (Overseas Economic Cooperation Fund and Japan International Cooperation Agency (JICA)) – attained the freedom to operate virtually unconstrained by legislative controls and political interests (Ahrens, 2002; Arase, 2005; Rodrik, 1996). This technocratic setting set the course, for better or worse, for Japan's developmentalist path into the 21st century including the emphasis on ODA-supported export promotion, FDI schemes, and regional production networks.

## China: state developmentalism and global silk road politics

Whether China also represents an ideal-typical example of a developmental state remains a matter of debate. It is possible, however, to highlight a set of features that resonate well with the developmentalist discourses surrounding East Asia's economic miracle which indicate strong similarities (as well as some differences) with Japan's post-war experience.

'Starting with the fact that post-1978 China has been an East Asian developmental state with a long socialist legacy', Mao et al. (2017: 17) note, 'China's economic planning agencies too have been trying to create (and pick) winners, just as their counterparts in Japan, Singapore, South Korea, and Taiwan have done.' Several empirical studies suggest that Chinese state bureaucracy has been instrumental in identifying promising sectors, special economic zones, and promising technologies (Haggard, 2015; Mao et al., 2017).

Beginning in 1978, Deng Xiaoping's economic reforms paved the ground for China's transformation into a modern market economy with a socialist underpinning. State bureaucracies were called upon to modernize and prepare domestic industries for international trade and investment. In this transition period, China encountered challenges that were similar to those encountered in post-war Japan and Korea.[6] Against this background, China's policy-makers were receptive to and strongly influenced by the developmental state model (Haggard, 2018; Mao et al., 2017). While China's policy regime is certainly not identical to those of its neighbours – viewing it as a socialist (rather than a capitalist) pathway to modernization – it nonetheless resonates in many ways with other East Asian experiences. As Boltho and Weber (2015: 267) summarize it:

> China, since reforms began in the late 1970s, has shared some of [the developmental state] characteristics, but not all. In particular, it is still much more of a command economy than the other [East Asian] countries have ever been, yet, at the same time, has embraced globalization with, arguably, much greater enthusiasm than was done, in earlier times, by Japan, Taiwan or Korea. If China's experience, however, is compared with that of other, more or less successful, developing countries, the similarities with the East Asia development model would seem to dwarf such differences.

Explicit similarities are also evident in China's emulation in the field of public planning and coordination. Drawing on the experiences of coordinating bodies in Japan (MITI), Korea (EPB), and Taiwan (Industrial Development Bureau, IDB), China set up a planning and steering board, the 'National Reform and Development Commission' (NDRC), to facilitate public–private sector collaboration and policy harmonization. In close collaboration with China's Ministries of Commerce (MOFCOM), Foreign Affairs (MFA), Finance (MOF), and other key ministries, NDRC's central task was to strengthen and steer industrial and development policies. This included the streamlining of fiscal measures (subsidies and tax breaks), import substitution in heavy industries, promoting exports in light industries, and supporting state-owned enterprises (Baek, 2005; Zhang, 2018). Over time, China adopted a more ambitious agenda of industrial catch-up that emulated the national innovation system in other advanced economies (Mao et al., 2017). Particular attention was focused on promoting 'strategic emerging industries' and technological innovation. The key objective of Chinese state agencies (including NDRC) was to devise concerted policies that allowed for rapid industrial development and technological leap-frogging. This required not only the streamlining of bureaucratic policies, but also the intensive collaboration with private sector actors (Chen and Naughton, 2016).

Institutional similarities can also be observed in the ways in which industrial policies are combined with development cooperation efforts. In 2018, the government established the China International Development Cooperation Agency (CIDCA). This newly institutionalized agency is similar to, but ultimately more powerful than Japan's JICA and Korea's International Cooperation Agency (KOICA). It facilitates the identification, planning, and evaluation of China's foreign development programmes – in close cooperation with key state agencies (including MOFCOM, MFA, MOF, and NDRC). Moreover, to enhance funding mechanisms and endorse its multilateral commitment, China has established the Asian Infrastructure Investment Bank (AIIB) since 2015. With more than 100 member countries and an initial capitalization of US$100 bn, the organization and governance structure of the AIIB is comparable to other leading multilateral development banks (Broz et al., 2020; Hameiri and Jones, 2018). By establishing a multilateral development bank in Beijing – which complements and occasionally competes with regional funding schemes of the Asian Development Bank (traditionally under Japanese leadership) and the World Bank (traditionally under US leadership) – China has assertively expressed the institutional commitment and ambition to promote its development model in Asia and beyond.

Similar to Japan and Korea, this development model is informed by China's own economic transformation. Looking back at a long track record of ODA programmes, the former recipient country has emerged as a key development donor – and is bound to surpass many traditional DAC members in the years to come. According to Bräutigam et al. (2019), China's foreign aid programme in 2016 accounted for $6.6 bn in concessional grants and loans (ODA) and roughly $9.3 bn in export credits (other official flows (OOF)).[7] Similar estimates emerge from a study of the JICA Research Institute (Kitano, 2019) which assesses Chinese foreign development commitments over time and highlights a continuous rise of bilateral and multilateral ODA (see Figure 2.3). Tracing ODA/OOF flows between 2000 and 2014, Dreher et al. (2017, 2021) estimate that China has disbursed approx. $350 bn in more than 4,300 projects in 140 countries and, in doing so, has emerged as the second largest development donor in the world.

The rapidly expanding scope and scale of China's foreign development assistance is, to a large extent, driven by the Belt and Road Initiative (BRI), a signature policy initiative that was officially launched by Xi Jinping in 2013. The key objective is to forge two transcontinental connectivity corridors towards Eurasian and African economies. The land-based corridor (Silk Road Economic Belt) envisions the construction of connected railways, highways, logistic facilities, and

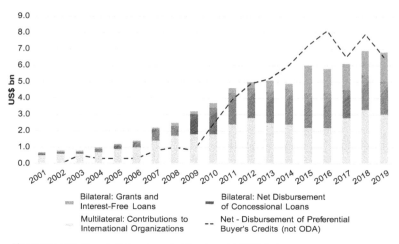

**Figure 2.3** China's net disbursement of foreign aid (US$ bn)
*Source*: Author's figure based on data from Kitano and Miyabayashi (2020)

energy plants that interconnect East Asia with Central Asia and Europe. The maritime corridor (21st Century Maritime Silk Road) comprises the construction of deep-sea ports and trans-shipment harbours along the Indian Ocean that enhance trade and energy ties – primarily between China, South/Southeast Asia, and Africa. While budget estimates of this multi-trillion infrastructure programme vary,[8] China's New Silk Road undoubtedly constitutes one of the largest development initiatives in modern history.

Without a doubt, the BRI, with its large-scale infrastructure, energy, and digitalization projects, has become the keystone of China's emerging foreign development cooperation. According to President Xi's speech at the 19th National Congress in 2017, China is setting out to 'actively promote international cooperation through the Belt and Road Initiative. In doing so, we hope to achieve policy, infrastructure, trade, financial, and people-to-people connectivity and thus build a new platform for international cooperation to create new drivers of shared development' (Flint and Zhu, 2019: 99). Assuming the Chinese economy and BRI implementation regains its (pre-pandemic) momentum, it is hence likely that China's infrastructure loans will outperform comparable commitments of leading Western donors for many years to come.

'The key challenge for the US [and other Western donors]' Bräutigam et al. (2019: 2) note, 'is that China is an East Asian developmental state. This means that like Japan, Korea, and Taiwan, China's instruments for fostering trade and investment overseas are far more developed and far better funded than Washington's.' These developmental instruments transcend ODA and build on strong public–private sector collaboration that 'undermines traditional donor's efforts to promote neoliberal and liberal-democratic' agendas (Rosser, 2020: 293). Against this backdrop, democracy promotion efforts and aid conditionalities fostering liberal-democratic ideas are increasingly losing traction in regions like Africa and Central Asia.

## Prospects of a developmentalist consensus

Whether development cooperation practices in Japan, China, and Korea will converge and give rise to what may be described as a 'new developmentalist consensus' remains an interesting and challenging question. The ability to inform and influence international policy debates will depend on the ability of East Asian policy-makers to showcase their shared experience as a desirable pathway to economic and social development. It will also depend on the willingness of all involved parties to cooperate as well as the political clout they have to reach out to regional and international audiences. In other words, the prospects of an emergent consensus can be assessed by considering three key aspects: *convergence, reception, and leverage.*

### Convergence: similarities of East Asian development practices and interests

The foregoing discussions show that East Asia's development practices are converging in a number of respects. This seems to be true in terms of sectoral priorities, funding modalities, and the emphasis on strong state–business relations (Stallings and Kim, 2017; Mao et al., 2017; Haggard, 2018). Compared to prevailing standards in Western DAC countries, East Asian donors have placed greater emphasis on physical infrastructure (rather than social development), concessional loans (rather than grants), and state-led private sector partnerships (rather than deregulated markets). Moreover, while East Asian development funds have traditionally been directed to Asia (and, in recent years, Africa), Western ODA commitments tend to flow to the least developed countries – without any discernible regional pattern.

Large infrastructure programmes have been a pragmatic means to provide international public goods and, at the same time, promote national commercial interests. Against this background, China's *Belt and Road Initiative*, Japan's *Partnership for Quality Infrastructure* and, initially, Korea's *Eurasia Initiative* are prime examples of what we may call 'ODA with benefits' – a developmentalist approach that blurs the lines between providing foreign aid and promoting national industries. President Xi, for instance, has repeatedly emphasized the objective of 'mutual economic benefit' in the context of advancing China's BRI programmes. Meanwhile, former Prime Minister Abe has openly conceded that efforts to secure 'national interests' will be reflected in Japan's development cooperation (Sato, 2018). This official endorsement[9] of commercial synergies marks a turning point in the way Japan frames its regional cooperation and sheds its former 'reticence about self-promotion' (Wallace, 2019: 863).

Overall, the successful interweaving of domestic and foreign ODA objectives is a challenging task that requires substantial state capacities. East Asian bureaucratic systems – initially in Japan, later in Korea, and more recently in China – all display a track record of seamlessly synchronizing industrial and development policies. This synchronization, as outlined in the foregoing discussion, is predicated on technocratic skills, bureaucratic autonomy, and strong state–business relations. The powerful position of lead agencies, which operate without notable legislative and societal interferences, has been another corresponding feature in Japan, Korea, and China's developmental experience. Prominent examples include Japan's Ministry of International Trade and Industry (Johnson, 1982), Korea's Economic Planning Board (Woo-Cumings, 1991), and, in a similar vein, the recent formation of China's National Reform and Development Commission (Gore, 2011; Zhang, 2018).

In sum, East Asian development practices indicate a convergence in their development assistance practices. Although Japan and Korea are official DAC member countries – and geopolitically closer aligned with Western nations – there are nonetheless notable similarities in both countries' sectoral priorities, funding modalities, and state–business relations.[10] Equally noteworthy are China and Japan's state-sanctioned infrastructure programmes, which feature similar levels of public–private collaboration and have raised much attention, as well as contention, in the region and beyond. Whether Japan and China will be inclined to collaborate – or compete – in Asian and African infrastructure programmes is hard to predict. Historically embedded tensions render an official endorsement of Sino-Japanese collaboration susceptible to political resistance in both countries. This may also explain why Japan has remained quiescent in BRI Forums and has yet to join the China-led AIIB.

Yet, while state-level commitments may take time, there are numerous less formalized formats of triangular ODA cooperation. According to Sato (2018), Japan's development administration (JICA/MOF) has met with its Chinese counterparts (CIDCA/MOFCOM) regularly since 2010 to discuss joint priorities and potential areas of collaboration. Correspondingly, Korea and Japan have conducted joint annual trainings/workshops through their respective ODA agencies, KOICA and JICA (Cools, 2016). Moreover, irrespective of political complexities, China and Japan have begun to jointly implement large infrastructure and transportation projects in Central Asia – most notably in Tajikistan and Kyrgyzstan (Kitano, 2012; cited in Sato, 2018: 123).

Whether Japan, Korea, and China will elevate collaborative development efforts to a more institutionalized and internationally visible level will also depend on the interplay of domestic and international politics (including respective relations with future US administrations). Perhaps the most promising venue would be a joint promotion of ideas and interests in multilateral platforms (e.g. AIIB, Asian Development Bank, BRI Forum), regional platforms (including the successful launching of the Regional Comprehensive Economic Partnership, the Asia-centred free trade agreement), and trilateral platforms (such as the Trilateral Cooperation Summit). Thus, a gradual and multilateral approach to demonstrate East Asia's consensus might prove more feasible than any unilateral effort to do so.

### Reception: track record in regional and international recipient countries

The reception of East Asia's developmental model and its advocacy of large-scale infrastructure projects has been mixed. Similar to other donors' construction of large-scale dams, ports, highways, railway connections, and energy plants, China/Korea/Japan's economic infrastructure projects have also received their share of criticism. The fact that the lion's share of 'infrastructure investment is a for-profit activity that private companies have been willing to [conduct]' (Ogawa, 2019: 14) raises concerns of an increasing commercialization of East Asia's foreign assistance. Given its enormous scope and geo-economic impact, China's Belt and Road has attracted particular attention. Some Eurasian and African BRI projects have raised issues of environmental degradation and social displacement (Renliang, 2016; Rüland, 2020). Another point of contention is China's disbursement of large non-concessional loans which thus elevates the risks of increasing public debt. Sri Lanka's Hambantota project is a case in point. Unable to repay the $1.5 bn loan for a deep-sea port, Sri Lanka ultimately agreed to sign over the Hambantota port area to China on a 99-year lease (Heiduk and Sakaki, 2019).

Although Japanese infrastructure programmes have drawn less criticism, in comparison, Tokyo's push for 'quality infrastructure' has nonetheless raised concerns. Accelerated by the increasingly nationalist tone of the second Abe administration (Sakaki, 2019), Japan's infrastructure diplomacy has become more commercialized, more politicized, and less pro-poor (Jiang, 2019; Yoshimatsu, 2017). By endorsing a strong symbiosis of economic statecraft and national business interests, Ogawa (2019) argues, Japan's government may resurrect its former image as a 'rogue donor' and risks reverting to early post-war practices.

Economic assessments about East Asian infrastructure programmes have, in contrast, been more upbeat. A review of recent empirical studies indicates that China's *Belt and Road* and Japan's *Quality Infrastructure* initiatives are widely seen as accelerators for foreign investment, trade, and economic growth (Chung, 2018; Iqbal et al., 2019; Jiang, 2019). Impact assessments of BRI-funded infrastructures, conducted by the World Bank, arrive at similar results. Summarizing their findings, the authors note that:

> Countries that lie along the Belt and Road corridors are ill-served by existing infrastructure ... BRI transport corridors will help in two critical ways—lowering travel times and increasing trade and investment. Along economic corridors, the study estimates that travel times will decline by up to 12 percent once completed. Travel times with the rest of the world are estimated to decrease by an average of 3 percent, showing that non-BRI countries and regions will benefit as well. Trade will also increase sharply, if unevenly, for Belt and Road corridor economies. The study estimates that trade will grow from between 2.8 and 9.7 percent for corridor economies ... Importantly, low-income countries are expected to see a significant 7.6 percent increase in foreign direct investment due to the new transport links. Expanded trade and investment will increase growth in most corridor economies. Real income gains could increase by up to 3.4 percent at the high end of the study's estimates (World Bank, 2019: xiii).

Overall, it seems fair to say that the perception of East Asia's developmental model, exemplified by its promotion of large-scale infrastructure programmes across Eurasia and Africa, points in different directions. While social and environmental problems undoubtedly persist, economic assessments are by and large more optimistic and highlight the potentials of economic trade, investment, and income growth. This mixed picture, where economic benefits eclipse social and environmental ones, was a common feature in East Asia's early industrialization. It resonates closely with the technocratic trade-offs during Japan, Korea, and China's industrial catch-up phase and, hence, is consistent with East Asia's developmentalist model.

### Leverage: East Asia's weight in regional and global policy arenas

The third aspect that needs to be considered is the notion of political leverage. To what extent is East Asia in a powerful position to showcase its development model? Do China, Japan, and Korea have sufficient political influence in global policy arenas? To be sure, it is not the first time that an East Asian donor has sought to advocate ideas and experiences to a global audience. In the early 1990s, Japan, which had emerged as the world's largest ODA donor and second largest economy, was ultimately unsuccessful in its effort to establish a counter discourse. The World Bank study, *The East Asian Miracle* (1993), was intentionally commissioned and funded by Japan to shed empirical light on Asia's heterodox success story. Yet, the final study paid little, if any, homage to the region's promotion of industrial policies and state-led coordination (Fine, 1999; Wade, 1996), perhaps unsurprising in view of the World Bank's neoliberal tendencies. And although Japan's developmentalist advocacy received notable support from Southeast Asia's (mostly authoritarian) leaders – including Singapore's Lee Kuan Yew and Malaysia's Mahathir Mohamad – the Washington consensus and its neoliberal framework remained largely intact; not least, because the Asian financial crisis in 1997/98 cast considerable doubt on Asia's state-led governance.[11]

Today, 30 years later, the ripples of the Asian crisis have subsided, while the Global Financial Crisis of 2008 has eroded confidence in the neoliberal model. Meanwhile, Asia remains a centre of economic gravity, Japan continues to be the world's third-largest economy, and China has become an economic superpower. Arguably, this creates substantial political momentum for change – perhaps larger than ever before – and, with it, new opportunities to engage in global policy debates. Overall, it seems fair to say that the changing zeitgeist of a less Anglo/Euro-centric world bodes well for more heterodox and diverse ideas on development cooperation.

East Asian donors' rising financial commitments to building public infrastructures and services generate additional leverage. A closer look into global ODA flows (see Figure 2.4) indicates that Japan, China, and Korea's combined commitments (on the order

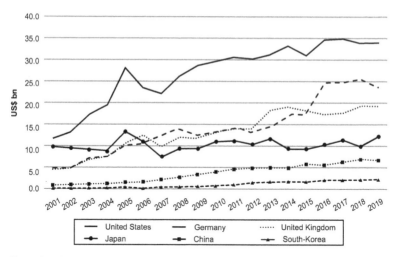

**Figure 2.4** Gross ODA flows from DAC countries to emerging donors (US$ bn)
*Source*: Author's figure based on data from Kitano and Miyabayashi (2020)

of $20 bn and rising) are bound to surpass leading donors such as the UK and Germany. Once non-concessional flows and export credits (OOF) are added to the equation, this trend will gain further momentum (see Figure 2.3). This serves to illustrate East Asia's dominant position in loan-based funding schemes and, implicitly, its capacity to support transcontinental infrastructure development across Eurasia and Africa.

Will East Asia's infrastructural megaprojects and connectivity corridors across Eurasia and Africa generate sufficient political momentum for an emergent developmental consensus to form? The jury is still out as to how and when an Asian donor model will be accorded centre stage in global development debates. Clearly, a policy shift in developmentalist directions would be contested and, hence, slow and incremental. What is clear, however, is that the changing zeitgeist of a less Anglo/Euro-centric world opens policy spaces for more heterodox and diverse ideas on development cooperation. Some of these spaces are bound to be occupied by Asian policy entrepreneurs who leverage China and Japan's infrastructure drive and/or multilateral alignments to global policy debates and, in doing so, elevate the developmental profile.

## Notes

* Professor of Southeast Asian Studies at the University of Applied Science Konstanz (HTWG), Germany. cluebke@htwg-konstanz.de

1. For a detailed discussion of Weber's ideal-typical categories of meritocratic bureaucratic power see for instance Weber (1925, 1947).
2. In view of Britain's economic rise during the Industrial Revolution, Hamilton was a key proponent of protecting US 'infant industries' by introducing protectionist measures (tariffs and quotas) that would prevent British imports from dominating the US market (McKee, 1934: 189–256).
3. Between 1954 and 1967, the Japanese government signed and disbursed reparation agreements that amounted to US$1.83 bn. Among the signatory countries were Myanmar (1954, $340 m); Thailand (1955, $26.7 m); Philippines (1956, $550 m); Indonesia (1958, $223 m); Laos (1958, $2.8 m); Cambodia (1959, $4.2 m); South Vietnam (1959, $390 m), South Korea (1965, $300 m); Singapore (1967, $8.2 m); and Malaysia (1967, $8.2 m). For a discussion on post-war reparations see Arase (1995: 29) and Takagi (1995: 11).
4. For a detailed review of Akamatsu's 'flying geese' paradigm and the progression of Asia's regional industrialization and economic integration, see also Kojima (2000) and Ozawa (2006).
5. Kohli (1994), for instance, notes that Japan's colonial influence on Korea's developmental state has not received enough attention. He argues that

> Japanese colonial influence on Korea in 1905–45, while brutal and humiliating, was also decisive in shaping a political economy that later evolved into the high-growth South Korean path to development. More specifically, three state-society characteristics that we now readily associate as elements of the South Korean 'model' originated during the colonial period: Korean state under the Japanese influence was transformed from a relatively corrupt and ineffective social institution into a highly authoritarian, penetrating organization, capable of simultaneously controlling and transforming Korean society; production-oriented alliances involving the state and dominant classes evolved, leading up to considerable expansion of manufacturing, including 'exports;' and the lower classes in both the city and the countryside came to be systematically controlled by the state and dominant classes. While there were important discontinuities following World War II, when the dust settled, South Korea under Park Chung-Hee fell back into the grooves of colonial origins and traveled along them, well into the 1980s (Kohli, 1994: 1269).

A contrasting and more sceptical view of Japan's 'colonial developmentalism' is presented in Booth and Deng (2017).
6. South Korea's post-war economic miracle is often interlinked – especially during the Cold War presidencies of Park and Chun

(1962–88) – with narratives of the developmental state. Key elements of these authoritarian developmentalist regimes, as many have outlined (Amsden, 1989; Haggard, 1990; Woo-Cumings, 1991), included a strong and meritocratic bureaucracy, a state-led coordination of private sector conglomerates and emerging industries, and the repression of labour unions and societal interests.

7. The OECD-DAC defines ODA (official development assistance) as a 'government aid designed to promote the economic development and welfare of developing countries ... [including] grants, 'soft' loans (where the grant element is at least 25% of the total) and the provision of technical assistance.' The category of OOF (other financial flows), in turn, is defined as 'official sector transactions that do not meet official development assistance (ODA) criteria ... [including] grants to developing countries for [commercial] purposes; official bilateral transactions intended to promote development, but having a grant element of less than 25%; and, official bilateral transactions, whatever their grant element, that are primarily export-facilitating in purpose.' Further details can be found on the OECD-DAC website at https://doi.org/10.1787/d5eccaf3-en.

8. According to the American Enterprise Institute, China's public–private push for overseas infrastructure commitments has exceeded $1 tn (Mayer and Zhang, 2020: 5). Other studies estimate announced BRI investment volumes upwards of $8 tn (Hurley et al., 2019). The policy think-tank MERICS, which monitors actual implementation, estimates that *completed* BRI projects amount to roughly $100 bn (https://www.merics.org/en/tracker/mapping-belt-and-road-initiative-where-we-stand).

9. The confluence of commercial interests is also readily observable in Japan's 2015 ODA Charter, which emphasizes that development cooperation 'will lead to ensuring Japan's national interests such as maintaining its peace and security [and] achieving further prosperity' (MOFA, 2015: 3).

10. Admittedly, this chapter presents a somewhat simplified framing of South Korea's ODA. For a more comprehensive and nuanced discussion of Korean development cooperation, including its gradually changing sectoral priorities and institutional reforms, see Chapter 3, 'Decoding South Korea's development cooperation'.

11. Krugman summarized Washington's scepticism towards the Asian developmental model in the late 1990s by noting: 'the biggest lesson from Asia's troubles is not about economics, it is about government. When Asian economies delivered nothing but good news, it was possible to convince yourself that the alleged planners of these knew what they were doing. Now the truth is revealed, they do not have a clue' (Krugman, 1997: 27).

## References

Ahrens, J. (2002) *Governance and Economic Development: A Comparative Institutional Approach*, Edward Elgar, Cheltenham.

Akamatsu, K. (1962) 'A historical pattern of economic-growth in developing-countries', *Developing Economies* 62(1): 3–25 <https://doi.org/10.1111/j.1746-1049.1962.tb01020.x>.

Amsden, A.H. (1989) *Asia's Next Giant: South Korea and Late Industrialization*, Oxford University Press, New York.

Arase, D. (2005) *Japan's Foreign Aid: Old Continuities and New Perspectives*, Routledge, London, New York.

Baek, S.-W. (2005) 'Does China follow the East Asian development model?' *Journal of Contemporary Asia* 35(1): 485–98 <https://doi.org/10.1080/00472330580000281>.

Bates, R. (2008) *When Things Fell Apart. State Failure in Late-Century Africa*, Cambridge University Press, Cambridge and New York.

Boltho, A. and Weber, M. (2015) 'Did China follow the East Asian development model', *The European Journal of Comparative Economics* 6(2): 267–86 <https://doi.org/10.1017/CBO9781139962858.009>.

Booth, A. and Deng, K. (2017) 'Japanese colonialism in comparative perspective', *Journal of World History* 28(1): 61–98 <https://doi.org/10.1353/jwh.2017.0002>.

Bräutigam, D., Akpaninyie, M. and Rudyak, M. (2019) 'China is upping its aid and development game. How should the U.S. respond?' *ChinaFile Conversation*, 15 February, New York.

Broz, J.L., Zhang, Z. and Wang, G. (2020) 'Explaining foreign support for China's global economic leadership', *International Organization* 74(3): 417–52 <https://doi.org/10.1017/S0020818320000120>.

Buckley, R. (1998) *Japan Today*, Cambridge University Press, Cambridge.

Burnell, P. (1997) *Foreign Aid in a Changing World*, McGraw-Hill Education, London.

Chen, L. and Naughton, B. (2016) 'An institutionalized policy-making mechanism: China's return to techno-industrial policy', *Research Policy* 45(10): 2138–52 <https://doi.org/10.1016/j.respol.2016.09.014>.

Chung, C.-P. (2018) 'What are the strategic and economic implications for South Asia of China's Maritime Silk Road initiative?' *The Pacific Review* 31(3): 315–32 <https://doi.org/10.1080/09512748.2017.1375000>.

Coates, D. (2000) *Models of Capitalism: Growth and Stagnation in the Modern Era*, Polity Press, Cambridge.

Cools, L. (2016) 'South Korea's foreign aid: evolution and potential' [online], Australian Institute of International Affairs, Canberra <http://www.internationalaffairs.org.au/australianoutlook/south-korean-foreign-aid-evolution-and-potential> [accessed 13 September 2020].

Dreher, A., Fuchs, A., Parks, B., Strange, A. and Tierney, M.J. (2017) *Aid, China, and Growth: Evidence from a New Global Development Finance*

*Dataset*, AIDDATA Working Paper No. 46, AidData at William & Mary, Williamsburg, VA.

Dreher, A., Fuchs, A., Parks, B., Strange, A. and Tierney, M.J. (2021) 'Aid, China, and growth: evidence from a new global development finance dataset', *American Economic Journal: Economic Policy* 13(2): 135–74 <https://doi.org/10.1257/pol.20180631>.

Ehrke, M. (1996) 'Die japanische Entwicklungspolitik', in J. Betz (ed.), *Jahrbuch Dritte Welt*, pp. 34–53, Beck, München.

Ensign, M. (1992) *Doing Good or Doing Well? Japan's Foreign Aid Program*, Columbia University Press, New York.

Evans, P.B. (1995) *Embedded Autonomy: States and Industrial Transformation*, Princeton University Press, Princeton, NJ.

Fine, B. (1999) 'The developmental state is dead long live social capital?' *Development and Change* 30(1): 1–19 <https://doi.org/10.1111/1467-7660.00105>.

Flint, C. and Zhu, C. (2019) 'The geopolitics of connectivity, cooperation, and hegemonic competition: the Belt and Road Initiative', *Geoforum* 99: 95–101 <https://doi.org/10.1016/j.geoforum.2018.12.008>.

Foerster, A. (1994) *Japans Zusammenarbeit mit der Dritten Welt zwischen Entwicklungsorientierung und außenwirtschaftlichen Prioritäten*, Deutsches Institut für Entwicklungspolitik, Bonn.

Gore, L. (2011) *China's 'Mini-State Council': National Development and Reform Commission*, East Asian Institute, National University of Singapore.

Haggard, S. (1990) *Pathways From Periphery: The Politics of Growth in the Newly Industrializing Countries*, Cornell University Press, Ithaca, NY.

Haggard, S. (2015) 'The developmental state is dead: long live the developmental state!' in: J. Mahoney and K. Thelen (eds), *Advances in Comparative-Historical Analysis*, pp. 39–66, Cambridge University Press, Cambridge.

Haggard, S. (2018) *Developmental States: Elements in the Politics of Development*, Cambridge University Press, Cambridge.

Hameiri, S. and Jones, L. (2018) 'China challenges global governance? Chinese international development finance and the AIIB', *International Affairs* 94(3): 573–93 <https://doi.org/10.1093/ia/iiy026>.

Heiduk, F. and Sakaki, A. (2019) 'Introduction to the special issue— China's Belt and Road Initiative: the view from East Asia', *East Asia* 36(2): 93–113 <https://doi.org/10.1007/s12140-019-09312-y>.

Hurley, J., Morris, S. and Portelance, G. (2019) 'Examining the debt implications of the Belt and Road Initiative from a policy perspective', *Journal of Infrastructure, Policy and Development* 3(1): 139–75 <https://doi.org/10.24294/jipd.v3i1.1123>.

Iqbal, B.A., Rahman, M.N. and Sami, S. (2019) 'Impact of Belt and Road Initiative on Asian economies', *Global Journal of Emerging Market Economies* 11(3):260–77<https://doi.org/10.1177/0974910119887059>.

Jiang, Y. (2019) 'Competitive partners in development financing: China and Japan expanding overseas infrastructure investment',

*The Pacific Review* 32(5): 778–808 <https://doi.org/10.1080/095127 48.2019.1569117>.

Johnson, C. (1982) *MITI and the Japanese Miracle: The Growth of Industrial Policy, 1925–1975*, Stanford University Press, Stanford, CA.

Kevenhörster, P. (1993) *Japan: Außenpolitik im Aufbruch*, VS Verlag für Sozialwissenschaften, Opladen.

Kitano, N. (2019) *Comparing Development Cooperation of Northeast Asian Countries*, JICA Research Institute, Tokyo.

Kitano, N. and Miyabayashi, Y. (2020) *Estimating China's Foreign Aid: 2019–2020 Preliminary Figures*, JICA Research Institute, Tokyo.

Kohli, A. (1994) 'Where do high growth political economies come from? The Japanese lineage of Korea's "developmental state"', *World Development* 22(9): 1269–93 <https://doi.org/10.1016/0305-750X(94)90004-3>.

Kojima, K. (2000) 'The "flying geese" model of Asian economic development: origin, theoretical extensions, and regional policy implications', *Journal of Asian Economics* 11(1): 375–401 <https://doi.org/10.1016/S1049-0078(00)00067-1>.

Koppel, B. and Orr, R.M. (1993) *Japan's Foreign Aid: Power and Policy in a New Era*, Westview Press, Boulder, CO.

Krueger, A.O. (1974) 'The political economy of the rent-seeking society', *The American Economic Review* 64(3): 291–303.

Krueger, A.O. (1978) *Liberalization Attempts and Consequences*, Ballinger, for the National Bureau of Economic Research, Cambridge, MA.

Krugman, P. (1995) *Development, Geography and Economic Theory*, MIT Press, Cambridge, MA.

Krugman, P. (1997) 'Whatever happened to the Asian miracle?' *Fortune* 136(4): 26–28.

Leftwich, A. (1995) 'Bringing politics back in: towards a model of the developmental state', *Journal of Development Studies* 31(3): 400–27 <https://doi.org/10.1080/00220389508422370>.

Lie, J. (1998) *Han Unbound: The Political Economy of South Korea*, Stanford University Press, Palo Alto, CA.

List, F. (1841) *Das Nationale System der Politischen Ökonomie* [trans. The National System of Political Economy, Longmans, Green and Co., London, 1841], Kyklos, Basel.

Mao, J., Tang, S. and Zhi, Q. (2017) *China as a 'Developmental State' Miracle: Industrial Policy, Technological Change, and Productivity Growth*, Fudan University, Shanghai.

Mass, W. and Miyajima, H. (1993) 'The organization of the developmental state: fostering private capabilities and the roots of the Japanese "miracle"', *Business and Economic History* 22(1): 151–68.

Mayer, M. and Zhang, X. (2020) 'Theorizing China-world integration: sociospatial reconfigurations and the modern silk roads', *Review of International Political Economy*. Epub ahead of print 30 March 2020 <https://doi.org/10.1080/09692290.2020.1741424>.

McKee, S. (1934) *Papers on Public Credit, Commerce and Finance*, Colombia University Press, New York.

Ministry of Foreign Affairs (MOFA) (2015) *Cabinet Decision on the 2015 Development Cooperation Charter*, MOFA, Tokyo. Available from: https://www.mofa.go.jp/files/000067701.pdf [accessed 13 September 2020].

Ogawa, H. (2019) 'Normality of international norms: power, interests, and knowledge in Japan's ODA politics', *Journal of International Development Studies* 28(3): 5–18.

Ozawa, T. (2006) *Institutions, Industrial Upgrading, and Economic Performance in Japan: The 'Flying-Geese' Paradigm of Catch-Up Growth*, Edward Elgar, Cheltenham.

Renliang, L. (2016) *Dancing with the Dragon: The Trans-Asia Railway and its Impact on Thailand*, ISEAS Yusof Ishak Institute, Singapore.

Rodrik, D. (1994) 'King Kong meets Godzilla: the World Bank and the East Asian miracle', in: A. Fishlow, C. Gwin, S. Haggard and D. Rodrik (eds), *Miracle or Design? Lessons from the East Asian Experience*, Overseas Development Council, Washington, DC.

Rodrik, D. (1996) 'Understanding economic policy reform', *Journal of Economic Literature* 34(1): 9–41.

Rosser, A. (2020) 'The changing aid landscape and the political economy of development in Southeast Asia', in T. Carroll, S. Hameiri and L. Jones (eds), *The Political Economy of Southeast Asia*, pp. 293–314, Springer, Cham.

Rüland, J. (2020) 'Old wine in new bottles? How competitive connectivity revitalises an obsolete development agenda in Asia', *Journal of Contemporary Asia* 50(4): 653–65 <https://doi.org/10.1080/0047233 6.2019.1705878>.

Sakaki, A. (2019) *Japan-South Korea Relations: A Downward Spiral*, SWP Comment 2019/C 35, German Institute for International and Security Affairs, Berlin.

Sato, J. (2018) Triangular cooperation in East Asia: challenges and opportunities for Japanese official development assistance', *IDS Bulletin* 49(3): 111–28 <https://doi.org/10.19088/1968-2018.151>.

Sheridan, K. (1998) *Emerging Economic Systems in Asia: A Political and Economic Survey*, Allen & Unwin, London.

Shimomura, Y., Page, J. and Kato, H. (2016) *Japan's Development Assistance: Foreign Aid and the Post-2015 Agenda*, Palgrave Macmillan, New York.

Shleifer, A. and Vishny, R.W. (1998) *The Grabbing Hand: Government Pathologies and their Cures*, Harvard University Press, Cambridge, MA.

Srinivasan, T.N. (1985) 'Neoclassical political economy, the state and economic development', *Asian Development Review* 3: 38–58.

Stallings, B. and Kim, E.M. (2017) *Promoting Development: The Political Economy of East Asian Foreign Aid*, Springer, Singapore.

Takagi, S. (1995) *From Recipient to Donor, Japan's Official Aid Flows, 1945 to 1990 and Beyond*, Essays in International Finance, No. 196, Princeton University, Princeton, NJ.

Von Lübke, C. (1999) *Japan's Development Cooperation in Southeast Asia: An Assessment of the ODA Practice in Indonesia* (Master's thesis), University of Münster, Münster.

Wade, R. (1996) 'Japan, the World Bank, and the art of paradigm maintenance: the East Asian miracle in political perspective', *New Left Review* 217: 3–37.

Wallace, C. (2019) 'Japan's strategic contrast: continuing influence despite relative power decline in Southeast Asia', *The Pacific Review* 32(5): 863–97 <https://doi.org/10.1080/09512748.2019.1569115>.

Weber, M. (1925) *Wirtschaft und Gesellschaft*, Paul Siebeck Verlag, Tübingen.

Weber, M. (1947) *The Theory of Social and Economic Organization*, Oxford University Press, New York (trans. A. Henderson and T. Parsons).

Woo-Cumings, M. (1991) *Race to the Swift: State and Finance in Korean Industrialization*, Columbia University Press, New York.

World Bank (1993) *The East Asian Miracle: Economic Growth and Public Policy*, Oxford University Press, New York.

World Bank (2019) *Belt and Road Economics: Opportunities and Risks of Transport Corridors*, World Bank Group, Washington, DC.

Wunsch, J.S. and Olowu, D. (1990) *The Failure of the Centralized State: Institutions and Self-governance in Africa*, Westview Press, Boulder, CO.

Yasutomo, D.T. (1986) *The Manner of Giving: Strategic Aid and Japanese Foreign Policy*, Free Press, New York.

Yoshimatsu, H. (2017) 'Japan's export of infrastructure systems: pursuing twin goals through developmental means', *The Pacific Review* 30(4): 494–512 <https://doi.org/10.1080/09512748.2016.1276953>.

Zhang, F. (2018) 'The Chinese developmental state: standard accounts and new characteristics', *Journal of International Relations and Development* 21(2): 739–68 <https://doi.org/10.1057/s41268-017-0085-1>.

CHAPTER 3

# Decoding South Korea's development cooperation through the lens of developmental state politics: in search of symbiotic embeddedness

*Marieline Bader\* and Taekyoon Kim\*\**

## Introduction

The Republic of Korea (hereafter Korea or South Korea) can now look back at its first decade as a member of the Organization for Economic Cooperation and Development (OECD) Development Assistance Committee (DAC), which is not only an exclusive donor club of advanced economies but also a powerhouse in terms of creating international norms for development cooperation. Drawing on its own developmental path, in which the country made the successful transformation from aid recipient to donor country, Korea is recognized as a unique and impressive case, receiving much praise for achieving both rapid economic growth and democratic governance in a short period of time. The entailing increase in aid volume since Korea joined the OECD DAC in 2010 shows its proactive commitment to adhere to the international norms prescribed by the DAC. However, Korea's quantitative increase in official development assistance (ODA) is at odds with its qualitative and substantial performances. Korean ODA chronically suffers from the fragmentation among its planning and implementation agencies, weak or limited communication and engagement with civil society, a low ODA/gross national income (GNI) ratio, a comparatively high proportion of concessional loans and tied aid, as well as regional allocation preference over actual need-based geographical allocation.

The plethora of previous literature represents a growing interest in critically analysing Korea's aid policy, particularly in the course of its becoming an official member of the OECD DAC and afterwards. While some scholars analyse the quality and characteristics of Korean ODA (Chun et al., 2010; Patterson and Choi, 2019), others target the organizational and management culture, focusing on the fragmented aid architecture, the low qualities of Korean ODA, and limited aid effectiveness (Kim, 2011, 2016). An important common finding across the current research is that Korea's domestic and strategic interests seem to clash with the cosmopolitan visions of ODA policies, thereby generating dissonance between national interests and global norms, and making Korean ODA subject to criticism and constraints in terms of achieving aid effectiveness and taking up international norms (Marx and Soares, 2013). Other studies (e.g. Kalinowski and Park, 2016) have found that Korea's contemporary ODA system is still structured along the lines of the old and ongoing strong state–business alliance under state leadership. It could therefore be assumed that the 'old habits' of the Korean developmental state persist, and that the ODA thus helps to pursue the country's own national interests.

Despite the contention that Korea's developmental habitus, coupled with strong government intervention, spawns such discords between national interests and global aid principles, identifying how the underlying mechanisms of Korean developmentalism and supervised ODA projects have actually performed is a hitherto unexplored field. Both ideological and organizational fragmentation in the planning or implementing of Korea's ODA strongly point to a set of chronic problems inherent in its domestic developmental politics. This calls for the need to further identify the *institutional* sources for these persisting challenges.

Building upon the abovementioned setbacks and critics, this study contributes to the existing literature by placing Korea's ODA performance and fragmentation problems within the larger historical context of its own domestic developmental politics, specifically by viewing it through the lens of state–society relations whose institutional settings have evolved but remain stubbornly rigid. In reviewing the seeping of Korea's deep-seated developmentalism into its ODA policies at critical historical junctures, the present study detects Korea's developmental drift with regard to state–society dynamics. Specifically, this study includes the sociological concepts of 'embedded autonomy' and 'developmental citizenship' as theoretically central foundations which play an important role in understanding Korea's domestic developmental experiences and the working mechanisms within which its ODA policies were unconsciously framed. The paper also employs a critical review of Korea's developmental state at four historical stages. This functions as an effective filter for the country's ODA policies which can be seen as Korea's 'unfinished business', with the spectre of its own developmental past continuing to linger.

## Analytical framework: symbiotic embeddedness and historical institutionalism

The historically reproduced symbiosis between Korea's developmentalism at the national level and its development cooperation at the international level paved the way for the existing gap between Korea's global mission to comply with DAC rules and its actual implementation. The notion of 'symbiotic embeddedness' engendered between the developmental state and development cooperation is built conceptually as an institutional platform combining *reciprocity* exchanging conditions necessary to complement the activities of each partner and different *entrenchment* interlocking systems in the context of the developmental politics. The analytical strength of symbiotic embeddedness can be seen when two different systems are closely interconnected and mutually reinforcing for the sake of stable co-existence and development in a long-term relationship. These two systems involve multi-stakeholders, including the state, market, and civil society, beyond traditional symbiotic agents such as bureaucracies and the business sector, both of which much of the previous developmental state literature has taken for granted (Evans, 1995; Woo-Cumings, 1999; Kohli, 1999).

Accordingly, the symbiotic embeddedness contributes to expanding its conceptual inclusiveness, incorporating not only the notion of 'embedded autonomy', through which Evans (1995) highlights the combination of coherent internal private firms and the government's close links to business, but also 'mixed governance', thus confirming the hybrid effects of state–society relations on the institutional statecraft of the developmental government (Kim et al., 2011; Gainsborough, 2009). This concept eventually integrates another sociological concept, the concept of 'development citizenship', which marks an intersubjective intervention by the development state in the sense of the state's social engineering programme to drive its citizens into a pro-growth agenda and market-based citizenship (Chang, 2014; Lazar, 2015).

This study takes an interpretive approach, based on the framework of the symbiotic embeddedness, looking into the historical evolution of Korea's ODA in association with developmental politics to contextualize state–society relations embedded in its aid-induced developmental path. Such a middle-range method leads to the identification of historical institutionalism where Korea's aid agencies have reciprocated with developmental institutions and entrenched themselves under developmental politics either voluntarily or under duress. Analysing institutional arrangements, which were constructed at historic critical

**Table 3.1** Three dimensions and four critical junctures

| Historical junctures | Dimension | | |
|---|---|---|---|
| | Foreign aid as a discourse: how ODA visions are presented, politicized, and imposed | Structure of state apparatus: institutional processes for ODA decision-making | Composition of ODA: what ODA consists of |
| The formation of the Korean developmental state (1960–1986) | The birth of the Korean developmental state and the features of its success story. | | |
| ODA as a replication of developmental politics (1987–2004) | State–society relations during democratization process and the official creation of a legal basis for Korea's current ODA apparatus. | | |
| Unqualified ODA towards the OECD DAC (2005–2009) | ODA becomes an important foreign policy goal, strategic documents are developed, and civil society starts to get involved. | | |
| Consolidating the developmental power of economic developers (2010 and beyond) | Korea is committed to the global standards provided by the DAC, but the developmental habitus is still embedded in its ODA. | | |

*Source*: The authors

junctures, is an indispensable step towards recognizing the hybridity of developmental politics and developmentalist patterns in Korea's ODA policies, uncovering how the underlying apparatuses were created, and thus sustaining the symbiotic embeddedness of the country's development cooperation.

As can be seen in Table 3.1, three major dimensions – foreign aid as a discourse, structure of state apparatus, and composition of ODA – are used as a means to provide a fuller picture of the institutional mechanisms and developmental practices of Korea's ODA decision-making body. These in turn are analysed over four major historical periods covering the history of Korea's ODA: 1) the formation of Korea's development state (1960–1986); 2) the democratic transition and consolidation period (1987–2004); 3) the preparation period for DAC membership (2005–2009); and 4) the modernization period after Korea became a member of the DAC (2010 and beyond). In summary, the aim of this study is to provide a comprehensive historical overview of the symbiotic embeddedness of Korea's development cooperation and developmental politics, which, as far as we are aware, has not been attempted in any previous study.

## The formation of the Korean developmental state

The success of Korea's remarkable economic miracle and modernization is due to a committed and capable 'developmental state', a term coined by Johnson (1982) to describe a state employing policies primarily targeting economic growth. A key ingredient in Korea's developmental success was the strategic use of 'embedded autonomy' which determined how the Korean government coordinated the large foreign capital infusions it obtained as a recipient of development assistance. The state prioritized increasing production and providing subsidies for selected industries, while businesses benefited from the close cooperation with the state. While the state tried to lure businesses to support its developmental policies via preferential policies and programmes, which gave them exclusive rights to dominate a market and thus establish a monopoly, *chaebols*, large industrial conglomerates run by an individual or family, acted as strategic instruments of the government's industrial policies. Such a symbiotic alliance between the state and the *chaebols* is precisely what made Korea's developmental path so effective, as it established a triangular relationship between the state and the *chaebol* and was financed by the political and strategic marriage between these two players, both seeking economic transformation. Evans (1995: 234) wrote that 'in developmental states, connectedness has meant ties with industrial elites'; however, his idea of embedded autonomy is limited to a business-focused symbiosis and fails to include the other stakeholders in civil society.

A well-functioning financial management apparatus must be in place in order to acquire and distribute large sums of foreign capital loans. While the war-torn Rhee Syngman administration (1948–1960) lacked the institutional capacity and commitment to handle such foreign funds, the Park Chung-hee administration (1961–1979) was more determined in its efforts to effectively manage foreign assistance (Kim, 2013). Accordingly, Park reorganized the state bureaucracy and, with the primary objective of economic development, introduced the Five-Year Economic Development Plans and nationalized the banks. Park also centralized the procedural and policy framework, establishing the Economic Planning Board (EPB) and its Bureau of Economic Cooperation. The establishment of the EPB, together with the existing Ministry of Finance (MOF) and the Ministry of Trade and Industry (MOTI), created a three-pillar apparatus with the responsibility of orchestrating Korea's capital and industrial development policies. Strongly backed by Park, the EPB remained the most powerful and privileged ministry in regard to the handling and controlling of foreign concessional loans or foreign direct investments while the other two ministries functioned as backup in support of the EPB.

The EPB leadership was further consolidated by merging various government departments. This gave the EPB more power to manage financial resources, and Park appointed an assistant minister to the EPB who was soon promoted to deputy prime minister. EPB managers were given leadership positions in other planning ministries, which ensured a widespread and publicly accepted power over budgetary processes on economic policies (Evans, 1995). In short, combining the bureaucratic tradition and some cohesive power among elitist state officials empowered the EPB as an effective powerhouse over financial resources. The dynamic of Korea's strategic set-up went as far as to incorporate 'quasi-governmental research institutes', particularly the Korean Development Institute (KDI), to advance the government-led national development plans. The KDI, established by the EPB in 1971, received government funding in order to support the government's and businesses' symbiotic partnerships for growth-led developmentalism.

Korea's obsession with achieving economic growth during Park's military rule fostered a very particular form of interaction between the state and its citizens. An overarching concept that explains this particular relationship in Korea is related to developmental citizenship as a feature of developmentalist regimes in which the state constantly ensures economic growth, new markets, and jobs for its citizens, while only providing limited social rights and social welfare protection (Chang, 2014). This leaves both state officials and citizens in a mode in which their foremost concern is centred on achieving economic development and attaining material success. This is known as developmental politics. Citizens' values, activities, and rights become dependent on the all-out mobilization for economic development, while the state has the unspoken duty to ensure this development, thereby turning into a 'de facto political contract between citizenry and the state' and providing grounds for legitimizing the state's repressive, authoritarian rule (Chang, 2012: 188). Development citizenship goes hand-in-hand with a government's ability to co-opt even foreign charity organizations, which helped Korea's government to share the public burden of welfare provision after the Korean War.

Another aspect of this particular state–citizen relationship was the inability of civil society to challenge the repressive, authoritarian state and fight for social justice and welfare provision (Amsden, 1989: 423). Park's authoritarian government used the Korea Central Intelligence Agency and police force to maintain tight control over labour groups, students, and intellectuals. Historically, civil society has had a hard time voicing their opinions and thus influencing the government's decision-making processes. The reasons for this are, on the one hand, because of the top-down, non-democratic, and repressive governments of the past, and, on the other, because there was limited political space for civil society in a domestic political structure that favoured state–business ties (Kalinowski and Cho, 2012).

Indeed, during the phase of planned economic growth since the 1960s, the Korean developmental state has come to govern its people in terms of developmental arrangements between the state and society. The two concepts of embedded autonomy and developmental citizenship play a crucial role as key mechanisms for Korea's rapid economic growth. They not only determined the way Korea executed its financial and industrial policies, namely by using an authoritarian, top-down style and state–market symbiosis, but also created a peculiar relationship between the state and the citizenry. In this relationship, the majority of the people became dependent on the state's focus on economic growth which restricted the political space for welfare policies and participatory democracy.

## ODA as a replication of developmental politics

The Korean government's official version of the origin of the contemporary ODA system highlights that the country started giving aid in the 1960s as part of a USAID triangular cooperation programme. The real origins, however, can be found in the Chun Doo-hwan administration (1980–1988), during which the government not only used South–South Cooperation as a 'tool for the Cold War statecraft to compete against North Korea in an effort to secure official diplomatic ties', but also performed 'aid-like' activities to secure political and economic interests for themselves, such as export markets for Korea's businesses (Kim, 2016: 92). However, it was not until 1987 that the MOF first established the Economic Development Cooperation Fund (EDCF) to handle concessional loans and entrusted the EDCF to the Export-Import Bank of Korea (Eximbank), thus laying the first legal basis for Korea's current ODA apparatus. The government funnelled KRW 30 bn (US$38 m) to the public policy fund mainly for the purpose of assisting industrialization and economic development in low-income countries (Chun et al., 2010: 791). Later, in 1991, the Korea International Cooperation Agency (KOICA), a government agency under the Ministry of Foreign Affairs and Trade (MOFAT) in charge of grants-based projects, was established. The KOICA, together with the EDCF, marked the beginning of the two-pillar system that divided aid into grants and loans.

Korea's ODA activities started to emerge in a political setting marked by growing protests from civil society against the oppressive state. The social and political developments demanded by civil society posed a threat to the capitalist *chaebols*, as ordinary citizens started not only to insist on fair democratic elections, but also to seek justice and better working conditions for all citizens. 1987 marked the end of military rule and the beginning of the democratization process. While pro-democratic movements were mainstreamed within civil society, the Roh Tae-woo regime (1988–1993) did not push for any changes in the mutually reinforcing state–business relationship and the state's pro-business approach. With the onset of economic liberalization under the Kim Young-sam administration (1993–1998), Kim pledged fearless targets for economic reform, reminiscent of the authoritarianism period, but carelessly deregulated financial flows, allowing *chaebol*-affiliated enterprises to recklessly borrow and invest, thereby driving Korea into the 1997 financial crisis. With the shift towards neoliberal policies and the acceptance of IMF structural reforms, the theory and model of the interventionist developmental state seemed doomed to collapse (Woo-Cumings, 1999). Some scholars even predicted the end of the Korean developmental state altogether (Pirie, 2008).

In 1994, the former EPB merged with the MOF. This meant that the responsibility for handling Korea's foreign aid budget was transferred from the triple economic group – EPB, MOTI, and MOF – to two major ministries, MOFAT (today's Ministry of Foreign Affairs (MOFA)) and MOF (today's Ministry of Strategy and Finance (MOSF)). The establishment of the two agencies, EDCF under MOF and KOICA under MOFAT, laid the foundation for Korea's ODA apparatus. However, the merging of EPB and MOF ended up engineering MOF as the big brother in terms of handling of foreign budget-related affairs. Lumsdaine and Schopf (2007) claim that the low quality and quantity of Korea's ODA resulted from the negative combination of Korea's weak emphasis on humanitarian motives as a rationale for giving aid and the underdevelopment of its own civil society, which was still green in the civic value of giving. This combination created incentives for aid to be solely a government affair connected with concrete strategic interests, such as gaining political support for entering the UN, its international status as a member nation, as well as establishing better trade relations with developing countries. Such commercialized incentives became noticeable in the way concessional loans were distributed by Eximbank's non-ODA specialists, with less favourable loan terms than those of other OECD DAC members and with aid being funnelled towards social overhead capital projects – mainly to Korea's trading partners and Southeast Asia – in order to spur Korea's exports.

Korea remained an ODA recipient until as late as 2000 when it was removed from the DAC's ODA recipient list, having been taken off the World Bank lending list in 1995. Another driving force behind Korea's increased ODA after the turn of the century was as an exchange for US security (Kim, 2011). Highly reliant upon the US security umbrella, Seoul had little choice but to adhere to Washington's expectations, which explains Korea's increasing ODA flows to Afghanistan and Iraq at the start of the new millennium. However, a major shift in thinking occurred among democratic governments in favour of increasing ODA as a result of the more humanitarian and progressive policies under the Kim Dae-jung (1998–2003) and Roh Moo-hyun (2003–2008) administrations (Lumsdaine and Schopf, 2007). While Kim advocated a 32:68 grant-loan ratio in 2002, the ratio under the Roh administration shifted to 59:41 in 2005 and reached a 73:26 grant-loan ratio in 2007. Similarly, the untied aid ratio from 2001 to 2006 never rose above 5 per cent, but jumped to 24.7 per cent in 2007 and has been increasing ever since (Prime Minister's Office, 2014).

In essence, the democratic progression of developmental politics was reproduced within the contentious politics of Korea's ODA policy. Although democratic governments seized power in the late 1990s and civil society organizations (CSOs) have been mushrooming since then, Korea's political, social, and economic settings blew hot and cold, and administrations were preoccupied with the handling of the economy to secure stable growth. Saving the economy at all costs remained the primary goal of the state, which invoked the ghost of developmental politics, and thus reinforced the power of *chaebols* and directly influenced the everyday lives of citizens. Developmental citizenship led state–society relations to be tailored, above all, for the maintenance of Korea's economic sustainability and also left little space for citizens to advocate for philanthropic donations or develop any systematic notion of ODA as global social assistance. As such, even in the post-financial crisis era, Korean ODA remained a state-only affair, used as a means of pushing political and economic national interests for both the state and businesses. At this historical juncture, Korea's ODA was regarded as an extended arm of its developmental politics, where ODA appeared reactive to the internally democratized circumstances of the 'democratic developmental state', whereby CSOs were more broadly being included in ODA-related activities (Robinson and White, 1998).

## Unqualified ODA towards the OECD DAC

The years following 2005 provided new momentum for Korean ODA. With the Roh government actively seeking OECD DAC membership, ODA was repositioned as an important foreign policy goal. Another factor was civil society's recognition of the qualitative and quantitative shortcomings of Korean ODA. This led to the establishment of the Korean NGOs' Network Against Global Poverty in June 2005, whose common goal was to pressure the government to improve its ODA policies (Kim, 2006). In November 2005, the government took the initiative in preparing the Comprehensive Plan for Improving ODA, which laid out major ODA policy directions and strategies and proposed establishing the ODA Framework Act as well as setting up a coherent and integrated ODA system. Based on this Comprehensive Plan, in January 2006 the Roh government formed the Committee for International Development Cooperation (CIDC) under the Prime Minister's Office, with the Prime Minister acting as chair. This institutional arrangement was undertaken to overcome the fragmented ODA state apparatuses, with the CIDC becoming the overarching decision-making body. However, the ministerial selfishness of MOSF and MOFA, in the end, hampered the CIDC from living up to its initial purpose.

In 2006, Roh pushed for 'Korea's Initiative for Africa's Development' with the aim of diversifying the geographical concentration of aid towards African countries. This included a pledge to triple Korea's ODA to Africa to US$100 m by 2008 (Jung, 2006). While the government was expressing this ambitious plan to increase ODA to Africa, we suggest that the real purpose of the ODA might have been a means to tap Africa's natural resources under the emerging 'resource diplomacy' strategy. Despite some geographical reorientation and Korea's explicit wish to join the OECD DAC in the coming years, Korean ODA at that time deviated significantly from DAC norms and standards. Despite Korea's position as one of the largest economies in the world, its ODA contribution only amounted to 0.074 per cent of GNI in 2007, the lowest among all DAC member countries. Also, the low-quality characteristics of Korea's ODA – heavily bilateral, tied, and loan-based aid with a strong geographical priority for Asia – remained unchanged, which led to various Korean CSOs, such as People's Solidarity for Participatory Democracy, raising their concerns over Korea's stingy and negative image as a donor preoccupied with its own national interests.

When Lee Myung-bak (2008–2013) took office amid the 2007–2008 financial crisis, the general tone in domestic and foreign policies became more conservative. Lee's pro-business stance, giving beneficial tax rates to the high-income bracket (especially *chaebols*), focused on achieving national growth through corporate expansion and hoping for a trickle-down effect. Such economic-growth revitalization projects, such as the Four River Project and the Green Growth Strategy, however, not only resulted in the bipolarization of the economy – such as labour market liberalization vis-à-vis a worsening welfare system – but also further increased the wealth and power of the already super-wealthy *chaebols*. For this reason, Lee's presidential term came to be described as a 'new right-wing developmental state' (Suh and Kwon, 2014). His pledge that Korea would contribute to the global movement for peace and development by actively participating in UN peacekeeping operations and increasing its ODA to developing countries seemed in contrast with his administration's conservative tone. Korea promised to work cooperatively towards achieving the Millennium Development Goals (MDGs) via its foreign aid programmes. Yet it wanted to do so using 'our growing economic capabilities' and by strengthening 'economic cooperation with developing countries in a way that augments opportunities for Korean companies and for accessing energy and natural resources' (Office of the President, 2009: 30). This commercialized preference was in line with Lee's domestic and foreign policy as 'resource diplomacy', 'creative pragmatism' and his pro-business attitudes that rested on maximizing the benefits of invested costs and adopted the heavy use of loans and tied aid (OECD, 2018b: 9).

Lee also ambitiously promised to increase Korea's ODA to 0.25 per cent of GNI by 2015 to support the eradication of poverty and achieve the MDGs (MOFAT, 2009: 211). However, Lee's initiative ironically encountered strong resistance from MOSF, whose ministerial influences were strengthened by Lee's conservative developmentalism, thus giving it additional budgeting power thanks to the merger between the Ministry of Planning and Budget and MOF. MOSF's monopoly over budgetary power would coerce any budgetary decisions on ODA to meet due processes with MOSF, make it increasingly difficult for MOFAT to negotiate on equal terms, and worsen the already-existing fragmentation between MOFAT and MOSF. Such a fragmented structure was problematic as it hindered the institutionalization of a more integrated and effective aid system, thereby keeping developmental politics at the centre of Korea's ODA and enhancing MOSF's powerful position of stipulating commercial interests for ODA. This unequal power relationship also led to disagreements between government officials in MOSF and MOFAT regarding the willingness to join the DAC. MOSF, in particular, believed that complying with DAC norms seemed unrealistic, as Korean businesses specifically would not welcome untied aid (Kim, 2011: 815). Consequently, the structure of its ODA decision-making body rarely suggested that the internal 'embedded politics' should be removed from Korea's ODA.

Despite this, Korea's continued developmental politics, cultivated by MOSF and businesses, became more balanced as civil society became more interested and involved in ODA in the latter half of the 2000s. One of the influential CSOs and emerging development networks is the People's Solidarity for Participatory Democracy (PSPD), originally founded in 1994 to provide a civic voice for participatory democracy, promoting citizen's participation in government decision-making processes and socio-economic reforms. In 2008, the PSPD posted a collective position paper from Korean NGOs, co-written by multiple CSO representatives, in the *OECD DAC Special Review* focusing on several changes that would help civil society become more integrated in ODA decision-making and implementation processes (PSPD, 2008). Along with the PSPD, the People's Initiative for Development Alternatives (PIDA) is noteworthy. Originally established in 2009 as ODA Watch, PIDA closely monitors ODA policies and proposes alternative approaches to the government's aid policy. They proactively push for more accountable and effective ODA decision-making processes and have become a major watchdog regarding Korea's ODA. Despite these gains, such civic attempts to challenge developmental citizenship, however, still run on empty in Korean civil society, because only very few CSOs exert themselves on political advocacy confronting the nationalist developmentalism of Korea's ODA (Nauta et al., 2021).

### Consolidating the developmental power of economic developers

Korea's accession to the OECD DAC in January 2010 presented another critical juncture for scaling up its ODA. The membership not only set the legal basis for Korea conforming to DAC norms, but also provided the country with political opportunities for bigger spotlights of attention, both inside and outside Korea. Korea's entry into the DAC was publicly advertised as a success story: a country that made the transition from recipient to donor. In July 2010, the Framework Act on International Development Cooperation and the Presidential Decree on International Development Cooperation were promulgated, becoming the legal basis for establishing an integrated ODA policy-making and implementation system under the CIDC's legitimate power. Korea put development issues on the agenda of a G20 Summit for the first time in 2011, resulting in the adaption of the 'Seoul Development Consensus for Shared Growth' as well as the Multi-year Action Plan on Development. In that same year, Korea also took on a leadership role by hosting the Fourth High-Level Forum (HLF-4) on Aid Effectiveness in Busan.

This makes the contradiction between the legal set-up of Korea's ODA-related agencies and its qualitative performances even more puzzling. Korea's chronic problems, rooted in its fragmented ODA implementation structure and the low quality of ODA per se, have come to have direct constraints on aid effectiveness and account-ability. The *Shadow Report 2015*, a CSO report on Korea's progress and performance as an OECD DAC member, presented an overview of key findings and recommendations by comparing the *OECD DAC Peer Review 2012* with recent governmental implementation policies including the *Mid-term ODA Policy for 2016–2020*. This report also confirmed that the *OECD DAC Peer Review 2012* received only limited attention from the Korean government and led to very little progress, particularly in terms of policy coherence for development and fragmented aid systems (ODA Watch and ReDI, 2015). It is worthwhile to make note of the assumption that behind the chronic embeddedness of Korea's ODA development politics lie important economic reasons, institutions, and beliefs based upon Korea's unfinished business with its own developmentalism.

Korea's fragmented two-pillar architecture, which divided the management of loans and grants into MOSF and MOFA respectively, has long been a subject of concern. The establishment of the CIDC in 2006 failed to create any genuine effects on the coordination of policy between grants and loans, and the 2010 Framework Act, another legal attempt to concentrate a more coherent coordination mechanism for planning and budgeting on the CIDC, also has only limited capacity to regulate MOSF and MOFA via the CIDC. Korea's fragmented aid system not only suffers from this loan–grant division of labour by the two ministries, but also from an interlinked complex of fragmentation, which is characterized by a lack of coordination among decision-making bodies, ministries, and governmental and non-governmental organizations. This only aggravates the competition between agencies over financial resources and over the power to leverage the ODA budget. The lack of guidance and expertise in the CIDC eventually triggers them to avoid taking on responsibility as the highest priority.

More concretely, the MOSF, which is primarily staffed with financial experts, enjoys a super-ministry status to the extent that even the Prime Minister's Office is required to obtain MOSF approval for its management budget. The MOSF's super-power status goes so far that the MOSF-integrated Budget Office even has veto power on both grants and loans that do not match with MOSF's criteria. This powerful intervention directly impairs key CIDC functions as some ministries do not even attempt to get approval for their projects from inter-agency grant committees, but rather go directly to the MOSF for budget requests (OECD, 2012: 48). The MOSF's almighty power can be confirmed by the fact that MOSF modified KOICA's budgetary support for CSOs from 'endowments' to 'government subsidies' in order to be able to directly oversee civic engagement in ODA projects by bypassing MOFA and KOICA.

The centrality of MOSF and its resultant power struggle within the government mark the ingrained habitus of Korea's ODA architecture, which can be recapitulated with its view on loans for infrastructure development to achieve economic growth as a direct legacy from the developmental state era. Understanding these developmental dynamics requires us to further re-examine the consolidation of state power via the following two specific characteristics regarding the OECD DAC's far-off characterization of Korea's aid modalities.

The first character of MOSF's developmental hegemony is unravelled if we take a look at the Knowledge Sharing Program (KSP). In 2004, MOSF, in collaboration with KDI, launched KSP, which aimed to share Korea's development experience and knowledge with partner countries via policy consultations and capacity-building in the form of trainings, workshops, and seminars tailored to their specific needs. Beyond delivering aid on a large scale, proponents of this knowledge transfer characterize KSP as a distinctive form of Korea's ODA-based contributions and emphasize its missionary functions. Strategically speaking, KSP-based technical cooperation is designed to brand the distinctive Korean style of ODA in a world of competing ODA paradigms and construct a new unique identity as an aid-recipient-turned-donor. Both MOSF and KDI continued to upgrade KSP by modularizing its development experiences via documenting policies, implementation practices and their outcomes, and processes of institution building. All of this was meant to reflect Korea's economic development triumphs, particularly in the areas of economic policy, administration/ICT, agriculture, health and medicine, industrial energy, human resources, land development, and the environment (Lim, 2014).

What is at issue is that Korea's experiences are shared not only with the developing countries listed in the OECD DAC, but with all international players and donor countries interested in KSP, such as Saudi Arabia. The open selling of Korea's development experiences to non-developing countries, coupled with the fact that KSP is a grant-based programme under the auspices of MOSF (which is ordinarily responsible for loans), suggests strategic policy interests beyond development aid and a commercialized nature of KSP. While the *ODA White Paper 2014* lauds the plan to link KSP with concessional loans as an effort to integrate grants and loans for better aid effectiveness (Prime Minister's Office, 2014: 58), this linkage attempt is seen as more problematic as policy consulting would be combined with an actual loan project and sold as a 'package service' (Kalinowski and Cho, 2012). The trace of developmental politics is also corroborated by the fact that the main organizers of KSP are MOSF-appointed former economic policy-makers and former high-level investors. It is not surprising that the grant-based KSP would be criticized for being heavily focused on the economic aspects of Korea's development experience, while neglecting social aspects, and its lack of adequate responses to local needs (OECD, 2012: 30).

Second, Korea's high level of tied aid compared to its DAC peers has been viewed negatively by domestic NGOs and the international community. Generally, the problem with tied aid is donors' strategically using aid to achieve their own economic aims, as the tied funds favour businesses in the donor country in the process of procurement, thus giving the donor country more control over funds. In fact, Korea made continuous efforts to untie aid, by becoming a signatory to the 2005 Paris Declaration on Aid Effectiveness and the 2008 Accra Agenda for Action, both of which highlighted the importance of untying aid, and by hosting the HLF-4 with the Busan Outcome Document (BOD) which also encouraged donors to untie aid. Nevertheless, Korea fell short of meeting the pledged benchmark ratio of untied aid (75 per cent by 2015) to least developed countries and heavily indebted poor countries in 2014 (58 per cent), followed by an even lower ratio in 2015 (49 per cent), and is still far from meeting the DAC average (83.5 per cent) of untied aid (OECD, 2018a). Changing Korea's untied aid persistently proves to be a difficult task and has continually been a main target of reform efforts in DAC peer reviews as well as CSO statements (ODA Watch and ReDI, 2015).

Meanwhile, Korean aid has also been criticized due to its over-reliance on project aid. Project-based aid is problematic not only because the 'stand-alone' projects are implemented in an isolated manner without integrating the recipient's own institutions, but also due to its purpose-specific nature, such as seeking specific industries or sectors that would create export opportunities. Loan-based projects have received even stronger criticism in that developing countries are reduced to the status of debtors, while donors earn high profits by employing high power in the aid industry. The OECD DAC therefore recommended improving Korea's aid effectiveness by conducting more programme-based aid and enhancing country system-based aid (OECD, 2018a: 83). DAC recommendations remind us of the historically influential *chaebols* whose power persists today via tied and loan-based aid projects. Korea's consistently high ratio of loan-based projects is nothing more than a display of businesses' powerful position compared to civil society and the business-centric attitude of the government, which ultimately illustrates maintaining state–market symbiosis for strategic interests.

## Improved participatory approach while remaining top-down

Following Korea's DAC membership, the Korea Civil Society Forum on International Development Cooperation – consisting of inter alia PSPD and PIDA – was established in 2010 in order to provide a platform for CSOs to promote more effective and accountable development cooperation (Nauta et al., 2021). The golden age of Korean CSOs, associated with issues of development cooperation, came as late as the 2010s, particularly in relation to the 2011 HLF-4, which offered CSOs new opportunities to get their voices heard. The resulting BOD officially recognized the important role of CSOs in international development and promised to enable CSOs as actors in their own right. As a logical outgrowth of this trend, official government documents, such as the *Mid-term ODA Policy 2011–2015* and *ODA White Paper 2014*, clearly state that the Korean government recognizes civil society as partners on equal terms and holds regular policy meetings with groups in this sector as a means of increasing communication with the public. In 2018, CSOs and the government finally formed a mutual partnership by co-signing the long-awaited Policy Framework for Government-Civil Society Partnership in International Development Cooperation, which was presented as the formal beginning of a more structured and synergetic relationship between government and civil society.

The government's formal recognition of CSOs notwithstanding, Korean ODA is still criticized for not sufficiently integrating CSOs at both ends of the policy-making process and the project implementation. Although ODA channelled through and to CSOs has increased in terms of volume, it remains the same (2.3 per cent) as a share of bilateral ODA, which sharply differs from the OECD DAC average (17.4 per cent) (OECD, 2016). Indeed, the state–society synergy for Korean ODA still remains within the public authority, where purpose-specific and selective consultation with civil society is the norm. Despite some positive changes towards development CSOs, advocacy NGOs have yet to become fully involved in Korea's ODA policy-making and implementation processes, which is still far from being an approach based on truly inclusive multi-stakeholder partnerships.

Another characteristic of Korea's ODA institutions is exemplified by the rebirth of developmentalist memories from the developmental state era. Under the Park Geun-hye administration (2013–2017), the national policy paradigm shifted from Lee's 'resource diplomacy' or 'green growth' to Park's 'creative economy' or 'disciplined market economy', with the national goal being to create jobs and inclusive growth (MOFAT, 2014: 200). Although the underlying focus on developmental politics did not differ much from Lee's policies, Park's presidential vision for ODA, namely the revitalization of the Saemaul

Movement, rose to the top of the green-growth agenda in Lee's green ODA strategy. In fact, the new focus on the Saemaul Movement failed to present anything new other than renaming the already existing KOICA-led rural community development project as the Saemaul tradition for popularizing Park's agenda. Reincarnating the Saemaul Movement as the new ODA paradigm would not be interpreted as just an arbitrary decision if placed in a personal context with Park, as the campaign called to mind nostalgic memories of Park's late father, Park Chung-hee, who launched the rural-based modernization project during Korea's own developmentalist period. The Saemaul Movement was reborn as not only an international brand of 'Korean ODA', but as a flagship model to be transferred to developing countries.

While the Korean government was eager to sell the Saemaul Movement as a model which other developing countries could learn from, its marketable contents focused on Saemaul's philosophical values of 'diligence', 'self-help', and 'cooperation', all of which drove the development project back in the 1970s. Although developing countries are very enthusiastic about localizing the Saemaul project, the lessons learned and the marketization of the Korean model become more ambiguous when putting Korea's experience into various historical contexts (Douglass, 2014). The Saemaul project has been criticized for presenting mystifying ideas about its actual experience and thus remains largely a 'buzzword' without evaluating its clear position on Korea's ODA. While some come to hail the Saemaul experience and benefit from it, others experience it as a top-down and oppressive act by the government based on strategic and economic interests. Regardless of whether the developmental legacy of the Saemaul ghost is revived as a logical product of Park's intention to sell and justify its previous mobilization campaign, the modernized Global Saemaul Movement is an example of Korea's essential developmentalism. Accordingly, we now know the state remains at the centre of policy planning, as it is possible to redirect the focus of Korea's ODA policy with every new presidential election.

## Conclusion: symbiotic embeddedness in the developmental context

The symbiotic embeddedness between the state and businesses in the period of the Korean developmental state has been isomorphically replicated in a parallel form between Korea's aid policy and its developmental politics. Decoding the symbiotic embeddedness of Korea's ODA architecture in the developmental context requires a historical overview of how the developmental legacies were anchored in the democratized circle of governmental agencies designing and implementing ODA projects even after Korea had become a DAC member in 2010. This study is not aimed to belittle the Korean government's efforts to incorporate CSOs and civic networks as key stakeholders for inclusive partnerships, but was undertaken to verify the social origins of developmentalism within the area of Korea's ODA.

The new inclusive partnership paradigm after the Sustainable Development Goals of 2015 has made the development discourse more inclusive. Development becomes the business of a wider public, including CSOs and academia, but also of a wider private sector, given that it leaves enough space for governments to attempt to promote the interests of large-scale conglomerates and other Korean businesses. Since Korea is now being more and more pressured to adhere to the DAC standards by untying aid, public–private partnerships seem to offer a back door for private firms to sustain their involvement. At the same time, the inclusive partnership paradigm legitimizes Korea's win-win rhetoric, as private business involvement in development cooperation cannot possibly only be about non-profitable voluntary and generous acts. While benefits resulting from public–private partnerships are not exclusively a Korean matter, it nevertheless reaffirms Korea's developmentalist legacy of a market–state symbiosis that has never left the scene.

Consequently, escaping from developmentalism by inviting global universalism into Korea's ODA industry calls for a full-scale surgery, democratizing all players involved in Korea's aid projects, long tamed by developmental citizenship and the embedded autonomy of the state. However, it is an encouraging move that the active participation of CSOs in the state's once exclusive aid policies, offers civil society the opportunity to collectively challenge the lingering presence of developmentalism in the non-developmentalist agenda of helping low-income countries abroad. Despite the positive aspect of civic engagement, the Korean state still sustains developmental grounds to legitimize its interventionist top-down rule in development cooperation via the complementary symbiosis embedded in society for the state to achieve its developmental objectives by acting through non-state actors in the form of mixed governance.

## Notes

[*]    Responsible Programs and Project Manager of 'Refugees Go Solar+' at the Solafrica in Switzerland. marieline.bader@solafrica.ch

[**]    Professor of International Development at the Graduate School of International Studies, Seoul National University, South Korea. oxonian07@snu.ac.kr

# References

Amsden, A. (1989) *Asia's Next Giant: South Korea and Late Industrialization*, Oxford University Press, Oxford.

Chang, K. (2012) 'Predicaments of neoliberalism in the post-developmental liberal context', in K. Chang, B. Fine, and L. Weiss (eds), *Developmental Politics in Transition: The Neoliberal Era and Beyond*, pp 70–91, Palgrave Macmillan, New York.

Chang, K. (2014) *South Korea in Transition: Politics and Culture of Citizenship*, Routledge, Abingdon.

Chun, H., Munyi, E.N. and Lee, H. (2010) 'South Korea as an emerging donor: challenges and changes on its entering OECD/DAC', *Journal of International Development* 22(6): 788–802 <https://doi.org/10.1002/jid.1723>.

Douglass, M. (2014) 'The Saemaul Undong in historical perspective and in the contemporary world', in I. Yi, and T. Mkandawire (eds), *Learning from the South Korean Developmental Success: Effective Developmental Cooperation and Synergistic Institutions and Policies*, pp. 136–71, Palgrave Macmillan, Basingstoke.

Evans, P.B. (1995) *Embedded Autonomy: States and Industrial Transformation*, Princeton University Press, Princeton, NJ.

Gainsborough, M. (2009) 'The (neglected) statist bias and the developmental state: the case of Singapore and Vietnam', *Third World Quarterly* 30(7): 1317–28 <https://doi.org/10.1080/01436590903134957>.

Johnson, C. (1982) *MITI and the Japanese Miracle: The Growth of Industrial Policy, 1925–1975*, Stanford University Press, Stanford, CA.

Jung, Y. (2006) 'No bragging for Korea's Africa initiative', *Dong-A Ilbo*, 13 March [online] <http://www.donga.com/news/article/all/20060313/8284058/1> [accessed 5 January 2021].

Kalinowski, T. and Cho, H. (2012) 'Korea's search for a global role between hard economic interests and soft power', *European Journal of Development Research* 24(2): 242–60 <https://doi.org/10.1057/ejdr.2012.7>.

Kalinowski, T. and Park, M.J. (2016) 'South Korean development cooperation in Africa: the legacy of a developmental state', *Africa Spectrum* 51(3): 61–75 <https://doi.org/10.1177/000203971605100303>.

Kim, D. (2006) 'Concrete action needed on domestic social welfare and foreign aid policies', *Social Watch's National Reports*, Social Watch, Montevideo.

Kim, S. (2011) 'Bridging troubled worlds? An analysis of the ethical case for South Korean aid', *Journal of International Development* 23(6): 802–22 <http://doi.org/10.1002/jid.1811>.

Kim, S. (2016) 'Tracing the roots and domestic sources of Korea's ODA: Aid as a Cold War statecraft for a middle income country', *Journal of International Cooperation Studies* 24(1): 87–102 <https://doi.org/10.24546/81009638>.

Kim, T. (2013) 'Translating foreign aid policy locally: Korea's modernization process revisited', *Asian Perspective* 37(3): 409–36 <https://doi.org/10.1353/apr.2013.0016>.

Kim, T., Kwon, H., Lee, J. and Yi, I. (2011) 'Poverty, inequality, and democracy: "mixed governance" and welfare in South Korea', *Journal of Democracy* 22(3): 120–34 <https://doi.org/10.1353/jod.2011.0037>.

Kohli, A. (1999) 'Where do high-growth political economies come from? The Japanese lineage of Korea's "developmental state"', in M. Woo-Cumings (ed.), *The Developmental State*, pp. 93–136, Cornell University Press, Ithaca, NY.

Lazar, S. (2015) 'Citizenship quality: A new agenda for development?', in T. Kontinen and H. Onodera (eds), *Citizenship, Civil Society and Development: Interconnections in a Global World*, pp. 7–24, Routledge, Abingdon.

Lim, W. (2014) 'Beyond one-time, one-sided knowledge transfer: KSP with the Dominican Republic', *Analysis of Development Policy and International Cooperation* 1(1): 95–119.

Lumsdaine, D. and Schopf, J.C. (2007) 'Changing value in Korean development assistance', *The Pacific Review* 20(2): 221–55 <https://doi.org/10.1080/09512740701306881>.

Marx, A. and Soares, J. (2013) 'South Korea's transition from recipient to DAC donor: assessing Korea's development cooperation policy', *International Development Policy* 4(2): 107–42 <https://doi.org/10.4000/poldev.1535>.

Ministry of Foreign Affairs, Republic of Korea (MOFAT) (2009) *Diplomatic White Paper 2009*, MOFAT, Seoul.

MOFAT (2014) *Diplomatic White Paper 2014*, MOFAT, Seoul.

Nauta, W., Han, J. and Kim, T. (2021) 'Inspiring democratic progress in development assistance: South Korea's aid policy reforms via civic engagement', *Forum for Development Studies* 48(2): 309–30 <https://doi.org/10.1080/08039410.2021.1907784>.

ODA Watch and ReDI (2015) *Shadow Report: On Korea's Progress in the OECD Development Assistance Committee (DAC), Peer Review Recommendations*, ODA Watch and ReDI, Seoul.

Organisation for Economic Co-operation and Development (OECD) (2012) *Korea – DAC Peer Reviews of Development Co-operation, 2012*, OECD Development Co-operation Directorate, Paris.

OECD (2016) *Development Co-operation Report 2016: The Sustainable Development Goals as Business Opportunities*, OECD, Paris.

OECD (2018a) *OECD Development Co-operation Peer Reviews: Korea 2018*, OECD, Paris.

OECD (2018b) *DAC Special Review: Development Cooperation of the Republic of Korea*, OECD, Paris.

Office of the President (2009) *Global Korea: The National Security Strategy of the Republic of Korea*, Office of the President, Seoul.

Patterson, D. and Choi, J. (2019) 'Policy and practice in ODA disbursements: an analysis of changes in South Korea's official development assistance'. *Journal of East Asian Studies* 19(2): 239–64 <https://doi.org/10.1017/jea.2019.17>.

People's Solidarity for Participatory Democracy (PSPD) (2008) *Position Paper of Korean NGOs*, PSPD, Seoul.

Pirie, I. (2008) *The Korean Developmental State: From Dirigisme to Neo-liberalism*, Routledge, Abingdon.

Prime Minister's Office (2014) *ODA White Paper 2014*, Prime Minister's Office, Seoul.

Robinson, M. and White, G. (1998) *The Democratic Developmental State: Political and Institutional Design*, Oxford University Press, Oxford.

Suh, C. and Kwon, S. (2014) 'Whither the developmental state in South Korea? Balancing welfare and neoliberalism', *Asian Studies Review* 38(4): 676–92 <https://doi.org/10.1080/10357823.2014.963509>.

Woo-Cumings, M. (1999) 'Introduction: Chalmers Johnson and the politics of nationalism and development', in M. Woo-Cumings (ed.), *The Developmental State*, pp. 1–31, Cornell University Press, Ithaca, NY.

# CHAPTER 4

# The Belt and Road Initiative and the role of the Chinese developmental state

*Meibo Huang\* and Zhaoli Shen\*\**

## Introduction

During a visit to Kazakhstan in September 2013, Chinese President Xi Jinping proposed an initiative to build the 'Silk Road Economic Belt'.[1] At a meeting of the Association of Southeast Asian Nations (ASEAN) countries in October of the same year, Xi proposed the idea of building the '21st Century Maritime Silk Road'. These initiatives led to the formation of the Belt and Road Initiative (BRI), a Chinese-led policy involving the expansion of regional cooperation in response to the changes in China's domestic situation as well as in the international economic situation. In promoting the construction of the Belt and Road, the Chinese government provides guidance and financial support to Chinese state enterprises and performs the role of a developmental state in international economic cooperation. This chapter analyses the role of the Chinese developmental state in promoting bilateral trade and investment, providing financial support, strengthening bilateral tourism cooperation, as well as facilitating human resource exchange. The chapter tries to depict how the Chinese government has used the Belt and Road Initiative to promote shared prosperity among countries along the route. The initiative epitomizes China's developmental state policy extended to bolster economic cooperation with developing countries.

## The developmental state and economic growth: theoretical and empirical analysis

### The developmental state and its role in the economy: theoretical mechanisms

The concept of the developmental state emerged in the 1980s. The term, which developed in the field of economics, was originally coined by Chalmers Johnson (1982) in his book on Japan's economic growth after World War II. Johnson's work opened a new research area looking into the role of government intervention and economic growth in the 'East Asian Economic Miracle'. According to Johnson, the developmental state makes economic development its top priority, making sure that nothing else interferes with this goal. Governments that pursue this strategy play a decisive role in the process of economic development, planning the development process and formulating and achieving a large number of social and economic goals, rather than relying on market forces to determine the best allocation of resources. Subsequently, different scholars have carried out research on the developmental state including South Korea (Amsden and Euh, 1993), emphasizing the government's role in economic growth. Other scholars have conducted comparative studies looking at East Asian countries and other developing countries around the world. These studies propose four main characteristics of the developmental state.

First, economic development is the top priority for the developmental state. As Amsden (1991) shows, in order to achieve this goal, the government generally sets ambitious economic and social targets, such as increasing the country's productivity and improving residents' living standards, narrowing the economic gap with developed countries. She asserts that, in order to achieve these goals, the state is more likely to actively intervene in market operations, rather than only formulating market operation rules or arranging the sequence of development.

Secondly, the developmental state refers to a state that promotes growth through economic and industrial policies. Johnson (1982) pointed out that the developmental state usually uses these policies to intervene in the market and guide the flow of resources. White and Wade (1988) summarized the economic policies in the East Asian developmental state as the use of national policies to promote domestic industrial investment and channel the investment into industries that are vital to the country's future economic growth; the use of protective measures to help create a series of internationally competitive industries; strengthening the financial system via banks; and taking specific steps to promote trade freedom, while prioritizing the development of export industries.

Thirdly, the developmental state involves establishing an autonomous and rational economic bureaucracy. Chibber (2002) believes that such bureaucratic rationality is an important factor in maintaining the capacity of a developmental state. It enables a developmental state to avoid predatory behaviour and wasting resources. In such a state, a group of elites detached from the influence of social forces or interest groups have a strong desire for development. These groups can independently formulate far-sighted development strategies, mobilize limited resources, and, by implementing industrial policies, promote the industrial development and economic growth of a country or region. Chan et al. (1998) see the benefits of this type of bureaucracy in the ability to resist various social groups' myopia and rent-seeking behaviour, as well as overcoming the problems of collective action. This allows the state to isolate itself from special interests, and develop and implement a national development plan.

Fourthly, the developmental state promotes the close cooperative relationship between the government, private capital, and enterprises. Evans (1996) writes that the developmental state presents a relative cooperative relationship with 'embedded autonomy'. Weiss and Hobson (1995) describe the developmental state as a 'managed interdependence'. Under such a government-led development strategy, the government and the market are the two basic forces that regulate economic operation. The government as a whole takes on a leading and organizing function, coordinating the role of the market, mobilizing society from top to bottom, and targeting a planned modern development, such as promoting trade and investment, and infrastructure construction, and even, when necessary, acting as the main force of economic development.

The developmental government's strategy in economic development has been questioned by Western mainstream economics because of its excessive emphasis on the role of government. However, there are many successful examples of government-led development models in history, from Russia and Prussia in the 19th century to the East Asian miracle in the mid-20th century, followed by the miracle of China's economic growth in the 21st century. The developmental state's role in economic development in these countries and regions should not be underestimated.

### The East Asian government-led development model and the East Asian miracle

After World War II, as many developing countries got rid of the shackles of colonialism one after another, they gradually moved towards political independence and sought their own economic development. However, due to their huge populations, as well as the relative scarcity of arable land and natural resources, the development prospects of East Asia were not viewed favourably. However, in the 40 years after the war, East Asian countries, represented by Japan, Korea, Chinese Taiwan, Hong Kong, and Singapore, not only realized economic growth, but also improved people's lives and achieved social progress. Therefore, the remarkable achievement of East Asian economic development has been hailed as the 'East Asian miracle'.

Since Johnson (1982) put forward the concept of the 'developmental state', the theory has continued to be refined and has become the theoretical cornerstone for exploring government-led development.

In the context of the 'developmental state' theory, the Japanese government's industrial policy was the impetus for the country's economic miracle. Subsequently, Johnson (1982) and Amsden (2001), using the cases of South Korea and Chinese Taiwan, show the importance of the state as a force in economic development beyond free market mechanisms. In 1997, the World Bank outlined its 'five points' on the role of the government in economic development (World Bank, 1997). The first point is to establish a framework for rule of law, that is, legislation and law enforcement, especially to safeguard property rights and contract systems, and provide institutions for normal market operation. The second aspect is to implement correct macroeconomic policies, especially fiscal policy, monetary policy, exchange rate policy, and foreign investment policy, to maintain the stability of market operations as much as possible. The third is to provide public goods to establish a solid material basis for market operations, such as infrastructure and public facilities. The fourth is to control the externalities of market activities, including the promotion of positive externalities by improving education and health care, as well as environmental protection to reduce negative externalities. The fifth is to promote social justice, not only by providing a social safety net, but also by implementing redistribution policies.

Although many scholars believe this 'government-led development strategy' can be used to explain the 'East Asian miracle', voices of doubt have also emerged. Some authors have argued that the developmental state is not actually the reason behind the East Asian miracle. According to this group, while adopting industrial policies is an important contributor, it is not an economic booster, but at best a lubricant (White and Wade, 1988; Amsden, 2001). Other scholars (e.g. Aoki et al., 1997) emphasize the condition and stage of a particular developmental state. They acknowledge that a high degree of government intervention in the economy has a positive effect on economic development, but they also point out that the effectiveness of the developmental state is more strongly influenced by a series of non-institutional factors. That is, the application of the developmental state theory is conditional (Hayashi, 2010). The World Bank (1993) posited that the prerequisites for an effective government-led development policy are normally functioning market mechanisms, the vitality of private enterprises, as well as the institutionalized channels for constructive cooperation between government and enterprises. Only under these conditions can a government-led development strategy come to fruition. At the same time, the World Bank pointed out that the type of active government interventionism advocated by the developmental state theory, especially trade and industrial policies related to specific industries, has historical roots, such as the cold war.

### China's developmental state model after its reform and opening up

China can be regarded as a developmental state. The planned economy model slowly emerged in the early days after the founding of the People's Republic of China, while the formal developmental state model began to arise after the reform and opening up. The formation and development of this model is not accidental, but the result of a combination of specific historical conditions and strategic choices. According to Johnson's theory, the developmental state model, a model of a market economy with state intervention, is located somewhere between the market economy model and the planned economy model, with the state formulating some targeted economic and industrial policies to guide economic development. Lin et al. (1999) argue that, since the early days of the founding of the People's Republic of China, Chinese society quickly embarked on the path of modernization and developmentalism and resorted to planning and rational means to promote social and economic development.

With the continuous deepening of reform and opening up, China's developmental state has gradually manifested characteristics similar to the East Asian developmental model. Firstly, the Chinese government has focused on economic development and attached great importance to the formulation of industrial policies. At the same time, China has established an economic management institution with strong capabilities and efficiency. Wang (2008) noted that the Chinese government uses policy tools to adjust the industrial structure and coordinate the balance of supply and demand. Secondly, the Chinese government has established a close cooperative relationship with private capital and enterprises. Oi (1995) pointed out that the local government influences the local economy more like the board of directors of an enterprise. They provide information, financial and technical support, and channel resources from more prosperous enterprises to newly established enterprises as well as poorly run village enterprises.

Ramo (2004) referred to the Chinese development model as the 'Beijing Consensus', in which the Chinese government pioneered the establishment of special economic zones, development zones, and industrial parks, implemented preferential tax policies, actively improved the investment environment, guided the development of key industries, and promoted economic development. In addition, politically, it firmly defended its national sovereignty and interests, and handled the Taiwan issue properly. Thus, this development model not only focuses on economic development, but also on many additional aspects, such as society and politics. It is a development approach that seeks just and high-quality growth. The Chinese government's active innovation and bold practice has led to a development model suited to its own national conditions.

## The Belt and Road Initiative and the role of the developmental state

We now turn our attention to the Belt and Road Initiative (BRI), the new model of regional economic cooperation proposed by China to further promote the development of economic globalization. In this section, we will use developmental state theory to analyse the Chinese government's role in promoting BRI construction.

Firstly, the government set goals for regional economic cooperation. On 27 March 2015, the National Development and Reform Commission of China, the Ministry of Foreign Affairs, and the Ministry of Commerce jointly issued the 'Visions and Actions for Promoting the Joint Construction of the Silk Road Economic Belt and the 21st Century Maritime Silk Road' (hereinafter referred to as 'Visions and Actions') (National Development and Reform Commission et al., 2015). The BRI takes peace, cooperation, development, and mutual benefit as the core concepts, and focuses on policy communication, unimpeded facilities, unimpeded trade, financial integration, and people-to-people bonds.

Secondly, the government provided strategic guidance and cooperation mechanisms for the BRI. According to Gao (2015), the 'One Belt One Road' construction project is led by the government. From the perspective of the development stage, at the initial stage of BRI economic cooperation, the parties involved in the cooperation face large investment risks due to the large gap in capabilities and the imperfect investment environment in most developing countries. This means that the government's role needs to be fully brought into play. The five BRI cooperation priorities can be explained in terms of the 'five connectivities', of which 'policy connectivity' reflects the role of the government. Kong (2014) pointed out that the role of the government in the BRI is mainly to guide the direction of cooperation and establish a coordination mechanism. In the process of advancing the BRI, the Chinese government has thus indeed played a guiding role. Through intergovernmental policy connectivity, the government has managed to guide the direction of the BRI and establish a coordination and communication platform or mechanism for cooperation (Kong, 2014).

At the same time, China's foreign aid has played an important role in several aspects of promoting the five connectivities and in terms of development financing. Developing countries are often faced with large infrastructure investment gaps, and a large amount of development financing is needed to support infrastructure construction ('facility connectivity' and 'financial connectivity'). After the level of infrastructure in developing countries has been improved, thereby enhancing the business environment, the overall cooperation between China and the BRI countries enters a relatively free and effective market stage, allowing the market to fully play its role (Cui and Liu, 2004). Liu and Liu (2019) believe that the cooperation framework of the Chinese foreign cooperation mechanism should be continuously improved. Wen and Shen (2019) suggest that it is necessary to explore the idea of setting up an investment and financing cooperation model of 'benefit sharing and risk sharing', and build a sustainable debt assessment evaluation system and financial security system that are compatible with the development of the BRI.

Thirdly, in the Belt and Road construction, the Chinese government has played a coordinating role and established close cooperative relations with private capital and enterprises. Deng (2016) pointed out that the BRI emphasizes the coordinated development of the government and the market, in which the scope of government guidance is defined in terms of policy support, carrier platform construction, and quasi-public welfare projects. Lv et al. (2017) argued that the BRI should adopt a dual government and enterprise coordination mechanism. Yang (2018) believes that the efficient interaction between the government's macro-economic adjustments and the market's resource allocation would be an effective measure to accelerate the construction of the BRI. Sheng and Quan (2018) asserts that, in the BRI project, the functions and values of government, cities, parks, and enterprises do not exist in isolation, but instead form a symbiotic relationship with each other. Therefore, the construction of the BRI must give full play to the forces of multiple parties and move from government-led to diversified linkages. Wang (2019) proposed that 'The Belt and Road Initiative' still needs to adhere to the principles of market players' dominance, government promotion, and market operation. The government builds a stage for enterprises from various countries to cooperate, and these enterprises then play the main role in terms of achieving economic benefits.

### The policy coordination role of the Chinese government

BRI is an open and inclusive platform for regional economic cooperation. China has always adhered to the principles of extensive consultation, joint construction, and joint sharing, and insists on an enterprise-oriented and market-oriented operation. BRI construction projects are mainly commercial projects. However, due to the fact that some BRI countries take relatively high investment risks, policy guidance from the government becomes an essential part. The government can pave the way for effective markets via policy coordination and communication, foreign aid, and development finance.

When President Xi Jinping visited Kazakhstan in 2013, he spoke about the policy communication of the 'Silk Road Economic Belt'. In his speech, he said:

> When strengthening policy communication, related countries can fully communicate on economic development strategies and countermeasures, and follow the principle of seeking common ground while reserving differences. The planning and measures for regional cooperation will give the green light to regional economic integration in terms of policies and laws (Bie, 2010: 3).

The 'Visions and Actions' (2015) also included the content of the five connectivities, putting policy communication (connectivity) at the top of the list. The document pointed out that strengthening policy communication is an important guarantee for the construction of BRI. The focus of the communication and exchange content is based on economic development strategies and countermeasures between countries. Moreover, the policy communication of BRI does not deliberately pursue consistency, but can be highly flexible and a diversified and open cooperation process (Institute of International Trade and Economic Cooperation, 2020). Over the past few years, the gigantic BRI construction project has achieved remarkable results in terms of policy communication between governments. The following sections will describe some of these achievements.

*Promotion of bilateral and multilateral cooperation*
As of May 2020, China has signed 20 cooperation documents with 138 countries and 30 international organizations for the joint building of the BRI. These agreements cover infrastructure, investment, trade, finance, technology, society, humanities, people's livelihoods, and oceans, among other things. The signatory countries comprise 27 European countries, 37 Asian countries, 44 African countries, 11 Oceania countries, 8 South American countries, 11 Central American and Caribbean countries (Institute of International Trade and Economic Cooperation, 2020).

*Promotion of trade and investment*
By the end of 2019, China had reached 17 free trade agreements with 25 countries and regions, 12 free trade agreements were being negotiated or upgraded, and 10 free trade agreements were under joint

feasibility studies or upgrading studies (Institute of International Trade and Economic Cooperation, 2020). In 2019, China first adopted the negative list approach to carry out the second phase of the China-Korea Free Trade Area service and investment negotiations and China-Japan-Korea Free Trade Area negotiations, which shows that the construction of the free trade area had entered the era of high-standard 'negative list' stage, leading to a more standardized operation of trade and investment. In October 2019, China and Mauritius signed a free trade agreement, which was the first free trade agreement between China and an African country. In addition, China and New Zealand concluded negotiations on upgrading their own free trade agreement. China is also pushing to sign and enter into the second phase of a free trade agreement with Pakistan, while at the same time putting forward the free trade area upgrading protocol with ASEAN, Singapore, and Chile.

### Strengthening tourism cooperation

China has also developed tourism cooperation agreements with many countries. These agreements have promoted the facilitation of visas and transportation from these countries to China, leading to an increase in the number of direct flights to the country. As of January 2019, China has achieved full mutual visa exemptions with 14 countries, while 15 other countries unilaterally grant visa-free entry to Chinese citizens. Another 44 countries unilaterally grant visas upon arrival to Chinese citizens. At present, Chinese citizens holding ordinary passports can travel to 72 countries and regions without any visa or visa on arrival requirements. In addition, China has reached 71 agreements or arrangements to simplify visa procedures with 42 countries. China has opened direct flights with 45 countries and regions along the BRI route, thus simplifying travel between these countries (Institute of International Trade and Economic Cooperation, 2020).

### Increasing educational exchange

There have also been achievements in educational exchange programmes. One example is the establishment of the 'Silk Road' Chinese Government Scholarship Programme, and Hong Kong and Macao Special Administrative Regions scholarships related to the joint construction of the BRI. In addition, as of April 2019, China has signed agreements on mutual recognition of higher education qualifications with nearly 30 BRI countries, and 60 Chinese universities have launched overseas education programmes in 23 related countries. In terms of talent training, as of August 2019, the 'Belt and Road Connectivity' talent development project has trained 33 international public management masters and Chinese law masters from 22 countries around the world, organized six advanced seminars and trained 240 senior government officials, business executives, and scholars from 20 countries and regions. In addition, China also provides professional skills training for BRI countries, covering various fields such as poverty reduction, agriculture, health care, and education (British Chamber of Commerce in China, 2019).

*Promoting cultural exchanges*
Cultural exchange is another important feature of the BRI. China has formulated a series of directives, such as 'Guiding Opinions on Strengthening the Construction of "Belt and Road" Soft Power', 'Guiding Opinions on Promoting the Reform and Development of Confucius Institutes', and '"Belt and Road" Cultural Development Action Plan (2016–2020)', among others, as guidelines for cultural exchanges between China and the Belt and Road countries (Ministry of Culture, 2016). China has signed inter-governmental cultural exchange and cooperation agreements with all countries along the BRI; signed agreements on the mutual translation of literary classics with more than 50 countries; and signed cultural heritage cooperation documents with Indonesia, Myanmar, Serbia, Singapore, Saudi Arabia, and other countries. In addition, China has set up 17 Chinese cultural centres in countries along the BRI; it has mutually hosted cultural years, tourism years, art festivals, film festivals, seminars, book fairs, sports events, think-tank dialogues and other activities with relevant countries. At the time of writing, there were 310 members of the cooperative network of non-governmental organizations along the Silk Road. Programmes such as 'The Belt and Road' library cooperation project, copyright trade cooperation programme, 'Silk Road Young Scholars Funding Programme', publishing cooperation, and documentary academic community have been established and implemented respectively.

### International assistance facilitated to BRI countries

South–South Cooperation is China's basic position for its international development cooperation. The White Paper on China's International Development Cooperation (State Council Information Office of *China*, 2021) claims that China is still in the primary stage of socialism at present and will remain so for a long time. The international development cooperation provided by China to other developing countries involves mutual help between developing countries and belongs to the category of South–South Cooperation. In the process of building the BRI, China will continue to assume international responsibilities commensurate with its own development stage and actual capabilities, and promote the sustainable development of other developing countries.

The joint construction of the BRI is an important platform for China to carry out its new stage of international development cooperation. The Silk Road Economic Belt and the 21st Century Maritime Silk Road are important public products for China to provide to the world. Since the BRI was put forward, China has increased its development assistance to other developing countries based on their development needs, to promote policy communication, facility connectivity, unimpeded trade, capital financing, and people-to-people bonds, which play an important role in deepening the BRI, as well as to cultivate space for sustainable development in all countries.

In terms of policy communication, in order to encourage BRI countries to strengthen mutual trust, carry out pragmatic cooperation, and deepen the integration of interests, China has promoted understanding with the BRI co-founding countries, and has established an exchange platform for policy communication between countries. From 2013 to 2018, China organized more than 4,000 official training programmes for relevant countries. At the same time, China has also dispatched expert consultants to provide technical consulting services. Through deepening the under-standing of the national conditions and policies and legal systems of the BRI countries, China has proposed practical development plans to lay the foundation for national security and effective cooperation.

In terms of facility connectivity, infrastructure connectivity is the key to the joint construction of the BRI. Through development assistance projects in infrastructure, such as Pakistan's Peshawar–Karachi highway, Karakoram highway and other related road reconstruction and expansion projects, Kyrgyzstan's north–south highway construction and Tajikistan road repair project, the Mauritania Friendship Port expansion project, and airport upgrades and expansion projects in Pakistan, Nepal, the Maldives, Cambodia, Zambia, Zimbabwe, Togo, and other countries, China actively supports the joint construction of the BRI countries' highways, railways, ports, bridges, and communication networks and so on. These infrastructure projects are helping to build the 'six corridors, six routes, multi-country, multi-port' interconnection pattern, which has brought more convenience to cross-border personnel movement, and created more opportunities for integration into the BRI.

In order to enhance the competitiveness of developing countries in the global supply chain, China helps relevant countries improve their terms of trade through trade promotion assistance (aid for trade), actively helps countries to jointly build BRI projects, improve trade infrastructure, and promote the modernization of trade circulation to enhance trade development capabilities, which, combined, lay a solid foundation for unimpeded trade between countries. From 2013 to 2018, China organized more than 300 trade-related seminars for relevant countries, including trade facilitation, international logistics and multimodal transport services, e-commerce, entry-exit health and quarantine, entry-exit animal and plant inspection and quarantine, and import and export food safety, promoting the coordination of trade policies and integrating into the multilateral trading system (Institute of International Trade and Economic Cooperation, 2020).

In terms of development financing, on the one hand, China provides government concessional loans to BRI developing countries. On the other hand, China actively supports BRI countries to optimize their domestic financial environment, improve financial systems, establish finance cooperation platforms, and facilitate their participating in the international financial system. In April 2018, China established a joint capacity development centre with the International Monetary Fund which provides intellectual support for the joint construction of BRI countries to improve their macroeconomic and financial framework.

In terms of people-to-people bonds, China has, through development assistance, increased people-to-people and cultural exchanges and cultural cooperation among members. Firstly, this has led to the implementation of a number of livelihood aid projects in BRI countries, involving the areas of housing, water supply, medical care, education, rural roads, and assistance for vulnerable groups, to help fill in the gaps of infrastructure and basic public services. Representatives from Sri Lanka, Pakistan, Kazakhstan, and other countries involved in joint BRI projects were invited to China for exchanges to enhance their knowledge and understanding of China's national conditions and culture. This has deepened non-governmental exchanges. The young volunteers become a bridge to promote people-to-people bonds. China has also carried out 33 cultural relics aid projects with 17 countries that jointly built the BRI. In addition, China is implementing the 'Ten Thousand Villages' project, which involves installing digital TVs in 10,000 villages in more than 20 African countries. As a whole, these undertakings help to build a solid social foundation for the joint construction of the BRI.

### Development financing and infrastructure connectivity

*The policy and development financial institutions' role*
Chinese funding plays an important role in the construction of the BRI. So far, the financial support for the construction of the BRI has mainly come from policy finance and development finance sources, with a relatively small proportion from commercial finance sources.

Because of this, many Western countries accuse the BRI of being led by the Chinese government rather than being market-oriented (Shapiro, 2016). Chinese banks currently involved in financing the construction of the BRI mainly include the China Development Bank, the Export-Import Bank of China, and a few commercial banks. These banks differ in the focus of their financing support, ranging from facilities connectivity, economic and trade cooperation, industrial investment to resource cooperation. The China Development Bank and the Export-Import Bank of China, as a development bank and policy bank, respectively, rank in the forefront in terms of contracted projects and investment funds. In terms of loan funds, as of the end of 2019, the Export-Import Bank of China has implemented more than 1,800 projects under the BRI, with a loan balance of more than RMB 1 tn (US$141.2 m), distributed in more than 50 countries (China Export-Import Bank, 2019). The China Development Bank (CDB) is the world's largest development financial institution, China's largest foreign investment and financing cooperation bank, as well as a medium and long-term credit bank and bond bank. As of the end of 2019, CDB had issued BRI special loans of more than RMB 240 bn for more than 600 projects (China Development Bank, 2020) to finance the infrastructure interconnection, production capacity cooperation, financial cooperation, and medium-sized enterprises development, among others, and to promote the economic and social development of partner countries, industrial transformation and upgrading, and people's livelihood improvement in BRI countries. In comparison, the four major Chinese commercial banks are far behind the China Development Bank and the Export-Import Bank of China in terms of the total number of projects supported. Among these four banks, the Industrial and Commercial Bank of China, Bank of China, and China Construction Bank have been the most active, while the Agricultural Bank of China has been the least active.

In terms of financing the construction of the BRI, policy banks and development banks are currently the mainstay, with commercial banks making up a relatively small proportion of the total. The reasons for that are, first of all, that infrastructure interconnection is a priority area in the construction of the BRI and that infrastructure is a non-exclusive and non-competitive public product, providing long-term social benefits. The second reason is that the private sector and enterprises are reluctant to invest in infrastructure projects. Most infrastructure projects are therefore led and supported by government departments. Third, due to the huge investment funds in infrastructure, it is still difficult to support it only by relying on the strength of countries along the Belt and Road, and external forces such as financial institutions are needed to participate in the construction. However, at present, external financial institutions cannot provide sufficient financial services and support by themselves. Multilateral development banks, such as the World Bank and the Asian Development Bank, cannot meet the infrastructure construction funding needs of developing countries and regions for economic development along the BRI (Liu, 2016). Therefore, in this market environment, the Asian Infrastructure Investment Bank, the China Development Bank, and the Export-Import Bank of China, which are dominated by developing countries such as China, have to come forward and use their investment and financing functions to guide China's private capital to contribute to the BRI route. Their investments in infrastructure construction projects in these countries and regions can alleviate this problem.

*International competitiveness of Chinese commercial banks*
As the main project cooperation of the BRI is concentrated in the fields of infrastructure construction and resource exploration, the project funds have the characteristics of large investments, with low rates of return and long payback periods. The 2020 China Overseas Investment National Risk Rating Report, issued by the Institute of World Economics and Politics of the Chinese Academy of Social Sciences (2020), listed five major indicators to rate the 51 countries along the BRI from the perspective of Chinese enterprises and sovereign wealth overseas investment. These indicators include: economic foundation, debt solvency, social resilience, political risk and relationship as well as 42 sub-indicators. The report pointed out that the investment risk for emerging economies is relatively high. According to the report, most of the countries in the BRI region are medium-risk, while only a small number of countries are considered high- and low-risk. Compared to other BRI regions, East Asian countries represent a relatively low level of investment risk. Some South Asian and Commonwealth of Independent States countries are considered a generally higher investment risk. Commercial bank investments therefore face greater risks and uncertainty, which undoubtedly increases the resistance of such banks to invest in development projects in these countries, and leads to higher risk control requirements.

Up to now, the international competitiveness of Chinese commercial banks along the Belt and Road has been insufficient. The first reason for this is the dominant role played by five state-owned banks compared to the joint-equity commercial banks. The five state-owned banks, the Industrial and Commercial Bank of China, Agricultural Bank of China, Bank of China, China Construction Bank, and Bank of

Communications, which represent the main commercial banks in Belt and Road countries, have bank branches throughout the BRI regions. These banks have the most primary institutions across all regions, and they are the main players in the international market among the Chinese commercial banks. The joint-equity commercial banks have only a limited involvement in BRI construction projects; their market is concentrated in the Asia-Pacific region, such as Singapore and South Korea (Wei and Tang, 2020). The second reason is the Chinese commercial banks' uneven distribution between BRI regions, and their low level of financial interconnection. Due to their limited business and service capabilities and lack of international market development capabilities, the Chinese commercial banks are mainly located in the Asia-Pacific region, Europe, and West Asia. In addition, they also have low coverage and uneven distribution in Central Asia, South Asia, and Africa. The third reason is that the business variety is not perfect. China's commercial banks that focus on foreign investments guarantee more traditional business. Internal and external linkage, multi-currency liquidation, and other kinds of structured products are not yet offered, because it is difficult to establish multi-currency, cross-agency, and collaborative integrated service mechanisms, coordinate joint projects, effectively implement marketing mechanisms, and promote the competitiveness of the service.

As Table 4.1 shows, despite the uncontrollable factors involved in BRI construction projects, including exchange rate risks and policy risks, a number of commercial banks, including the Bank of Communications, China Merchants Bank, China CITIC Bank,

**Table 4.1** Current layout of Chinese commercial bank overseas branches (as of the beginning of 2018)

| Region | Number of state-owned large-scale commercial bank branches | Number of joint-equity commercial bank branches | Total number of commercial bank branches |
|---|---|---|---|
| Asia-Pacific | 37 | 5 | 42 |
| Central Asia | 2 | 0 | 2 |
| West Asia | 14 | 0 | 14 |
| South Asia | 4 | 0 | 4 |
| Europe | 20 | 1 | 21 |
| Africa and Latin America | 5 | 0 | 5 |

*Source*: Figures compiled from the official website of the Belt and Road Initiative (https://www.yidaiyilu.gov.cn/) and the annual reports of major banks

Industrial Bank, Ping An Bank, and Shanghai Pudong Development Bank, are currently participating in and increasing their investments in BRI construction along with the four state-owned banks. However, there is still a huge gap between the amount of these banks' investments and the number of their investment projects in BRI countries compared with the Industrial and Commercial Bank of China and Bank of China, and most of these commercial banks are still at the stage of setting up overseas branches. The other small and medium-sized commercial banks are still in their infancy, and their participation in BRI activities is relatively low. As a whole, however, China's major commercial banks are now familiarizing themselves with the international market and consolidating international competitiveness in the construction of the BRI. And while their current overall financing percentage is still quite low, in the future, these commercial banks will gradually increase their financial coverage in countries along the Belt and Road to help promote the overall layout and construction of the BRI.

## BRI's achievement in regional economic cooperation

According to the 'Visions and Actions' of the Chinese government (Ministry of Foreign Affairs of the People's Republic of China, 2015), the BRI aims to promote the orderly and free flow of economic factors, the efficient allocation of resources, in-depth market integration, to develop larger, higher-level, and deeper regional economic cooperation, and jointly create an open, balanced, and inclusive regional economic cooperation framework. This shows that the Chinese expect to be more deeply integrated into the global economic system under the premise of conforming to the current world development mechanisms and trends, and to play a more active role in leading global economic development (Liu, 2015). Viewed from the perspective of principles and coverage, the BRI is a market-based project, supplemented by the guidance of the Chinese government, and covers regional economic cooperation activities mainly in developing countries. As far as the authors understand it, the BRI is China's globalization policy adjustment in a new era. From this point on, China has shifted its international economic cooperation policy from the stage of focusing on trade globalization to the stage of emphasizing trade and investment equally, and shifted its investment perspective from attracting foreign direct investment to going out and investing outside its borders. From a market perspective or from the perspective of a global cooperative country, China has moved from relying heavily on developed countries to being a liaison between developed and developing countries. Although the BRI represents China's regional economic cooperation initiative in a new era, the initiative still emphasizes the core principle of adhering to global markets. That is to say, the BRI is fundamentally a market-oriented, not government, project. Wang and Zhang (2018) believe that the resources and comparative advantages possessed by Chinese companies are the basis for regional economic cooperation in the BRI, and the economic cooperation is also the result of market selection based on maximizing benefits. Zhou and Wen (2019) studied the cooperation mechanism of corporate creative innovation in the context of the BRI from the perspective of the dynamic game of the industrial value chain, and suggested that companies should make full use of market advantages to increase the cohesiveness of cooperation.

The BRI is essentially a regional economic cooperation act that promotes the cross-border flow of economic factors and economic cooperation between countries, and it is an economic globalization promoted by China. As China continues to deepen economic and trade cooperation with countries along the BRI, the level of trade and investment liberalization and facilitation between China and the BRI countries has continued to increase, and the degree of opening to the outside world has also increased.

### Growth in trade

From 2013 to 2019, China's total trade in goods with 65 BRI countries increased from US$1.04 tn to $1.34 tn (see Figure 4.1), and its share in China's total trade in goods rose from 25.0 per cent to 29.4 per cent. In 2019, China's total trade in goods with the 138 countries that signed BRI cooperation agreements reached $1.90 tn, accounting for 41.5 per cent of China's total trade in goods, of which exports were $983.76 bn and imports $913.79 bn (Institute of International Trade and Economic Cooperation, 2020).

### Expansion of foreign investment

The investment vitality of China and the countries along the route has continued to increase since 2013. And at the same time, this has promoted the industrialization process of related countries and provided new opportunities for common development. As Figure 4.2 shows, from 2013 to 2019, China's cumulative direct investment in BRI countries was $117.31 bn, with an average annual growth rate of 6.7 per cent, which was 2.6 per cent higher than the average level of

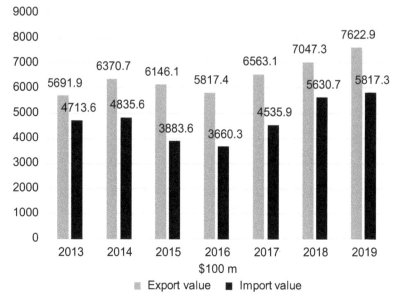

**Figure 4.1** The volume of trade in goods between China and 65 countries along 'The Belt and Road' (2013–2019) (Unit: $100 m)
*Source*: Figures compiled from 'China's Belt and Road Trade and Investment Development Report' of the Ministry of Commerce of the People's Republic of China (2019) <https://www.caitec.org.cn/upfiles/file/2021/11/20211208103423002.pdf>.

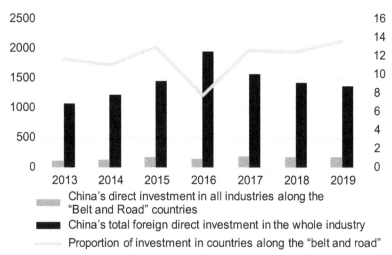

China's direct investment in all industries along the "Belt and Road" countries

China's total foreign direct investment in the whole industry

Proportion of investment in countries along the "belt and road"

**Figure 4.2** China's industry-wide direct investment flows in 65 countries along the BRI (2013–2019) (Unit: $100 m)
*Source*: Figures compiled from 'China's Belt and Road Trade and Investment Development Report', 2021 <https://www.caitec.org.cn/upfiles/file/2021/11/20211208103423002.pdf>.

China's overall outward direct investment in the same period. In 2019, China directly invested $18.69 bn in the Belt and Road countries, accounting for 13.7 per cent of the total during the same period and an increase of 1.2 per cent, mainly in Singapore, Indonesia, Vietnam, Thailand, the United Arab Emirates, Laos, Malaysia, and Kazakhstan, Cambodia, and other countries (Institute of International Trade and Economic Cooperation, 2020).

### Advance in international project contracting

Countries along the BRI have become important destinations for Chinese companies' foreign contracted project cooperation (Institute of International Trade and Economic Cooperation, 2020). As Table 4.2 shows, from 2015 to 2020, the value of new contracts signed by China in the 65 BRI countries has rapidly increased from $92.64 bn to $141.46 bn, with an average annual growth rate of 8.7 per cent. Completed turnover has rapidly increased from $69.26 bn to $91.12 bn, with an average annual growth rate of 5.2 per cent. In 2019, companies signed 6,944 new foreign contracted engineering project contracts in BRI countries, with a newly signed contract value of $154.89 bn, accounting for 59.5 per cent of the newly signed contract value of China's foreign contracting projects in the same period, a year-by-year increase of 23.1 per cent. The total turnover was $97.98 bn, accounting for 56.7 per cent of the total in the same period, an increase of 9.7 per cent per year, which is higher than the overall growth rate of the industry (Ministry of Commerce of the People's Republic of China, 2020).

Since the BRI was put forward, state-owned key enterprises and private enterprises have responded actively and become actors and

**Table 4.2** China's project contracting in 65 BRI countries (2015–2020)

| Year | Number of newly signed project contracts | Newly signed contract amount ($100 m) | Complete turnover ($100 m) |
|------|------|------|------|
| 2015 | 3,987 | 926.4 | 692.6 |
| 2016 | 8,158 | 1,260.3 | 759.7 |
| 2017 | 7,217 | 1,443.2 | 855.3 |
| 2018 | 7,721 | 1,257.8 | 893.3 |
| 2019 | 6,944 | 1,548.9 | 979.8 |
| 2020 | 5,611 | 1,414.6 | 911.2 |

Source: Ministry of Commerce of the People's Republic of China (2020: 20) 'The Belt and Road Trade and Investment Development Report' (2020: 20).

new forces in BRI construction projects. As of April 2019, China's key state-owned enterprises have undertaken a total of 3,120 BRI projects. Among the infrastructure projects that have been started or are scheduled to start, the number of projects undertaken by key state-owned enterprises has accounted for more than 60 per cent, with the contract value representing nearly 80 per cent. At the same time, in deepening international capacity cooperation, state-owned key enterprises have successively carried out more than 60 oil and gas cooperation projects in about 20 countries (*China Daily*, 2019). These projects range from infrastructure construction and energy resource development to international production capacity cooperation and industrial park construction. At the same time, private enterprises have also played an active role in the construction of the BRI. As of 2019, the total import and export volume between the Chinese private enterprises and the 65 BRI countries was $619.98 bn, accounting for 43.0 per cent of China's overall trade volume with countries along the BRI, representing a growth rate of 12.1 per cent (China Federation of Industry and Commerce, 2019).

## Conclusion: BRI, development cooperation, and the role of the developmental state

East Asian governments can be good models for developing countries. These governments have more experience in promoting economic development and investment than other developing countries. Their foreign aid is also mainly focused on the infrastructure and productive sectors. Most of the BRI countries are developing countries with weak market mechanisms. One of the goals of promoting cooperation with these countries is to help make up for the missing functions of their market. In the process of advancing BRI construction, the Chinese government can make full use of the comparative advantage of its developmental state experience and help the governments of developing countries nurture markets and improve their development capacities. The BRI's achievement and the Chinese government's role in it can be summarized in three ways.

First, the goal of the BRI is to promote regional economic cooperation and the shared development of countries along the road. At present, the BRI has attracted the participation of more than 100 countries and international organizations. China has signed the BRI cooperation framework agreements with more than 40 countries and international organizations, established comprehensive strategic partnerships, and entered into a large number of inter-governmental cooperation projects. The promotion of economic development in the areas along the route is the common denominator of these cooperation projects. For example, financial cooperation represented by the Asian Infrastructure Investment Bank and the Silk Road Fund, has continued to deepen, providing financial support for the economic development of these countries. The implementation of strategic plans, such as the six major economic corridors, has improved the infrastructure construction in the areas along the route, and at the same time promoted investment and industrial transfer in Southeast Asia, South Asia, Central Asia, Africa, and other regions. All these have gradually transformed the BRI from a strategic initiative into a real platform for promoting regional economic cooperation.

Second, the role of the Chinese developmental state in the BRI is defined in terms of its policy and financial support as well as the provision of quasi-public welfare projects. Economic development is a process of continuous advances in technology, industry, infrastructure, and institutional structures. With technological innovation and industrial upgrading, infrastructure and upper-level institutional arrangements must be continuously improved. However, these are not the types of things that enterprises alone can promote. The developmental state, in constructing the BRI, sets up institutional arrangements, signs trade agreements and memorandums of understanding with other countries through policy communication, encourages and supports private enterprises to use both international and domestic resources and markets, and actively guides enterprises to 'go global' (Xu, 2015). In terms of infrastructure investment, it is helpful for the development and policy bank to provide loans, and at the same time guide social capital and private forces to participate in the infrastructure construction of the BRI to help create a good business environment for the countries involved (Zhou, 2017).

Finally, the BRI has established a close cooperative relationship between the government, private capital, and enterprises. According to developmental state theory, the BRI is a product of the linkage between the developmental state and the market. On the one hand, during the construction of the Belt and Road Initiative, market, credit, and system construction will help create a good business environment, provide a solid guarantee for enterprises to go global, and form a benign interactive relationship between the government, private capital, and enterprises. On the other hand, the government can build a platform to facilitate the participation of social capital and private forces, and give full play to the decisive role of the market in resource allocation, achieving mutual benefits and win-win results. The scope of government guidance is defined by policy support, carrier platform construction, and quasi-public welfare projects, while the scope of market allocation is defined by investments and trade between the countries along the route, transformation of factor flow, and industrial chain integration (Deng, 2016). The construction of the BRI fundamentally adheres to the principles of market subject domination, government promotion, and market operation. The government builds a stage for cooperation between enterprises of various countries, while enterprises play the main role (Wang, 2019). From this perspective, the BRI is a bold attempt and a full manifestation of East Asian development-oriented governments to promote regional economic cooperation, especially promoting regional economic cooperation with developing countries.

## Notes

\*    Professor and the Director of the International Development Cooperation Academy at Shanghai University of International Business and Economics, China. mbh841123@163.com
\*\*   Research assistant at the International Development Cooperation Academy at Shanghai University of International Business and Economics, China.
1.   The Silk Road Economic Belt is a new economic development area formed on the basis of the ancient Silk Road concept. It includes the five north-western provinces, Shaanxi, Gansu, Qinghai, Ningxia, and Xinjiang, as well as the four south-western provinces, autonomous regions, and municipalities, Chongqing, Sichuan, Yunnan, and Guangxi.

## References

Amsden A.H. (1991) 'Diffusion of development: the late-industrializing model and greater East Asia', *American Economic Review* 81(2): 282–86.

Amsden, A.H. (2001) *The Rise of 'The Rest': Challenges to the West from Late-Industrializing Economies*, Oxford University Press, New York.

Amsden, A.H. and Euh, Y. (1993) 'South Korea's 1980s financial reforms: good-bye financial repression (maybe), hello new institutional restraints', *World Development* 21(3): 379–90 <https://doi.org/10.1016/0305-750X(93)90151-X>.

Aoki, M., Kim, H.K. and Okuno-Fujiwara, M. (eds) (1997) *The Role of Government in East Asian Economic Development: Comparative Institutional Analysis*, Oxford University Press, Oxford.

Bie, H. (2010) 'Zheng zhi gou tong fen xi: Bei jing, kuang jia yu ping jia' [Analysis of political communication: background, framework and evaluation], *Tribune of Social Sciences* 23: 32–38 <https://doi.org/10.14185/j.cnki.issn1008-2026.2010.23.018>.

British Chamber of Commerce in China (2019) *Education on the Belt and Road*. Available from: https://www.britishchamber.cn/wp-content/uploads/2019/02/Education-on-the-Belt-and-Road-Final-0219.pdf [accessed 1 March 2022].

Chan, S., Clark, K. and Lam, D. (1998) 'Looking beyond the developmental state', in S. Chan (ed.), *Beyond the Developmental State*, pp. 1–8, Palgrave Macmillan, London.

Chibber, V. (2002) 'Bureaucratic rationality and the developmental state', *American Journal of Sociology* 107(4): 951–89 <https://doi.org/10.1086/341010>.

*China Daily* (2019) 'Yang qi he min qi zai yi dai yi lu jian she zhong fa hui zhong yao zuo yong' [Central enterprises and private enterprises are playing an important role in the construction of the Belt and Road], 25 April [online] <https://baijiahao.baidu.com/s?id=1631754072690299760&wfr=spider&for=pc> [accessed 21 June 2022].

China Development Bank (2020) guo jia kai fa yin hang nian bao 2020 [Report on China Development Bank Annual 2020], 26 August [online] <http://www.cdb.com.cn/bgxz/ndbg/ndbg2020/> [accessed 21 June 2022].

China Export-Import Bank (2019) 'Yi dai yi lu xiang mu dai kuan yu e chao wan yi yuan' [The Belt and Road project loan balance exceeds one trillion yuan], 19 April [online] <https://baijiahao.baidu.com/s?id=1631228715520980013&wfr=spider&for=pc> [accessed 21 June 2022].

China Federation of Industry and Commerce (2019) *Zhong guo min ying qi ye yi dai yi lu ke chi xu fa zhan bao gao* [Report on the sustainable development of Chinese private enterprises along the Belt and Road], 24 August [online] <https://baijiahao.baidu.com/s?id=1642717143981311187&wfr=spider&for=pc> [accessed 21 June 2022].

Cui, W. and Liu, X. (2004). *Qu ji jing ji xue* [Interregional economics], Economic Science Press, Beijing.

Deng, Z. (2016) 'Yi dai yi lu zhan lue zheng fu yin dao yu shi chang pei zhi lu jing xuan ze yan jiu' [Research on the Belt and Road strategic government guidance and market allocation path selection], *Social Sciences in Ningxia* 195(2): 80–83.

Evans, P. (1996) 'Government action, social capital and development: Reviewing the evidence on synergy', *World Development* 24(6): 1119–32 <https://doi.org/10.1016/0305-750X(96)00021-6>.

Gao, D. (2015) 'Yi dai yi lu zhan lue: kua yue shi kong de li shi xing si kao' [The Belt and Road strategy: historical thinking across time and space], *Sub National Fiscal Research* 11: 4–9.

Hayashi, S. (2010) 'The developmental state in the era of globalization: beyond the Northeast Asian model of political economy', *Pacific Review* 23(1): 45–69 <https://doi.org/10.1080/09512740903398330>.

Institute of International Trade and Economic Cooperation, Ministry of Commerce of the People's Republic of China (2020) 'Zhong guo yi dai yi lu mao yi tou zi fa zhan bao gao 2020' [China's trade and investment cooperation under the Belt and Road Initiative 2020], 28 September [online] <https://www.caitec.org.cn/n5/sy_gzdt_xshd/json/5532.html> [accessed 21 June 2022].

Institute of World Economics and Politics of the Chinese Academy of Social Sciences (2020) Nian zhong guo hai wai tou zi guo jia feng xian ping ji bao gao [Report on the Country Risk Rating of China's Overseas Investment 2020] [online] <https://baijiahao.baidu.com/s?id=1733964073560399106&wfr=spider&for=pc> [accessed 21 June 2022].

Johnson, C.A. (1982) *MITI and the Japanese Miracle: The Growth of Industrial Policy, 1925–1975*, Stanford University Press, Stanford, CA.

Kong, G. (2014) 'Tui jin yi dai yi lu yi chu li hao ruo gan guan xi' [Promoting the Belt and Road should handle several relations], *China Investment* 10: 47–49.

Lin, Y., Cai, F. and Li, Z. (1999) *Zhong guo de qi ji: Fa zhan zhan lue yu jing ji gai ge [China's Miracle: Development Strategy and Economic Reform]*, Truth & Wisdom Press, Shanghai.

Liu, C. and Liu, B. (2019) 'Yi dai yi lu chang yi xia de zhong guo dui wai he zuo ji zhi jian she:Jin zhan, wen ti yu dui ce' [The construction of China's foreign cooperation mechanism under the Belt and Road Initiative: progress, dilemma and countermeasures], *Journal of Xi'an Jiaotong University (Social Science)* 39(2): 134–41 <https://doi.org/10.15896/j.xjtuskxb.201902015>.

Liu, G. (2016) 'Lun ya tou hang zai tui jin yi dai yi lu jian she zhong de jin rong zhi cheng zuo yong' [On AIIB's role of financial support in the Belt and Road Initiative], *Northeast Asia Forum* 25(2): 58–66 <https://doi.org/10.13654/j.cnki.naf.2016.02.006>.

Liu, W. (2015) 'Yi dai yi lu zhan lue de ke xue nei han yu ke xue wen ti' [Scientific understanding of the Belt and Road Initiative of China and related research themes], *Progress in Geography* 34(5): 538–44 <https://doi.org/10.11820/dlkxjz.2015.05.001>.

Lv, J.Z., Yang, H., Wang, Y.J., Zhao, X., Zhong, W.X. and Yu, G.M. (2017) 'Zai yi dai yi lu guo ji chan neng he zuo zhong jian li qi ye zhu dao yu zheng fu tui dong de xie tong ji zhi' [Establishing a collaborative mechanism between enterprise leadership and government promotion in the Belt and Road international production capacity cooperation]. *International Petroleum Economics* 25: 1–6.

Ministry of Commerce of the People's Republic of China (2019) *Zhong guo dui wai cheng bao gong cheng fa zhan bao gao* [China's Belt and Road Trade and Investment Development Report] [online]. Available from: https://www.caitec.org.cn/upfiles/file/2021/11/20211208103423002.pdf [accessed 21 June 2022].

Ministry of Commerce of the People's Republic of China (2020) *Zhong guo dui wai cheng bao gong cheng fa zhan bao gao* [Annual report on China international project contracting] [online]. Available from: http://images.mofcom.gov.cn/fec/202106/20210630085424891.PDF [accessed 21 June 2022].

Ministry of Culture of the People's Republic of China (2016) 'Wen hua bu yi dai yi lu wen hua fa zhan xing dong ji hua (2016–2020)' [The cultural development action plan under the Belt and Road (2016–2020)], 5 January [online] <http://www.gov.cn/xinwen/2017-01/05/content_5156933.htm> [accessed 21 June 2022].

Ministry of Foreign Affairs of the People's Republic of China (2015) 'Vision and actions on jointly building Silk Road Economic Belt and 21st century Maritime Silk Road' [website] <https://www.fmprc.gov.cn/eng/topics_665678/2015zt/xjpcxbayzlt2015nnh/201503/t20150328_705553.html#:~:text=The%20Chinese%20government%20has%20drafted,African%20countries%20more%20closely%20and> [accessed 21 June 2022].

National Development and Reform Commission, Ministry of Foreign Affairs, and Ministry of Commerce of the People's Republic of China (2015) 'Vision and actions on jointly building Silk Road Economic Belt and 21st-Century Maritime Silk Road', 1 October [online] <https://www.fmprc.gov.cn/ce/cggb/eng/gzgg/t1252730.htm> [accessed 21 June 2022].

Oi, J.C. (1995) 'The role of the local state in China's transitional economy', *The China Quarterly* 144: 1132–49 <https://doi.org/10.1017/S0305741000004768>.

Ramo, J.C. (2004) *The Beijing Consensus*, Foreign Policy Centre, London.

Shapiro, L. (2016) 'The planner in action: China's influence as a developing and non-market economy on the WTO' [online], *College Undergraduate Research Electronic Journal* <https://repository.upenn.edu/curej/201/> [accessed 21 June 2022].

Sheng, L. and Quan, H. (2018) 'Cong zheng fu zhu dao zou xiang duo yuan lian dong yi dai yi lu de shi jian luo ji yu shen hua ce lue' [From government domination to multiple actors initiation: practice logic and further development of the Belt and Road], *Academic Monthly* 50(4): 46–57 <https://doi.org/10.19862/j.cnki.xsyk.2018.04.004>.

State Council Information Office of China (2021) zhong guo guo ji fa zhan he zuo bai pi shu [The White Paper on China's International Development Cooperation] [online] <http://www.scio.gov.cn/zfbps/32832/Document/1696685/1696685.htm> [accessed 21 June 2022].

Wang, J. (2008) 'Yin shi li dao yun ping zhou qi wen jian fa zhan: tou shi gai ge kai fang yi lai de liu ci hong guan diao kong' [Taking advantage of the situation to smooth out the steady development of the ironing cycle-looking at the six macro-controls since the reform and opening up], *Qian Xian* 9: 4–6.

Wang, S. and Zhang, X. (2018) 'Yi dai yi lu bei jing xia hua qiao hua ren yu zhong guo qi ye zou chu qu he zuo ji zhi yan jiu' [A study on the cooperation mechanism of overseas Chinese and Chinese enterprises going global in the context of the Belt and Road], *Journal of Overseas Chinese History Studies* 2: 51–60.

Wang, W. (2019) 'Zou chu qi da ren shi wu qu gao zhi liang gong lian yi dai yi lu' [Getting out of the seven misunderstandings and building high-quality the Belt and Road], *Journal of International Economic Cooperation* 1: 80–91.

Wei, L. and Tang, Z. (2020) 'Zhong zi shang ye yin hang zai yi dai yi lu yan xian guo jia de fen bu ji qi ying xiang yin su' [The distribution and influencing factors of Chinese commercial banks in countries along the Belt and Road], *Economic Geography* 40(11): 10–17 <https://doi.org/10.15957/j.cnki.jjdl.2020.11.002>.

Weiss, L. and Hobson, J. (1995) *States and Economic Development: A Comparative Historical Analysis*, Polity, Cambridge.

Wen, H. and Shen, J. (2019) 'Guan yu yi dai yi lu tou rong zi mo shi yu he zuo ji zhi de zheng ce si kao' [Policy thinking on the Belt and Road's investment and financing model and cooperation mechanism], *Macroeconomic Management* 2: 54–61 <https://doi.org/10.19709/j.cnki.11-3199/f.2019.02.011>.

White, G. and Wade, R. (1988) 'Developmental states and markets in East Asia: An introduction', in G. White (ed.), *Developmental States in East Asia* (pp. 1–29), Palgrave Macmillan, London.

World Bank (1993) *The East Asian Miracle: Economic Growth and Public Policy*, Oxford University Press, New York.

World Bank (1997) *World Development Report 1997: The State in a Changing World*, Oxford University Press, New York.

Xu, N. (2015) 'Yi dai yi lu zhan lue xia zhong guo qi ye zou chu qu de si kao' [Thinking on Chinese enterprises going global under the Belt and Road Initiative], *Economic Science* 3: 17–19.

Yang, L. (2018) 'Yi dai yi lu jian she zhong zheng fu diao kong yu shi chang pei zhi de hu dong' [The interaction of government regulation and market allocation in the construction of the Belt and Road], *People's Tribune* 5: 72–73.

Zhou, X. (2017) 'Jian chi shi chang hua yun zuo que bao yi dai yi lu tou rong zi ke chi xu xing' [Adhere to market-oriented operation to ensure sustainable investment and financing of the Belt and Road] [online] <http://finance.sina.com.cn/roll/2017-05-15/doc-ifyfekhi7654518.shtml> [accessed 15 February 2021].

Zhou, Y. and Wen, J. (2019) 'Yi dai yi lu bei jing xia dong man qi ye chuang yi chuang xin he zuo ji zhi yan jiu: Ji yu chan ye jia zhi lian dong tai bo yi de shi jiao' [Research on the creative and innovative cooperation mechanism of animation enterprises under the background of the Belt and Road: based on the perspective of dynamic game analysis of industrial value chain], *Journal of Northwest University (Philosophy and Social Science Edition)* 49(2): 156–62 <https://doi.org/10.16152/j.cnki.xdxbsk.2019-02-018>.

## CHAPTER 5

# Japan's developmentalist cooperation for quality infrastructure

*Sanae Ito* *

## Introduction

The popularity of the concept of 'connectivity' in the recent development literature reflects a growing emphasis on infrastructure in international development. 'Connectivity' here refers to the transportation, energy and telecommunications infrastructure that links communities and countries. The drive to improve connectivity across countries and regions is especially pronounced in Asia, where China and Japan compete for investment opportunities with the help of the two financial institutions under their control, the Asian Infrastructure Investment Bank (AIIB) and the Asian Development Bank (ADB).

The Japanese government's programme, the 'Partnership for Quality Infrastructure' is one example in which the government, in partnership with the Asian Development Bank, promotes connectivity through infrastructure investment abroad. This chapter looks at this national initiative in order to examine the changing politics of Japan's development cooperation underlying its promotion of connectivity. In particular, it explores the political nature of the seemingly technical initiative surrounding infrastructure development, and shows how the export of *quality infrastructure*, as a form of development cooperation incentivised by the official development assistance (ODA), is legitimized in the language of the Sustainable Development Goals (SDGs). The chapter argues that the current global development discourse surrounding the SDGs serves to depoliticize the policy framework for *quality infrastructure* and makes it appear as if it is predominantly a technology-driven initiative with the purpose of advancing sustainable development. It also argues that *quality infrastructure* is the core of Japan's revived developmentalism and its developmentalist cooperation across Asia. The developmental donor–recipient partnership thus forged is mediated by the use of the ODA to facilitate state-led economic growth for both the donor and the recipient countries. The notion of development is equated here with the fulfilment of the SDGs to bring universal benefits to both rich and poor countries.

## Infrastructure, modernization, and international development

What is infrastructure anyway? According to Larkin (2013: 329), infrastructure refers to 'objects that create the grounds on which other objects operate', connecting things, people, towns, regions, and countries. Operating as systems, they are more than simply a collection of technologies. They construct 'the relation between things' by mobilizing not just materials and technologies, but an amalgam of administrative and financial techniques (Larkin, 2013: 329). The 'relation between things' thus constructed is expected to be in harmony with the local environment and to expand people's life opportunities. Infrastructures also distribute the important resources people depend on, such as energy, information, and time (Appel et al., 2018), so that the construction of infrastructure offers multiple sites where negotiations between state agencies and people with differential access to those resources can take place.

Questions inevitably arise as to how resources will be distributed and whose life opportunities will be expanded or even sacrificed. When infrastructures are built in developing countries through development cooperation, these negotiation sites become even more complex, involving not just state agencies and local people, but foreign aid agencies, international financial institutions, multinational companies, as well as domestic and international civil society organizations. Thus, infrastructure development in the context of international development weaves a complex web of conflicting interests and political consternations.

In the West, the construction and management of infrastructure has historically been driven by neoclassical or neoliberal economic policies. With its capacity to connect people and objects, well-functioning infrastructure was seen vital to support long-term productivity growth and international trade. In the Global South, infrastructure-led industrialization promoted by Western aid donors in the 1950s and 1960s was associated with modernization theory which viewed the use of technologies and the rational organization of social and economic activities as the sole path to achieving a Western-style modern, industrialized society (Corbridge, 1995: 1–4).

The recent shift back to infrastructure-led development, triggered by China's South–South Cooperation, can arguably be regarded as a new version of such modernization projects, this time led by interventionist East Asia (Mawdsley, 2012). Instead of trying to follow the same uniform path to development once trodden by Western countries, the developing countries with East Asian-financed public works projects, are now being offered an alternative path to development, one with a strong focus on industrial policy and state-led infrastructure development. Furthermore, China's impressive record in poverty reduction over the last 20 years renews developing countries' faith in the efficacy of prioritizing growth-oriented economic policies with their 'trickle-down' effects on the poor over targeted poverty reducing interventions. Moreover, the current infrastructure-led development promises multiple benefits not seen before. It promises not only to physically connect people and objects but to generate local employment, improve human capacities, and to ensure social and environmental sustainability (METI, 2018). The type of social and environmental damages caused by earlier modernization projects would be contained this time thanks to improved communication with local communities and to superior eco-friendly technologies.

The modernization projects of the 1950s and 1960s were severely criticized by dependency theorists[1] during the 1970s for failing to bring about sustainable economic growth with the promised trickle-down effects upon the poor in developing countries. Attacks were also directed at the idea of applying uniform Western-style solutions to the developing world where each country possessed a unique history and institutions (Corbridge, 1995). Modernization projects of today, in contrast, promise non-Western and technologically more sophisticated solutions to the perceived unsustainable development of the past. Being firmly integrated in the SDGs, these solutions moreover resuscitate the idea of development as an outcome of short-to-medium term technocratic planning,[2] following the general trend established during the era of the Millennium Development Goals.

This trend in development thinking is in sharp contrast to the historical turn in the post-development theories of the 1980s and 1990s. The post-development theories rejected the discourse underlying short-to-medium term 'development planning' (Escobar, 1992) born out of the West's ethnocentric assumptions (Sumner and Tribe, 2008). What is different this time is that the trend is associated with an alternative to the traditional Western-oriented view of development and is supposed to reflect a diversity of views including those of emerging donors as well as private businesses as non-state development actors. The infrastructure-led development in this new era can thus be defined in terms of advanced technologies, diversity, and sustainability.

## Japan and the 'Partnership for Quality Infrastructure'

'The Partnership for Quality Infrastructure' is a Japanese government flagship programme for promoting infrastructure investment overseas. Japan's *White Paper on Development Cooperation 2015* (MOFA, 2016) describes 'quality infrastructure' in terms of its usefulness, safety, resilience, and building quality. Investing in quality infrastructure should help developing countries to achieve inclusive, sustainable, and resilient 'quality growth' and serve Japan's national and regional strategic interests at the same time. While strengthening connectivity between countries and regions, quality infrastructure is also intended to be in harmony with the local environment, help transfer technology between countries, and improve local people's livelihoods by generating jobs.

To understand the background to the Partnership for Quality Infrastructure Programme, we need to look back at *Japan Revitalization Strategy – Japan is Back* (Provisional) (Cabinet Office, 2013), a policy document released two years prior to the Partnership for Quality Infrastructure as the third 'arrow' of *Abenomics*[3] that outlined Japan's strategy to recover from decades of economic stagnation. The strategy aimed to increase infrastructure sales from ¥10 tn (approximately US$70 bn) in 2010 to ¥30 tn (approximately US$210 bn) by 2020[4] (Figure 5.1) through an all-Japan, public–private partnership (PPP) that entailed the active use of ODA. Infrastructure here refers to integrated infrastructure systems, or the package-type infrastructure projects that include not only design, equipment and facility procurement, and construction, but also management, operation, and maintenance using trained human resources. These package-type infrastructure projects generate long-term revenues for Japanese contractors. For example, IHI Infrastructure Systems and Sumitomo Mitsui Construction, two of Japan's mid-tier construction companies, built the ODA-financed Vietnam–Japan Friendship Bridge (Nhat Tan Bridge) in 2014 as 'quality infrastructure' (MLITT, 2021). The ODA process began in 2006 and

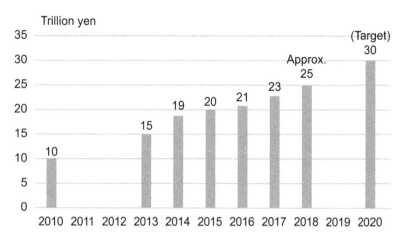

**Figure 5.1** Order volume for infrastructure systems export
*Source*: Translated and modified by the author based on METI, 2021: 3

lasted until 2013. The companies took full charge of the material procurement and labour management procedures, the key conditions for ensuring the effective deployment of advanced technologies and their smooth operations by well-trained technical staff.

The 'Partnership for Quality Infrastructure' is thus aligned with the Japanese government's economic revitalization strategy, and is built on four pillars (MOFA, n.d.). The first is the active involvement of Japan's aid agency, the Japan International Cooperation Agency (JICA), underscoring the conflation of infrastructure investment and foreign aid. The second is the close collaboration with the Asian Development Bank (ADB) whose president has traditionally been supplied by Japan's Ministry of Finance. The third is an increase in funding for relatively high-risk projects by the Japan Bank for International Cooperation (JBIC), a policy-based lending body that supports Japanese companies competing globally. The fourth is the marketing of 'Quality Infrastructure Investment' as an idea to establish an internationally accepted model (MOFA et al., 2015). The four pillars together outline the Japanese government's policy objectives for mobilizing Japan's ODA strategically to support its own companies investing in quality infrastructures across Asia.

In May 2016, Japan took the initiative to endorse the 'G7 *Ise-Shima* Principles for Promoting Quality Infrastructure Investment' at the G7 *Ise-Shima* Summit. The principles outlined in the agreement cover the issues of governance, economic efficiency, safety, resilience, job creation, capacity building, social and environmental impacts, and resource mobilization to be addressed through infrastructure projects (Kajikawa, n.d.). The then prime minister of Japan, Shinzo Abe, energetically campaigned for the idea of quality infrastructure investment at subsequent international conferences, pledging to spend US\$200 bn globally between 2017 and 2021 (Cabinet Office, 2022) (Figure 5.2). According to Ogawa (2019), Abe was intent on using his role as an international norm setter as leverage against China's growing influence in the region while domestic resources were increasingly constrained.

Quality infrastructure investment is commonly promoted through PPP which involves a risk-sharing mechanism between the public and private sectors. The mechanism requires setting up local private entities, or special purpose companies, in which governments and banks of both partner countries can invest. Figure 5.3 shows how Japan's ODA loans[5] offer comprehensive support to encourage Japanese businesses to form special purpose companies locally to participate in PPP infrastructure projects in developing countries. These special purpose companies are entrusted with project-related

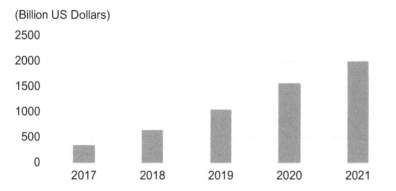

**Figure 5.2** Dollars spent on quality infrastructure investment worldwide
*Source:* Adapted from Cabinet Office, 2022: 1

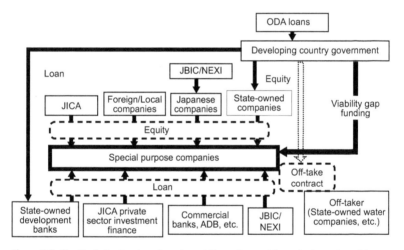

**Figure 5.3** Quality infrastructure investment through a public–private partnership
*Source:* Adapted from JICA, n.d.

infrastructural work such as design, construction, operation, maintenance, and financing. JICA provides developing country governments with ODA loans to assist these companies through a variety of funding and guarantee arrangements as long as the lead partner in these companies is a Japanese company. Apart from the ODA loans to the government, JICA can directly support the special purpose company through the Private Sector Investment Finance.[6] JBIC and Nippon Export and Investment Insurance (NEXI), an official export credit agency, provide financial support to mid-tier Japanese enterprises and small and medium-sized enterprises (SMEs)[7] as well as to their overseas affiliates to facilitate Japanese foreign direct investment in sectors related to quality infrastructure. JICA assists Japanese SMEs in particular to conduct feasibility surveys for project formulation and encourages them to disseminate their technologies in developing countries (JICA Philippines Office, 2017).

The quality infrastructure projects that appear in official documents are often described as part of Japan's efforts to fulfil the SDGs. For example, the MLITI (Ministry of Land, Infrastructure, Transport and Tourism, 2021: 1), which compiled a list of quality infrastructure good practices, explains that '[p]romoting quality infrastructure investment contributes to achieving international goals such as the 2030 Agenda for Sustainable Development'. The use of ODA for such efforts is seen as a means to attract Japanese commercial capital inflows in order to expand the total amount of financial resources available in developing countries to address the SDGs (Hataeda, 2019). In his presentation slides for Japanese investors, JICA's Hataeda (2019) explains that JICA will provide comprehensive support to *virtuous* companies willing to invest in SDG-related business projects in developing countries, including loans and funding for the special purpose companies they set up locally.

Such ODA funding schemes that assist the private sector in donor countries are not uncommon these days, as foreign aid is increasingly viewed as a catalyst for private financial flows (Kharas et al., 2011). The global development discourse associated with the SDGs encourages private sector investment in developing countries. In fact, there is a great deal of interest globally in 'blended finance', or the use of ODA to mobilize private capital for the purpose of international development (Development Initiatives, 2019). Building resilient infrastructure is an important part of the SDGs and, at the same time, is the prime focus of blended finance. According to the Organisation for Economic Co-operation and Development (OECD), in 2018–19 around US$50 bn were mobilized from the private sector by official development finance (OECD, 2021a: 3).

The use of ODA for blended finance is not without its controversies. Since the overall levels of ODA are not showing any signs of significant increase,[8] the growing use of ODA as part of blended finance for infrastructure projects would mean less ODA available for other types of development interventions. Moreover, the countries that receive such investments are not necessarily among the poorest. The OECD and the United Nations Capital Development Fund (UNCDF) published a joint report (2020: 20) to show that, between 2012 and 2018, the world's least developed countries received about $13.4 bn, or 6 per cent of the total private capital mobilized by official development finance. This compares with $84 bn received by upper middle income countries and $68 bn received by lower middle income countries (ibid.: 20). Further, the private capital thus mobilized was found to be concentrated in only a few economically promising sectors such as energy and financial services but not in sectors such as agriculture or water and sanitation that would have a direct impact on the lives of the poor.

The Japanese government's enthusiasm for catalysing development by mobilizing ODA to facilitate Japanese companies' investment in overseas infrastructure can be understood against this background. The enthusiasm contrasts with the historical trajectory Japan followed in order to catch up with the exemplary donors of the OECD's Development Assistance Committee (DAC) that were once suspicious of the close ties between aid and business. While the global context has changed dramatically in favour of private sector participation in development cooperation, the objective of development itself has often been confused with the achievement of the SDGs. Moreover, due to the fact that the SDGs are non-binding and universal, almost any individuals or groups can engage in activities related to any of the 17 SDGs, imagining that they are somehow contributing to international development. JICA's Private Sector Investment Finance that facilitates Japanese companies' investment in quality infrastructure projects is basically the same scheme that was discontinued in 2001 amid growing public criticisms over its non-transparent operations and questionable objectives unrelated to poverty reduction. When it was resumed in 2012, the NGO community strongly protested, arguing that the government made the decision in a non-transparent manner without paying attention to the problems it had raised once before.[9]

## Japan and the Easternization of Development[10]

As mentioned earlier, the 'Partnership for Quality Infrastructure' programme is often seen as a response to China's growing presence in infrastructure development through its Belt and Road Initiative. As a response, other Northern aid donors, too, are adjusting their foreign aid approaches to those of China and other emerging powers implementing South–South Cooperation. Japan, on the other hand, is arguably shifting its identity from Northern donor to East Asian donor. Despite the apparent gap between Japan's post-war record as a member of the Northern donors' club and China and South Korea's postcolonial history as aid recipients, commonalities within East Asia are not difficult to identify. These include their shared non-Western development experience, an emphasis on economic growth as opposed to social development, and the relative weakness of civil society, which have all been associated with the region's developmental state tradition in one way or another.

Japan's foreign aid programme officially started in 1954 when it joined the Colombo Plan to initiate economic cooperation with developing countries (MOFA, 2014a). In the same year, Japan signed a peace treaty with Burma (now called Myanmar) and started paying war reparations and setting up an economic cooperation with the country, later expanding this to other Asian countries. Kitano (2011: 28–29) explains that the notion of economic cooperation should be understood in terms of the obligation to pay reparations and that the term 'cooperation' may have been used instead of 'assistance' or 'aid' because Japan itself was at the time a developing country receiving foreign aid. 'Economic cooperation' in this context implied a broader framework than development assistance and was intended to encourage private sector investment in Asia's developing countries through a combination of ODA, export credit, and investment insurance (Kato, 1998: 84). Japan was one of the original members of the DAC and, when it started its economic cooperation for developing countries in the 1950s, it used ODA to mobilize additional private sector resources for development under this broader foreign aid concept of economic cooperation – an approach that strongly resonates with the recent global trend towards blended finance.

The strong focus on mercantilism that had evolved in that period then became the subject of intense debate throughout the 1980s and 1990s, drawing strong criticism from Japan's nascent civil society. The criticism was specifically directed at the government's narrow focus on economic infrastructure, the preferential use of loans rather than grants, and the close ties between aid and Japan's business community (Rix, 1993; Kitano, 2011: 137–69). While Japan was always regarded as something of 'an odd man out' among Western donors (Söderberg, 2010: 107), these characteristics of Japan's ODA were tolerated by the mainstream development community in the West as long as Japan was making progress, albeit slowly, in aligning its aid with partner countries' domestic priorities.

This has clearly changed, as the growth of the East and Southeast Asian economies appears to have vindicated Japan's aid approach, at least from the point of view of Asia's development communities. Rix cites Islam (1991) to point out that Japan's aid has recently been seen as 'unquestionably successful in assisting economic development, especially in Asia, because of the growth of the Asian economies resulting from Japanese aid support' (Rix, 1993: 170). Concomitantly,

South Korea and China rose as emerging powers and created a common interest in an East Asian modality of development cooperation outside Asia. A variety of explanations have been offered to explain China's growing presence in Africa in particular. This presence, in part, has been explained in terms of the lingering spirit of the 1955 Bandung Conference which discussed Afro-Asian solidarity based on their common identities as victims of colonialism (Shinn and Eisenman, 2012). It has also been explained in the context of the discussions held at the Fourth High Level Forum (HLF) on Aid Effectiveness held in Busan, South Korea, in 2011. The Busan Partnership for Effective Development Cooperation that resulted from these discussions marked a paradigm shift in foreign aid and endorsed a variety of development cooperation modalities including South–South Cooperation.

As it happens, much of what Western analysts attribute to the Chinese development approaches in Africa also applies to Japanese approaches in East and Southeast Asia. Thus, de Haan's (2011) characterization of Chinese aid strongly resonates with how Japanese aid used to be characterized by both domestic and international critics (Rix, 1993; Murai, 2006). The close ties between aid and business communities to promote industrialization through infrastructure building and investment has been said, at one time or another, to characterize Japan's ODA (Söderberg, 2010: 113–15). China's emphasis on supporting developing countries' 'self-reliance' (Brautigam, 2009: 35; de Haan, 2011: 887) has also been the fundamental pillar of Japan's ODA policy for the last 20 years (MOFA, 2014b).

One may argue that these characteristics are not unique to East Asian donors at all. Robb (2004: 22–29), in his analysis of the changing power relations in the history of foreign aid, describes how some Western donors used foreign aid as technical, rather than social interventions in order to open markets for commercial interests in the post-World War II period up to the end of the 1960s. From this perspective, the so-called East Asian model of foreign aid is simply a passing phase that will be gradually upgraded to what has become known as the mainstream Western development paradigm endorsed until recently by the OECD-DAC. Yet, as China's and South Korea's presence in developing countries grows, the new discourse of development cooperation has gathered force in East Asia and, as discussed earlier, is now viewed as an alternative to the traditional model of development assistance saturated with strong neoliberal and moral orientation. In fact, many of the traditional Western donors themselves have begun swapping their conventional approaches for ones that are more in line with the East Asian approach, a phenomenon that Mawdsley (2018) calls the 'Southernization' of development. Since many of the features now ascribed to China as the champion of the South equally apply to Japan and South Korea, the phenomenon may more appropriately be referred to as the 'Easternization' of development.

## Quality infrastructure and Japan's revived developmentalism

Japan's 'Partnership of Quality Infrastructure' should thus be understood within the context of Japan's historical experience as a foreign aid donor and its more recent realignment with other East Asian development cooperation partners. Yoshimatsu (2017) analyses the Japanese government's policy initiatives which use ODA strategically to promote quality infrastructure exports, and argues that the export of quality infrastructure systems has clearly become a new policy field where the government pursues its developmentalist policy in order to assist the country's construction industry.

The debate about Japan's developmental state policies was originally instigated by Chalmers Johnson in the 1980s. Johnson (1982) analysed the growth of industrial policy in Japan between the period of 1925 and 1975 and argued that Japan's powerful bureaucracy, i.e. the Ministry of International Trade and Industry (MITI), took strong initiatives to steer its economy towards developing nascent industries while taking measures to reduce the negative impact of shifting from old to new industrial structures. After the late 1990s, the Japanese government arguably resorted to neoliberal reform programmes consisting of deregulation and privatization, discarding what was seen by Johnson (1982) as its developmental state policies (Yoshimatsu, 2017). Besides, Japan, along with other East Asian developmental states, is seen as having 'graduated' from the level of development at which such developmental state characteristics work effectively. Many would also argue that the role of the developmental state in general has become largely irrelevant amid the rapid progress of globalization (see Fine et al., 2013). In Asia in particular, the experience of the Asian financial crisis in 1997 cast a long shadow on the effectiveness of the developmental state policy instruments used to make adjustments with global capital markets (Fine et al., 2013).

What may be viewed more recently as the revival of developmentalist policy formation in Japan is thus a relatively new phenomenon, and one that should be understood against the backdrop of intensified global economic competition gradually eroding Japan's strength in formerly competitive manufacturing industries (Yoshimatsu, 2017). The revival is demonstrated not so much by state-led industrialization per se, but more so by state-led revitalization of old industries, such as the construction industry, via the promotion of trade and foreign direct investment. Infrastructure business in particular is seen as 'a seed to refuel Japan's exports and stimulate a growth engine' (Yoshimatsu, 2017: 509). The state moreover has embarked on reforming ODA loan and investment mechanisms so that foreign aid can serve as a catalyst for encouraging Japanese companies to form public–private partnerships for infrastructure export. Yoshimatsu (2017: 502) observes that 'the government offers selective means such as foreign aid, public finance, and trade insurance in order to facilitate private actors' overseas business, and senior government leaders play a prominent role in creating the foundation for business expansion towards target countries'.

The discursive framing of 'partnership' in the *quality infrastructure* programme is in line with the notion of development cooperation between equal partners seeking mutual economic benefit. As Fukuda-Parr and Shiga (2016) argue, the implementation of mutually beneficial economic cooperation has been part of Japan's economic strategy since the 1960s, built on the complementarity of the Japanese economy with those of its Asian neighbours. Earlier, though, such economic cooperation was implemented more explicitly through a specific form of industrial policy involving aid, trade, and investment as a package, which was referred to as the 'trinity approach' (*sanmi-ittai*), and was a hallmark of Japan's development assistance to East and Southeast Asia (Fukuda-Parr and Shiga, 2016). Arase argued back in 1995 that Japan's foreign aid was indeed an essential part of its developmentalist policy packages. He went on to describe how the Japanese bureaucracy, coordinated mainly by the then Ministry of International Trade and Industry (MITI), guided the private sector through its foreign aid policy into moving 'manufacturing with declining competitiveness to lower-cost production sites in Asia' (Arase, 1995: 249). Around the same time, Robert Wade (1996) wrote a detailed account of Japan's battle with the World Bank over its interventionist development policies and particularly over its policy of providing directed credit, i.e. subsidized and targeted or earmarked credit, to Southeast Asia. In doing so, Japan encouraged recipient governments to 'think more strategically and in more interventionist terms than can be accommodated by World Bank ideas', and to 'articulate national objectives and policy choices, to catalyse market agents, and to assist some industries more than others' (Wade, 1996: 5). As Japan historically outsourced less technology-intensive production to countries in Southeast Asia, they were in turn willing to adopt *appropriate* local industrial policies.

The recent revival of Japan's developmentalism involving quality infrastructure exports has reinvigorated the old practice of the 'trinity approach' to foreign aid, supported by the resumption in 2012 of

JICA's Private Sector Investment Finance mentioned earlier. While the ensuing revival of Japan's developmentalist cooperation is in part a competitive response to China's global expansion through the Belt and Road Initiative, it also plays a part in reinventing the *Eastern* approach to development.

## Conclusion

This chapter has argued that the Partnership for Quality Infrastructure occupies the central place in Japan's revived developmentalism and its developmentalist cooperation across Asia. The discourse surrounding the SDGs helps provide a conducive environment in which the political and economic nature of developmentalist cooperation is significantly neutralized by the global efforts to achieve the SDGs. Quality infrastructure is strongly associated with the language of the SDGs with frequent references to such concepts as resilience, sustainability, and inclusive growth. Thus, building quality infrastructure becomes almost synonymous with contributing to sustainable development. The SDGs' emphasis on universality and national contexts adds to the notion that a wealthy country that addresses particular goals and targets domestically, such as job creation and industrial upgrading, simultaneously contributes to sustainable development globally. The increased role of the private sector in the SDGs framework accelerates this tendency, allowing for the view that Japanese businesses investing in quality infrastructures in developing countries should be given ODA financed incentives.

Japan can readjust its foreign aid approaches to the current global context relatively more easily than some of its Western counterparts which are also trying to reconnect foreign aid with national interests.[11] This is because China and South Korea are recognized as influential Southern development partners engaged in similar practices, and Japan, together with the two other East Asian countries, can easily recast itself as representing an alternative, non-Western approach to development. Thus, the narrative that there are diverse, non-Western paths to development allows Japan to reframe the purpose of its development cooperation in line with its traditional developmentalist policy practices. What this East–South ideological partnership seems to resuscitate then is the once-popular discourse of development associated with state-led economic growth presented as the alternative to the neoliberal development model. Quality infrastructure as a public good gives such development discourse a clear focus around which mutually beneficial developmentalist cooperation can be organized. Development as defined in such terms assumes that poverty eradication in its partner countries is intrinsically linked to Japan's industrial revival and its trickle-down effects across borders.

## Notes

* Professor of development studies at the Graduate School of International Development, Nagoya University, Japan. ito@gsid.nagoya-u.ac.jp
1. Hans Singer, Raúl Prebisch, Andre Gunder Frank, and Immanuel Wallerstein, among others, contributed to the formation of dependency theory in the1960s and 1970s. Frank's *Capitalism and Underdevelopment in Latin America* (1967) was one of the most influential dependency school works to explain why poor countries stayed poor in the global capitalist system.
2. Sumner and Tribe (2008: 11–16) identified three discernible definitions of 'development', one of which is a 'short- to medium-term outcome of desirable targets' (13). It represents the narrower, and technocratic, view of development with a relatively short-term outlook.
3. *Abenomics* refers to an economic policy package implemented by the Japanese Government under the leadership of Shinzo Abe, who served as Prime Minister from 2012 to 2020. It consists of 'three arrows': monetary easing, fiscal stimulus, and structural reforms.
4. The total amount of infrastructure orders Japan received has reportedly reached ¥25 tn (about US$227.27 bn) in 2018.
5. Japan's bilateral aid consists of finance and investment cooperation (ODA loans and private sector investment finance) and grant aid and technical cooperation (JICA, 2021).
6. Private Sector Investment Finance is a policy-based lending scheme intended to 'stimulate economic activity and improve the living standards of people in developing countries through equity investments and loans for projects undertaken in developing countries by the private sector' (JICA, 2016: 131).
7. In the Japanese context, mid-tier companies are capitalized at roughly ¥100 m to ¥10 bn while SMEs are capitalized at ¥10 to 100 m. The majority of the SMEs are small-scale companies.
8. According to Development Initiatives (2021), overall levels of foreign aid have generally flatlined since 2016. In 2020, however, Covid-19 spending helped to push it up to an all-time high (OECD, 2021b).
9. Thirteen development and environmental NGOs jointly submitted a statement to the government, then led by Prime Minister Naoto Kan, to oppose the resumption of the Private Sector Investment Finance, criticizing the way the decision was made without

adequately consulting with civil society organizations (Friends of the Earth Japan, 2011).

10. This section draws on my article, 'Teaching development studies in Japan: navigating between Eastern and Western discourses of development' (Ito, 2017) published in the *Journal of International Development*.

11. According to the Principled Aid Rankings 2020 of the Overseas Development Institute that measure the degree of altruism in foreign aid, the UK and the US have both seen their scores fall, while France continuously ranks lowest (Gulrajani, 2021).

## References

Appel, H., Anand, N., and Gupta, A. (2018) 'Introduction: temporality, politics, and the promise of infrastructure', in N. Anand, A. Gupta, and H. Appel (eds), *The Promise of Infrastructure*, pp. 1–40, Duke University Press, Durham, NC.

Arase, D. (1995) *Buying Power: The Political Economy of Japan's Foreign Aid*, Lynne Rienner Publishers, Boulder, CO.

Brautigam, D. (2009) *The Dragon's Gift: The Real Story of China in Africa*, Oxford University Press, Oxford.

Cabinet Office, Japan (2013) *Japan Revitalization Strategy: Japan is Back* (provisional). Available from: https://www.kantei.go.jp/jp/singi/keizaisaisei/pdf/en_saikou_jpn_hon.pdf [accessed 30 September 2021].

Cabinet Office, Japan (2022) 'Shitsuno takai infra yushutsu kakudai initiative-no seika houkoku' [Outcome report on quality infrastructure export expansion initiatives], 3 June. Available from: https://www.kantei.go.jp/jp/singi/keikyou/dai54/kettei_4.pdf [accessed 5 August 2022]

Corbridge, S. (ed.) (1995) *Development Studies: A Reader*, Arnold, London.

de Haan, A. (2011) 'Will China change international development as we know it?', *Journal of International Development* 23: 881–908 <https://doi.org/10.1002/jid.1732>.

Development Initiatives (2019) *How Blended Finance Reaches the Poorest People: Theory and Practice*, Discussion Paper. Available from: https://devinit.org/documents/670/How-blended-finance-reaches-the-poorest_people.pdf [accessed 30 September 2021].

Development Initiatives (2021) *Aid Data 2019-2020: Analysis of Trends before and during Covid*, Briefing February 2021. Available from: https://devinit.org/documents/905/Aid_data_2019-2020_Analysis_of_trends_before_and_during_Covid.pdf [accessed 27 February 2022].

Escobar, A. (1992) 'Planning', in W. Sachs (ed.), *The Development Dictionary: A Guide to Knowledge as Power*, pp. 132–45, Zed Books, London.

Fine, B., Saraswati, J., and Tavasci, D. (2013) *Beyond the Developmental State: Industrial Policy into the Twenty-First Century*, Pluto Press, London.

Frank, A.G. (1967) *Capitalism and Underdevelopment in Latin America: Historical Studies of Chile and Brazil*, revised edn, Monthly Review Press, New York.

Friends of the Earth Japan (2011) 'Nihon no seifu kaihatsu enjo' [Japan's ODA] [website] <https://www.foejapan.org/aid/doc/110225.html> (posted 25 February 2011) [accessed 10 August 2021].

Fukuda-Parr, S. and Shiga, H. (2016) *Normative Framing of Development Cooperation: Japanese Bilateral Aid between the DAC and Southern Donors*, JICA-RI Working Paper 130. Available from: https://www.jica.go.jp/jica-ri/ja/publication/workingpaper/jrft3q0000005y6n-att/JICA-RI_WP_No.130.pdf [accessed 13 November 2022].

Gulrajani, N. (2021) 'World's wealthiest increasingly putting national interests over altruism when allocating aid', Overseas Development Institute [website] <https://odi.org/en/press/worlds-wealthiest-increasingly-putting-national-interest-before-altruism-when-allocating-aid/> [accessed 12 November 2021].

Hataeda, M. (2019) 'Kaigai toyushi-no gaiyo-to tenbo' [A summary of and prospects for private sector investment finance], JICA presentation slides, 25 January [online] <https://www.jica.go.jp/investor/bond/ku57pq00000r13n2-att/20190125_03.pdf> [accessed 26 July 2021].

Ito, S. (2017) 'Teaching development studies in Japan: navigating between Eastern and Western discourses of development', *Journal of International Development* 29(7): 981–92 <http://dx.doi.org/10.1002/jid.3043>.

Japan International Cooperation Agency (JICA) (2016) *ODA Loan and Private Sector Investment Finance*, JICA Annual Report 2016, pp. 130–31 [online] <https://www.jica.go.jp/english/publications/reports/annual/2016/c8h0vm0000aj21oz-att/2016_49.pdf> [accessed 1 August 2021].

JICA (2021) 'Official development assistance loans' [website] <https://www.jica.go.jp/english/our_work/types_of_assistance/oda_loans/overseas/index.html> [accessed 10 November 2020].

JICA (n.d.) 'PPP (public private partnership) shien' [Support for the public private partnership] [website] <https://www.jica.go.jp/activities/schemes/finance_co/about/ppp.html> [accessed 1 August 2021].

JICA Philippines Office (2017) 'JICA assistance program for quality infrastructure investment' [PowerPoint slides] <https://www.meti.go.jp/policy/mono_info_service/mono/waterbiz/kenkyukai/kaigai_infra/seminar-presen/PDFfiles/07_JICA.pdf> [accessed 1 August 2021].

Johnson, C. (1982) *MITI and the Japanese Miracle: The Growth of Industrial Policy, 1925–1975*, Stanford University Press, Stanford, CA.

Kajikawa, M. (n.d.) 'Promoting quality infrastructure investment – Japan's contribution to infrastructure development' [PowerPoint slides], Development Policy Division of the Ministry of Finance, Japan <https://www.oecd.org/daf/fin/private-pensions/Mitsutoshi-Kajikawa-Japan-MOF.pdf> [accessed 1 August 2021].

Kato, K. (1998) *Tsusho Kokka no Kaihatsu Kyouryoku Seisaku: Nichi Doku no Kokusaiteki Ichi to Kokunai Seido tono Renkan* [Development Cooperation Policies of Trading Nations: The Relationship between the International Status of Japan and Germany and their Domestic Institutions], Bokutakusha, Tokyo.

Kharas, H., Makino, K., and Jung, W. (eds) (2011) *Catalyzing Development: A New Vision for Aid*, Brookings Institution Press, New York.

Kitano, S. (2011) *Kokusai Kyoryoku no Tanjo: Kaihatsu no Datsuseijika wo Koete* [The Birth of International Cooperation: Beyond the De-Politicisation of Development], Soseisha, Tokyo.

Larkin, B. (2013) 'The politics and poetics of infrastructure', *Annual Review of Anthropology* 42: 327–43 <https://doi.org/10.1146/annurev-anthro-092412-155522>.

Mawdsley, E. (2012) *From Recipients to Donors: Emerging Powers and the Changing Development Landscape*, Zed Books, London.

Mawdsley, E. (2018) 'The 'southernisation' of development?', *Asia Pacific Viewpoint* 59(2): 173–85 <https://doi.org/10.1111/apv.12192>.

METI (2018) Committee on Trade and Investment, *APEC Guidebook on Quality of Infrastructure Development and Investment (revision)* [online]. Available from: https://www.apec.org/docs/default-source/Publications/2018/11/2018-CTI-Report-to-Ministers/TOC/Appendix-11---APEC-Guidebook-on-Quality-of-Infrastructure-Development-and-Investment.pdf [accessed 13 November 2022].

METI (2021) 'Keisansho infra FS support jigyo to infra system kaigai tenkai senryaku 2025' [METI infrastructure FS support projects and the global extension strategy for infrastructure systems 2025], Trade and Economic Cooperation Bureau [PowerPoint slides] <https://www.nedo.go.jp/content/100928533.pdf> [accessed 4 November 2021].

MOFA (2014a) 'History of Official Development Assistance' [website] <http://www.mofa.go.jp/policy/oda/summary/1994/1.html> [accessed 1 August 2021].

MOFA (2014b) *ODA Taiko Minaoshi ni Kansuru Yushikisha Kondannkai Hokokusho* [Recommendations by the expert's panel for the revision of the ODA charter]. Available from: http://www.mofa.go.jp/mofaj/gaiko/oda/about/kaikaku/taikou_minaoshi/files/yusikisya_report.pdf [accessed 1 August 2021].

MOFA (2016) *White Paper on Development Cooperation 2015: Japan's International Cooperation*. Available from: https://www.mofa.go.jp/files/000168443.pdf [accessed 30 September 2021].

MOFA (n.d.) 'Partnership for quality infrastructure' [PowerPoint slides] <https://www.mofa.go.jp/files/000117998.pdf> [accessed 30 September 2021].

MOFA, MOF, METI and MLIT (2015) 'Partnership for Quality Infrastructure: Investment for Asia's Future', 21 May [online] <https://www.mofa.go.jp/files/000081298.pdf> [accessed 30 September 2021].

Ministry of Land, Infrastructure, Transport and Tourism (MLITT), Japan (2021) *Nihon no Shitsuno Takai Infra Project: Good Practice Shu* [Japan's quality infrastructure projects: A collection of good practices]. Available from: https://www.mlit.go.jp/kokusai/content/001397310. pdf [accessed 28 February 2022].

Murai, Y. (ed.) (2006) *Tettei Kenshou: Nippon no ODA* [A Thorough Investigation of Japan's ODA], Commons, Tokyo.

Organisation for Economic Co-operation and Development (OECD) (2021a) *Amounts Mobilised from the Private Sector by Official Development Finance Interventions in 2018–19: Highlights.* Available from: https://issuu.com/oecd.publishing/docs/amounts-mobilsed-from-the-private-sector-by-dev-fi#:~:text=In%20 2018%2D19%2C%20direct%20investment,co%2Dfinancing%20 (4%25) [accessed 13 November 2022].

OECD (2021b) 'COVID-19 spending helped to lift foreign aid to an all-time high in 2020 but more effort needed' [website] <https:// www.oecd.org/newsroom/covid-19-spending-helped-to-lift-foreign-aid-to-an-all-time-high-in-2020-but-more-effort-needed. htm> [accessed 27 February 2022].

OECD/United Nations Capital Development Fund (UNCDF) (2020) *Blended Finance in the Least Developed Countries 2020: Supporting a Resilient COVID-19 Recovery,* OECD Publishing, Paris. Available from: https://doi.org/10.1787/57620d04-en [accessed 1 August 2021].

Ogawa, H. (2019) 'Normality of international norms: power, interests, and knowledge in Japan's ODA politics', *Journal of International Development Studies* 28(3): 5–18 <https://doi.org/10.32204/jids.28.3_5>.

Prahalad, C.K. (2005) *The Fortune at the Bottom of the Pyramid: Eradicating Poverty through Profits,* Wharton School Publishing, Upper Saddle River, NJ.

Rix, A. (1993) *Japan's Foreign Aid Challenge: Policy Reform and Aid Leadership,* Routledge, London.

Robb, C. (2004) 'Changing power relations in the history of aid', in L. Groves and R. Hinton (eds), *Inclusive Aid: Changing Power and Relationships in International Development,* pp: 21–41, Earthscan, London.

Shinn, D.H. and Eisenman, J. (2012) *China and Africa: A Century of Engagement,* University of Pennsylvania Press, Philadelphia.

Söderberg, M. (2010) 'Challenges or complements for the West: is there an "Asian" model of aid emerging?', in J.S. Sörensen (ed.), *Challenging the Aid Paradigm: Western Currents and Asian Alternatives,* pp. 107–37, Palgrave Macmillan, New York.

Sumner, A. and Tribe, M. (2008) *International Development Studies: Theories and Methods in Research and Practice*, SAGE Publications, London.

Wade, R. (1996) 'Japan, the World Bank, and the art of paradigm maintenance: the East Asian miracle in political perspective', *New Left Review* 1/217: 3–36 <https://newleftreview.org/issues/i217/articles/robert-wade-japan-the-world-bank-and-the-art-of-paradigm-maintenance-the-east-asian-miracle-in-political-perspective>.

Yoshimatsu, H. (2017) 'Japan's export of infrastructure systems: pursuing twin goals through developmental means', *The Pacific Review* 30(4): 494–512 <http://dx.doi.org/10.1080/09512748.2016.1276953>.

# CHAPTER 6

# Japan's developmentalist cooperation for the Joint Crediting Mechanism

*Kiyoshi Fujikawa\* and Sanae Ito\*\**

## Introduction

This chapter looks at Japan's developmentalist cooperation in areas related to climate change. Developmentalist cooperation is defined here as a form of development cooperation through which official development assistance (ODA) is used strategically as a policy instrument to facilitate Japanese business investment in developing countries. The chapter first gives an overview of how global climate change initiatives have connected the Global North and South, creating opportunities for the Global North to integrate their national interests in their environmental aid. It then explains the specific mechanisms by which the Japanese government tries to do so despite the discord it may create with the Organisation for Economic Co-operation and Development (OECD)-Development Assistance Committee (DAC) over its guideline on ODA eligibility.

Specifically, the chapter focuses on the Joint Crediting Mechanism (JCM), a bilateral scheme by which the Japanese government shoulders parts of developing countries' costs for their initial investments into low-carbon and zero emission technologies. The reduction of greenhouse gas (GHG) emissions achieved through this scheme is then recognized as a positive outcome by both Japan and its developing country partners. Here, Japan's ODA is used strategically to promote private sector participation and to achieve a triple benefit: for Japan, its developing country partners, and the environment. Domestically, three Japanese ministries have a stake in ensuring the success of the JCM: the Ministry of Economy, Trade and Industry, which promotes the export of *quality infrastructure*[1] associated with clean air technologies; the Ministry of Environment (MOE), which seeks to achieve Japan's emission reduction targets; and the Ministry of Foreign Affairs (MOFA), in charge of extending financial and technical assistance to developing countries. The chapter explores how the growing significance of the global climate change agenda has opened an opportunity for Japan to deploy developmental state policy instruments in its foreign aid programmes to provide public goods in the form of GHG emissions reduction.

## Japan's environmental aid

Japan first announced its environmental ODA policy at the G7 Summit held in Grand Arche, La Defense, France in 1989, pledging to disburse ¥300 bn (US$2.17 bn at the 1989 exchange rate) over three years through bilateral and multilateral assistance targeting environmental issues (JICA, 2001). In the early 1990s, the Japan International Cooperation Agency (JICA), a government agency in charge of delivering the bulk of Japan's ODA, set up an administrative section within the then Planning Department to address such issues. The section was later expanded to become the Environment, WID,[2] and other Global Issues Division. Simultaneously, the Overseas Economic Cooperation Fund (OECF), a government development finance institution reorganized in 1999 into the Japan Bank for International Cooperation, also started paying attention to environmental concerns. It formulated the OECF Guidelines for Environmental Considerations in 1989 to prevent its loan-financed infrastructure projects causing environmental damage. Japan expanded its financial commitment to environmental aid even further when it announced at the Rio Earth Summit in 1992 that the country would disburse ¥900 to 1000 bn over the following five years to address environmental challenges (MOFA, n.d.). The vast majority of this environmental aid was earmarked in the form of concessional loans, in contrast to other donor countries which provided a larger proportion of grants.

Thus, around 80 per cent of Japan's annual disbursement of environmental aid from 1994 to 2006 was in the form of ODA loans (Kim, 2012). The Environmental Policy Division of the Ministry of International Trade and Industry (MITI)[3] is said to have played a key role in these decisions. It especially underlined the need for technology transfer to developing countries to improve their environmental management processes (Dauvergne, 2001). MITI helped set up the International Centre for Environmental Technology Transfer in 1991 to export Japanese anti-pollution technologies to developing countries. As part of this initiative, MITI announced the Green Aid Plan in the following year to facilitate the diffusion of clean coal technologies in developing countries; 80 per cent of the funding for this plan came from MITI's non-ODA budget, while the remaining 20 per cent came from its ODA budget (Evans, 1999).

In 1995 Japan announced preferential conditions for ODA loans addressing environmental problems. Thus, potential recipient countries whose gross national product per capita had previously exceeded the eligibility criteria for ODA loans were now eligible for loans that would be used to mitigate environmental damage. This enabled countries like Mexico and Brazil to gain access to Japan's ODA loans. In 1997, amidst the financial damages wrought by the Asian financial crisis, Japan eased the conditions for ODA loans intended for environmental issues by lowering the interest rate to 0.75 per cent and instituting 40-year repayment and 10-year deferment periods (JICA, 2001). According to JICA (2001), this was a landmark change in the history of Japan's foreign aid because it allowed Japan to finance projects that had never previously been funded via ODA loans. These included projects for urban mass transportation systems such as subways, hydroelectric and natural gas power plants and their related facilities, as well as for retrofitting manufacturing facilities with energy-saving and resource-conserving devices (JICA, 2001).

This 'landmark' change in Japan's ODA loans to focus on environmental issues must be viewed against the backdrop that the country's environmental aid had always been characterized by an emphasis on its comparative advantage in anti-pollution and energy efficient technologies and infrastructure projects (Kim, 2012). Critics point out that this was a way of concealing the government's interest in supporting the Japanese companies specializing in capital-intensive technologies and accompanying services (Kim, 2012; Evans, 1999). Such technologies cannot be provided without involving the private sector, whose interest is in transferring technologies as a package with large-scale operating and monitoring systems to assess their impacts on the environment on a long-term basis. This was in contrast to other major DAC donors that allocated their aid primarily for sectoral institutional reforms and renewable energy development.

This was the context in which Japan took the initiative to host the Kyoto Protocol talks in 1997, wishing to highlight its commitment to climate change and boost its profile. Japan announced the 'Initiatives for Sustainable Development toward the 21st Century', commonly referred to as the Kyoto Initiative, at the Special Session of the United Nations General Assembly on Environment and Development. The initiative was intended to stimulate industrialized countries to develop technologies to reduce energy consumption and global warming and to transfer these technologies to developing countries. The concessional terms (a 0.75 per cent annual interest rate and a 40-year repayment period) announced by Japan were meant to support the country's efforts in this direction.

## Japan and the Kyoto Protocol

The Kyoto Protocol, which was adopted in December 1997 and went into force in February 2005, was the first addition to the United Nations Framework Convention on Climate Change (UNFCCC),[4] an international environmental treaty requiring its signatories to develop national programmes to reduce their emissions of GHGs. The Protocol rests upon the principle of 'common but differentiated responsibilities', recognizing that countries' varying capacities to tackle climate change depend on their level of economic development. Thus, most of the Annex I signatories[5] to the UNFCCC, industrialized (developed) countries held historically responsible for the present levels of GHGs in the atmosphere, were subject to mandatory emission-reduction targets. Developing country signatories, on the other hand, were not required to reduce their emissions, as their responsibility for the current levels of GHGs was considered negligible compared to the Annex I industrialized countries.

The protocol offered several means for industrialized countries to reach their targets. One of them was to use natural processes known as 'sinks', which include planting trees, to help remove GHGs from the atmosphere. Another is the so-called Kyoto mechanisms, which allow industrialized countries to meet some of their emission reduction targets outside their national borders through emissions trading, Joint Implementation, and the Clean Development Mechanism (CDM). Emissions trading, also known as 'cap and trade', involves participating countries trading their emissions rights as credits by placing an economic value on GHG emissions. Countries that succeed in reducing their carbon emissions below a certain baseline level could earn these credits and sell them to other countries. This is considered a cost-effective way of reducing emissions through the use of economic incentives and market mechanisms (United Nations, 1998).

Joint Implementation refers to emissions trading projects implemented jointly between two Annex I countries. In this scheme, one country may carry out a climate project in another country where the cost of reducing emissions is lower, and thus earn Emission Reduction Units to be counted towards meeting its own target. The CDM works in a similar way, but here emissions trading must take place between developed and developing countries. In industrialized countries, the marginal cost of GHG reduction is relatively high compared to developing countries. Thus, it is less costly and more efficient for industrialized countries to try to reduce emissions in developing countries. The CDM projects can therefore be carried out in developing countries without any reduction obligations. The emission savings that result from a CDM project are certified, and the units, called Certified Emission Reductions (CERs), can be claimed and used by the industrialized countries implementing the projects towards meeting their own reduction obligations. The CDM thus provides incentives for industrialized countries to invest in emissions reducing technologies

**Table 6.1** Kyoto Protocol achievement plan (original proposal)

| Reduction measures | Share against the total reduction target (%) |
| --- | --- |
| Domestic measures total | −0.5 |
|    $CO_2$ from energy consumption | +0.6 |
|    $CO_2$ of non-energy origin | −0.3 |
|    Methane | −0.4 |
|    Nitrous oxide | −0.5 |
|    CFC substitutes, etc. | +0.1 |
| Sinks | −3.9 |
| Kyoto Mechanisms (emissions trading) | −1.6 |
| Total | −6.0 |

Source: Author's compilation based on Kyoto Protocol Achievement Plan (Cabinet Office, 2008)

and infrastructures to be used in developing countries that often offer significant opportunities for emissions reduction. An investment in a rural electrification project in a developing country using solar panels would be one such example. According to the UNFCCC, a total of 7,846 CDM projects have been registered, with the total carbon dioxide ($CO_2$) reduction from these projects reaching almost 3 billion t-$CO_2$[6] as of January 2021 (UNFCCC, n.d.).

Table 6.1 shows the Kyoto Protocol Target Achievement Plan for Japan as formulated in 2005. The Japanese government at the time promoted a campaign called 'Team Minus 6%'. The 6 per cent target is misleading, however, since 'sinks' or the $CO_2$ absorption rate due to forest management (i.e. minus 3.9 per cent) were pre-determined during the negotiations for the Kyoto Protocol based on the assumption that Japan's forests had the capacity to absorb this amount. In other words, the minus 3.9 per cent was expected to be achieved automatically without the need for any extra effort. This meant that the amount that Japan actually needed to reduce was no more than 2.1 per cent. Of this amount, 1.6 per cent was achieved by emissions trading under the Kyoto Mechanisms. Thus, the Japanese government heavily relied on the Kyoto trading mechanisms from the start of the Kyoto Protocol process.[7]

## Japan and the Clean Development Mechanism

Just as Japan's environmental aid has been characterized by its focus on the country's comparative advantage in anti-pollution and energy efficient technologies and infrastructures, Japan's CDM approach is marked by an enthusiasm for supporting its private sector to transfer advanced technologies to developing countries through foreign aid schemes. According to Kim (2012), this is, in some ways, inevitable, due to the fact that the emissions reduction technologies are owned by the private sector and not the government. The government's natural instinct is to support private sector initiatives to provide technologies to developing countries in an infrastructural package that simultaneously requires managerial expertise, supporting services, and trained human resources. This, however, conflicts with the policy of the OECD's DAC. The proposal by the DAC Chair stipulates in Article 10 (Office of the DAC Chair, 2004: 3) that:

> 'ODA' measures donor effort *net of any returns to the donor* [original emphasis] from ODA expenditure. Such returns include loan repayments, recoveries on unspent grants and proceeds from equity sales. In line with this principle, CERs resulting from ODA-financed CDM projects should be considered as a return to the donor and give rise to a deduction from ODA flows. Conversely, if instead of receiving CERs, a donor has agreed with the host country not to receive any of the generated CERs, or if the project does not generate CERs (e.g. a capacity development activity), no deduction would be necessary.

Japan argued that the use of ODA could rectify the problem of CDM projects being concentrated in a few emerging powers, such as China, India, Mexico, and Brazil, by enabling it to reach poorer countries through financial and technical assistance. Kim (2012: 268) refers to Japan's 2006 ODA White Paper to illustrate Japan's position:

> While promoting measures against global warming on the one hand, CDM also promises to help developing countries secure additional investment in fields such as energy [conservation and efficiency], thus contributing to sustainable development ... Japan, which has made considerable progress through its existing energy conservation measures, will have difficulty achieving [its 2008–2012 Kyoto Protocol greenhouse gas reduction] target solely through these measures. For this reason, obtaining CERs through the use of CDM has considerable importance for Japan and, following international rules, Japan is promoting the effective use of ODA for CDM based on the consent of recipient countries.

This view mirrors Japan's conventional approaches to foreign aid where it capitalizes on the transfer of advanced technologies that have proved useful domestically. The idea behind Japan's ODA policy outlined in the above citation is to strategically use foreign aid to bring mutual benefit to both Japan and its partner countries, not only for GHG emissions reduction but for private sector development in both countries.

Funding the CDM project implementation with ODA, however, raised concerns among major international donors and civil society organizations who argued that funds allocated for CDM projects should not be seen as eligible for ODA as stipulated in the proposal by the DAC Chair (Office of the DAC Chair, 2004). Critics (e.g. Kim, 2012) argued that the ODA funds should be used to improve the capacity of the host country to reduce emissions in the public or the private sector, and not to pay for installing CDM project infrastructure or to pay for CERs. They also argued that the ODA funds being funnelled into the CDM projects would divert aid flows from important social sectors such as health, education, and rural development. The 2001 UN Climate Conference endorsed the Marrakesh Accords, emphasizing that 'public funding for clean development mechanism projects from parties in Annex 1 is not to result in the diversion of official development assistance and is to be separate from and not counted towards the financial obligations of Parties included in Annex 1' (UNFCCC, 2001).

In the meantime, serious concerns about the effectiveness of the CDM itself have been raised. Critics (e.g. Asuka, 2008) see three main problems. The first problem is the complexity of the project approval process. The process from project application to approval of carbon credit (CER issuance) is extremely complex and time consuming. Second is the uneven distribution of the host countries. The host countries have thus far been limited to emerging middle-income powers such as China, India, and Brazil at the expense of smaller and poorer developing countries. Third is the difficulty in proving 'additionality', that is, in identifying the difference the CDM projects have made financially, technologically, and environmentally to produce positive results. In order for an energy saving project to be approved as a CDM project, for example, it must be proven that the energy saving effects of the project could not have been possible without the CDM framework. It is quite difficult, however, to draw clear boundaries between CDM and non-CDM projects and to assess cost-benefit relationships.

While the CDM, in theory, is operational until it is officially discontinued, the emissions trading market has all but collapsed, and many CDM projects have been left with large volumes of unused credits (Kainou, 2021). The international community debated what to do with these credits at the 2019 COP 25 in Madrid but did not come to any conclusions. In the meantime, their attention has shifted to the discussion about Article 6 of the Paris Agreement adopted in

2015, which offers possibilities for a new international mechanism for preventing climate change substantially different from the Kyoto Protocol. The debate over Article 6 concerns the framework for the prospective carbon market, divided into decentralized bilateral cooperation mechanisms (Article 6.2) and a centralized governance mechanism to trade emissions reduction credits (Article 6.4). Giving up on the fragile multilateral crediting mechanism that it helped to create, Japan began implementing its own bilateral mechanism known as the Joint Crediting Mechanism (JCM) in 2013 (ADB, 2019).

## From the Clean Development Mechanism to the Joint Crediting Mechanism

The Joint Crediting Mechanism (JCM) was launched in 2013 as a bilateral crediting mechanism between Japan and its partner countries after the first commitment period of the Kyoto Protocol[8] ended in 2012. According to Japan's Ministry of Foreign Affairs (MOFA, 2020: 1), the JCM is 'a system to cooperate with developing countries for reducing greenhouse gas emissions, in which the result of reduction is assessed as contribution by both partner countries and Japan'. Its Ministry of Environment is a little more specific about Japan's own interest in the JCM, which is described as 'a means to facilitate the diffusion of [Japan's] leading low-carbon technologies, products, systems, services and infrastructure' and to 'evaluate contributions from Japan to GHG emissions reduction or removals in a quantitative manner and use them to achieve Japan's emissions reduction target' (MOE, 2016: 1).

The government estimates that the JCM projects can reduce emissions by 50 to 100 million t-CO$_2$ by 2030 (Agency for Natural Resources and Energy, 2018). The partner countries that enter into a bilateral agreement with Japan host and implement JCM projects with Japan's support, and the JCM issues credits for the approved emission reduction outcomes. Through the JCM projects, Japan's advanced low-carbon technologies are transferred as part of a package including supporting infrastructure and products as well as managerial and human resources support services. The Japanese government then purchases its share of the JCM credits resulting from the projects to meet its emissions reduction target. To date, the JCM is one of the few project-based national mechanisms that credit internationally transferred reduction outcomes under Article 6.2 of the Paris Agreement. The Asian Development Bank (ADB, 2019: xiii) reports that, as of October 2019, 17 partner countries are engaged in the JCM with 56 registered projects. Although the total volume of mitigation is still low, the Japanese government is confident that it will serve as a forerunner to Article 6.2 (ADB, 2019).

**Table 6.2** Differences between CDM and JCM

| | Clean Development Mechanism CDM | Joint Crediting Mechanism JCM |
|---|---|---|
| Governance | Centralized structure (UNFCCC of the CDM Executive Board) | Decentralized structure (governments of each country, Joint Committee) |
| Target sector/ project scope | Quite limited (Example: improving the efficiency of power plants is not covered) | Wider scope |
| Validation of project | Only designated operating organizations can carry out projects | SO14065 authenticated institutions can implement projects |
| | Evaluate the additivity of each project to the baseline | Check if the project meets the requirements that can be judged objectively |
| Calculation of emission reduction | Select from multiple formulas | Spreadsheet is provided |
| | Strict requirements on parameter estimates | Use conservative default values if the parameters have constraints |
| Project validation | The institution that has confirmed the validity of the project cannot implement the verification | The institution that has confirmed the validity of the project can implement the verification |
| | Validation and verification are performed separately | Validation and verification can be performed at the same time |

*Source:* Adapted from the Ministry of the Environment (Kawakami, 2015)

Table 6.2 summarizes the main differences between the JCM and the CDM. Despite being part of a system designed for international cooperation between developing and industrialized countries, the CDM ended up involving only a small number of middle-income developing countries that were capable of dealing with its complicated application procedure. This procedure ended up excluding many of the developing countries that lacked such capacity from the CDM projects, despite their greater need for technical assistance from industrialized countries. The JCM, on the other hand, makes it much easier for poorer developing countries to seek bilateral assistance from Japan as well as for Japan to justify the use of foreign aid to finance JCM projects.

A typical JCM project includes the project owner in the host country and a technology provider in Japan (ADB, 2016). The host country forms a Joint Committee which serves as the governing body for the project and includes representatives from the relevant ministries of

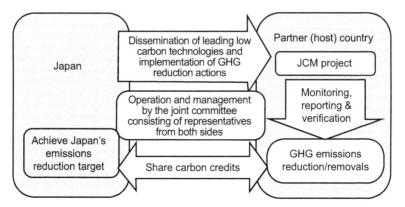

**Figure 6.1** Conceptual diagram of the JCM
*Source:* Adapted from Global Environment Centre Foundation (n.d.) 'Basic concept of the JCM'

both governments. The committee is co-chaired by the appointees of the two governments. The Japanese government works closely with the host country government, private companies, research organizations, and other public interest corporations throughout the project cycle to provide packaged support for technical transfer, institutional and administrative management, and capacity development in the host country.

Figure 6.1 illustrates how the JCM works. The Japanese government sets up an international consortium jointly with the host country, which is required to apply for JCM project registration and to monitor, report, and verify the project activities.[9] When the JCM credits are finally issued, the consortium must deliver at least half of them to the Japanese government.

As of June 2019, 17 countries have participated in the JCM, all recipients of Japan's ODA (see Table 6.3). They represent a broader section of the developing world compared to the CDM project participants. China is excluded since it no longer qualifies as one of Japan's ODA recipients.[10]

The JCM process begins with a Japanese private company applying for a public offering at the Global Environment Centre Foundation (GEC).[11] If approved, JCM projects are then implemented by an international consortium comprising a Japanese company, local companies or Japanese local subsidiaries in the host country as well as the local government in the host country. The international consortium receives half of the initial investment cost from the Japanese government, and the consortium delivers more than half of the $CO_2$ reduction achievements (carbon credits) to the Japanese government in return.[12]

**Table 6.3** JCM participating countries (as of June 2019)

| Participating countries | Start from | No. of projects under JCM financing programme |
|---|---|---|
| Mongolia | Jan 2013 | 8 |
| Bangladesh | Mar 2013 | 5 |
| Ethiopia | May 2013 | 1 |
| Kenya | Jun 2013 | 2 |
| Maldives | Jun 2013 | 3 |
| Vietnam | Jul 2013 | 37 |
| Laos | Aug 2013 | 6 |
| Indonesia | Aug 2013 | 43 |
| Costa Rica | Dec 2013 | 2 |
| Palau | Jan 2014 | 5 |
| Cambodia | Apr 2014 | 6 |
| Mexico | Jul 2014 | 6 |
| Saudi Arabia | May 2015 | 2 |
| Chile | May 2015 | 8 |
| Myanmar | Sep 2015 | 9 |
| Thailand | Nov 2015 | 45 |
| Philippines | Jan 2017 | 17 |
| **Total: 17** | | **205** |

*Source:* Adapted from Global Environment Centre Foundation (n.d.) 'Progress of the JCM in each partner country'

There are a number of advantages to JCM projects. While coordination among different stakeholders was difficult under the CDM because the United Nations CDM board of directors managed the projects collectively, it is significantly easier in the JCM because each country manages individual projects bilaterally with the host country. In addition, the sectoral scope of the projects was highly limited in the case of the CDM, but the JCM allows for a broader range of projects determined through bilateral agreements. In terms of calculating the reduction of GHG emissions, under the CDM, the operator had to select the most appropriate formulas from several options. In the JCM system, these reductions can be easily calculated using a prepared spreadsheet formula. While the CDM required a 'designated operating entity' determined by the United Nations to validate projects, the JCM permits any organization certified by ISO14065 to carry out the verification. Finally, the institution that confirmed the ex-ante validity cannot perform the ex-post verification in the CDM, while this institution can also perform the ex-post verification in the JCM. In general, the procedure required for the JCM is seen as simpler, more efficient, and more flexible (MOE, 2021).

## The JCM as part of Japan's developmentalist cooperation

The JCM is viewed by the Japanese government as an effective tool for obtaining relatively low cost carbon credits. Moreover, by strategically mobilizing its ODA, the JCM projects facilitate Japan's efforts to promote its environmental sector industries. Thirty years have passed since the first Japanese ODA Charter, which defined the basic principles of Japan's ODA, was released in 1992. The charter was revised in 2003 and then again in 2015, and given the new name, 'Development Cooperation Charter'. One of the significant changes in the Development Cooperation Charter is its incorporation of 'national interest' as an explicit objective underlying Japan's foreign aid. While national interest has always been part of its ODA policy, the Japanese government had avoided mentioning it explicitly until then. This changed attitude is in line with the paradigm shift that has occurred in global development, but it also reflects the Japanese government's long-standing view that ODA should be a diplomatic tool to advance its political, economic, and strategic interests, and which should simultaneously help developing countries resolve their own problems.

Japan's apparent comparative advantage in carbon reducing technologies may be a result of the country's historical experience in reducing industrial pollution. Promoting the use of these Japanese-owned technologies in developing countries supported by Japan's ODA fits the idea of national interest underlined in the 2015 Development Cooperation Charter. Besides, clean air is a globally recognized public good, the pursuit of which should be seen as a legitimate target for international cooperation. Where it involves developing countries, international cooperation becomes development cooperation in which Japanese experience can be usefully shared with the help of private sector participation. Japanese ODA has historically been strongly associated with infrastructure development, such as building roads and ports, and improving telecommunications, electricity, and water supply in developing countries. The Japanese government believes not only that such infrastructure development is the key to a country's economic development, but that it contributes to private sector development of the recipient countries at the same time. The JCM is the embodiment of this aid philosophy with an additional benefit for Japan in the form of carbon credits.

Japanese companies clearly benefit from JCM projects in three ways (Kawakami, 2015). First, they can expand their business opportunities in developing countries. Japanese ministries and aid agencies support Japanese companies' efforts to promote their technologies at the Joint Committee where they meet their counterparts in the host countries. Their official support facilitates these companies clearing the approval process for the JCM project. Second, their business risks are significantly reduced since the host country governments are involved in the project from the planning stage. If they experience any bureaucratic problems with the host country institutions, they can negotiate directly with the host government while the Japanese government oversees the negotiations. Third, the start-up costs for developing technologies are reduced significantly. These costs are usually very high, as are their operating costs, which makes it too costly for developing countries to use such technologies. Japanese private companies, however, can supply the advanced technologies at a relatively low initial cost when they use the JCM scheme. The Asian Development Bank (ADB) and Japan's Ministry of Environment (MOE) jointly set up a single-donor trust fund called the Japan Fund for Joint Crediting Mechanism in 2014. The Fund provides financial incentives for ADB member developing countries participating in ADB-financed projects associated with the JCM to adopt advanced low-carbon technologies developed by Japanese companies.

The JCM has received its share of criticism, however. Konishi (2011) questions the legitimacy of the JCM, arguing that there has never been clear international consensus for it, especially where it can act against the interest of internationally agreed-upon multilateral mechanisms such as the CDM. Since bilateral partners can make rules that suit their own needs, the additionality that is strictly assessed under the CDM may become compromised, and end up crediting commercial companies' business-as-usual activities. Here the financial incentives could be seen as de-facto subsidies to these companies. Moreover, if the scheme is successful, it could translate into reduced domestic efforts to cut GHG emissions. There is also the issue of double-counting when more than one international climate mitigation mechanism operates and where the same emissions reduction results may get credited multiple times to different bodies that run these mechanisms. Since the JCM has a wide range of projects, it is possible that $CO_2$ reductions in projects under different mechanisms may be registered in duplicate.

Questions have also been raised about the use of advanced technologies in the JCM projects in developing countries. Japanese companies take pride in supplying high-efficiency environmental technologies to developing countries, but whether expensive packages of sophisticated technologies are what developing countries actually need is debatable. Old questions about Japan's use of tied aid up to the 1980s to build expensive infrastructures that benefited Japanese companies have resurfaced with the government's growing enthusiasm for the JCM and the accompanying use of ODA (WWF Japan, 2010). The selection of host countries is another area of concern. Due to the complexity of its procedure, the CDM created a situation where developed countries' involvement concentrated in relatively better-off middle-income countries such as China, India, Mexico, and Brazil. The same could happen to the JCM since high energy consumption is more of a problem in emerging economies than in smaller, poorer countries.

## The case of a JCM project in Cambodia

Let us examine the case of a model JCM project implemented in Cambodia called 'High Efficiency LED Lighting Utilizing Wireless Network' to see how it is supposed to operate. The project overview can be seen in Figure 6.2. This project targeted Phnom Penh and Siem Reap, where infrastructure is being developed, and was intended to replace 5,672 conventional street lights with high-efficiency LED (light emitting diode) street lights to improve energy efficiency and reduce $CO_2$ emissions. The street lights are dimmed by adjusting to the brightness of the surrounding environment and information about the flow of people to further improve the energy saving efficiency. Since Cambodia is highly dependent on imported electricity, the project

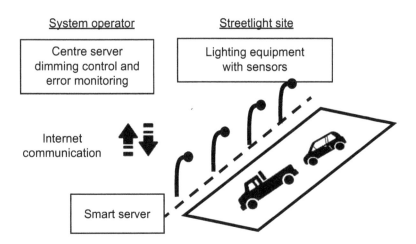

**Figure 6.2** Project overview
*Source:* Created by the authors based on Global Environment Centre Foundation (n.d.) 'Outline of GHG mitigation activity'

**Table 6.4** International consortium

| Role | Organizations / Companies |
|------|---------------------------|
| Representative company on the Japanese side | MinebeaMitsumi (Installation of street lights, development of wireless communication system) |
| Cambodian partners | Overseas Cambodian Investment Corporation (OCIC, private enterprise in Phnom Penh) |
| | Siem Reap Provincial Hall (municipality) |
| | The Authority for the Protection of the Site and Management of the Region of Angkor (APSARA, municipality) |
| Japanese providers | Iwasaki Electric (supplying LED street lights) |
| | NTT Communications (providing network services) |

*Source:* JCM Project Design Document Form, JCM_KH_F_PDD_ver03.0. [website] <https://www.jcm.go.jp/kh-jp/projects/66/pdd_file> [accessed 10 March 2022].

was expected to help reduce electricity consumption (in other words, electricity imports).

The international consortium involved in this JCM project is listed in Table 6.4. MinebeaMitsumi is a manufacturer of electrical parts, mainly bearings and motors, with headquarters in Nagano Prefecture, Japan. It has the largest share of the small ball bearing industry in the world, and most of its production is done in Southeast Asia. Overseas Cambodian Investment Corporation, the largest developer in Cambodia, constructs condominiums, hotels, and entertainment facilities, as well as public infrastructure for bridges and elevated roads. Siem Reap Provincial Hall and APSARA are the local governments in Siem Reap. APSARA is an organization that comprehensively handles archaeological site conservation, tourism development, and environmental conservation throughout the Siem Reap province.

This JCM project involved switching from conventional high intensity discharge (HID) lamp to LED street lights. The planned number of street lights to change in each area is displayed in Table 6.5.

According to data from the MinebeaMitsumi JCM Team (2017), the change to LED luminaires was expected to increase efficiency by about 55 per cent, with dimming expected to increase efficiency by an additional 15 per cent, resulting in a total energy reduction of approximately 70 per cent. The project estimated $CO_2$ credits (5,599 t-$CO_2$) for 11 years from 2018 to 2028. This project did not appear to be very effective when taking Cambodia's annual 10 million tonnes of $CO_2$ emissions into consideration, but it was significant when viewed as a pilot project for smart cities implemented within the JCM framework.

**Table 6.5** Project site

| Project site | Number of installations |
| --- | --- |
| Diamond Island (Phnom Penh) | 766 |
| Chroy Changvar (Phnom Penh) | 1,288 |
| APSARA area (Siem Reap) | 1,670 |
| Siem Reap Province Hall area (Siem Reap) | 1,948 |
| Total | 5,672 |

*Source:* JCM Project Design Document Form, JCM_KH_F_PDD_ver03.0. [website] <https://www.jcm.go.jp/kh-jp/projects/66/pdd_file> [accessed 10 March 2022].

MinebeaMitsumi's efforts in Cambodia can be evaluated as a demonstration experiment for the realization of a smart city. Residents from diverse backgrounds live in the city, and companies and organizations of various industries are active there. A smart city aims to increase energy efficiency, protect vulnerable people (such as elderly people and people living with disabilities), eliminate traffic congestion, and provide security maintenance, disaster countermeasures, and so on based on the activities of each inhabitant and each company/organization by utilizing information and communication technology (ICT). The ICT system that builds smart cities is called a cyber-physical system (CPS). A CPS is a system that optimizes activities in real space by collecting data that reflects the situation and movement of real space such as residential areas and street corners and analysing collected data in virtual space. Data is collected by various information terminals, and the data is sent to the server via a network. Big data analysis is performed in virtual space, and the analysis results are fed back to the real world.

MinebeaMitsumi's project in Cambodia is an example of a CPS. This JCM project involved the installation of energy-saving and long-life LED street lights, which serve as information terminals. Then, by analysing the sent information, the lighting/extinguishing/dimming status of LED street lights could be managed, while targeting further energy saving and operation cost savings. Such a system is highly expandable and is considered an important contribution to achieving smart cities.

## Environment, modernization, and developmentalist cooperation

As can be seen in the above example, the JCM is a mechanism by which Japan can combine its industrial policy for environmental technologies with its ODA policy in order to achieve mutual benefit for Japan and its developing country partners in areas related to the environment, infrastructure, and private sector development. MinebeaMitsumi, a manufacturer of electrical parts, was given financial incentives by the Ministry of the Environment to set up a cyber-physical system in Cambodia and thereby turn its cities into 'smart cities'. From a foreign aid perspective, this can arguably be seen as the latest version of Japan's modernization projects. As discussed in Chapter 5 of this book, modernization projects in the 1960s were largely discredited in subsequent decades for failing to bring about sustainable economic growth with the promised trickle-down effects for lower income groups and for damaging the environment. Modernization projects of today, on the other hand, promise superior technological solutions to sustainable development (Mawdsley, 2012). MinebeaMitsumi planned to reduce $CO_2$ emissions by 3,590 t-$CO_2$ annually (MinebeaMitsumi 2015). Part of the credits issued from these reductions would be passed over to MinebeaMitsumi. Cambodia benefits by reducing its power consumption thanks to greater efficiency, as well as by gaining access to the Japanese technological expertise necessary for building smart cities in Cambodia.

While enthusiasm for constructing smart cities is a global phenomenon, the Association of Southeast Asian Nations (ASEAN) has recently set up a collaborative platform called ASEAN Smart Cities Network in order to coordinate efforts to develop smart cities across the region. The network promotes regional cooperation and encourages private sector participation by mobilizing funds from within and outside ASEAN. Cambodia's cyber-physical system is part of the ASEAN Smart Cities Network. The Cambodian government approved three cities (Phnom Penh, Battambang, and Siem Reap) to join the ASEAN Smart Cities Network with some help coming from the Japanese government. JICA has approached Siem Reap's APSARA National Authority to join the efforts to turn Cambodia's ancient capital into a smart city (*Phnom Penh Post*, 2021), seeking opportunities for ODA-financed large infrastructural projects where the MinebeaMitsumi's JCM model project would fit in.

Like the Japanese government's 'Partnership for Quality Infrastructure' scheme,[13] the JCM was founded based on a partnership scheme called the 'JCM Global Partnership', whereby Japan aims to 'form partnerships with various stakeholders (partner countries, international organizations, local governments, NGOs and private companies) and to share information in order to realize decarbonized society' (Carbon Markets Express, n.d.). In addition to infrastructure, providing clean air is one of the most important of the Sustainable Development Goals (SDGs). International cooperation between rich and poor countries to facilitate providing the population with a global public good as important as clean air should by all means be promoted, particularly when it also encourages private sector participation as development partners. The strategic use of ODA to incentivize it is viewed in this context as an important means to achieve sustainable development globally as well as to enhance development effectiveness in Cambodia. Framing the discourse in this light, however, depoliticizes the developmentalist policy framework for the JCM, leading to the uncritical acceptance of the catalytic role of Japan's ODA in supporting its own private sector partners.

The developmentalist donor–recipient partnership forged through the JCM project reframes the notion of development as technologically driven, state-led economic growth in pursuit of public goods in the form of clean air and quality infrastructure. The construction of smart cities may be viewed as the latest version of modernization projects pursued through foreign aid. Only this time the intention is not to transform a traditional society into a liberal democratic society modelled on the West. Rather, it is to transform urban areas in developing countries into technologically advanced, futuristic cities through the developmentalist donor–recipient partnership originating in the East.

## Conclusion

This chapter has examined Japan's developmentalist cooperation in the area of climate change with a specific focus on the JCM. Through the bilateral crediting mechanism, the Japanese government provides financial incentives as well as institutional support to Japanese companies willing to install their clean air technologies in developing countries. Japan can promote the export of quality infrastructure associated with these technologies, seek to achieve its emission reduction targets, and provide financial and technical assistance to developing countries at the same time. Even before the introduction of the JCM, Japan's environmental aid was characterized by its focus on the country's comparative advantage in advanced environmental technologies. Yet its developmentalist tendencies have been strengthened in more recent years as the SDGs encourage private sector participation in universal efforts to mitigate climate change. The discourse surrounding the SDGs thus serves to depoliticize the developmentalist policy framework for the JCM, leading to the appreciation of the catalytic role of Japan's ODA in supporting its own private sector partners committed to sustainable development in the developing world.

## Notes

\* Professor of Economics at the Faculty of Economics, Aichi Gakuin University, Japan. fujikawakiyoshi@hotmail.com

\*\* Professor of Development Studies at the Graduate School of International Development, Nagoya University, Japan. ito@gsid. nagoya-u.ac.jp

1. One of the Japanese government's top priorities in reviving its economy is promoting quality infrastructure investment overseas. For detailed discussions on the subject, please see Chapter 5 (Japan's developmentalist cooperation for quality infrastructure) of this book.
2. WID refers to 'Women-in-Development'.
3. The former Ministry of International Trade and Industry (MITI) was renamed the Ministry of Economy, Trade and Industry (METI) in 2001.
4. The UNFCCC was signed by 197 countries globally.
5. Annex I countries include industrialized countries belonging to the OECD as of 1992 and such transition countries as the Russian Federation, the Baltic States, and several Central and Eastern European states.
6. This figure is rather large considering Japan's annual GHG emissions in 2019 were 1.2 billion $t\text{-}CO_2$.
7. The commitment period for the Kyoto Protocol was for a five year period from 2008 to 2012. During this time, Japanese GHG total emissions increased by 1.4 per cent compared to the base year of 1990, despite the fact that Japan's Kyoto target was a 6 per cent reduction. However, their Kyoto target was considered achieved because sinks from forests were calculated as 3.9 per cent and, thanks to the Kyoto mechanism, Japan was able to purchase overseas credits totalling 5.9 per cent.
8. The protocol's first commitment period was between 2008 and 2012.
9. The monitoring, reporting, and verification processes are jointly referred to as MRV. See Amellina (2017) for more information on MRV.
10. Support for JCM is provided to Japan's ODA target countries. China is not a target country for the JCM since Japan's ODA to China ended before FY 2021.
11. GEC is a Japanese public interest corporation founded in 1992 to help developing countries conserve the environment through Japanese knowledge and technologies. It also works closely with the Japanese government to help implement the JCM projects.
12. The Joint Committee determines the allocation of the remaining credits.
13. The Japanese government's scheme is to promote infrastructure exports.

## References

Agency for Natural Resources and Energy (2018) 'Nikokukan kredit seido wa nihon nimo tojokoku nimo chikyu nimo ureshii ondanka taisaku' [The bilateral credit system is a global warming countermeasure that is good for Japan, developing countries and the earth] [website] <https://www.enecho.meti.go.jp/about/special/johoteikyo/jcm.html> [accessed 16 February 2022].

Amellina, A. (2017) 'Enhancing the Joint Crediting Mechanism MRV to contribute to sustainable development', in J. Uitto, J. Puri and R. van den Berg (eds), *Evaluating Climate Change Action for Sustainable Development*, pp. 111–27, Springer, Cham <https://doi.org/10.1007/978-3-319-43702-6_7> [accessed 17 February 2022].

Asian Development Bank (ADB) (2016) *Handbook for Developing the Joint Crediting Mechanism Projects* [online] <https://www.adb.org/sites/default/files/institutional-document/219486/handbook-developing-joint-crediting-mechanism-projects.pdf> [accessed 17 February 2022].

ADB (November 2019) *Article 6 of the Paris Agreement: Drawing Lessons from the Joint Crediting Mechanism* [online] <https://www.adb.org/sites/default/files/publication/541116/article6-paris-agreeement-jcm.pdf> [accessed 17 February 2022].

Asuka, J. (2008) 'Kurin kihatsu mechanisumu no genjo to kadai' [The current situation and issues surrounding the Clean Development Mechanism], *Kagaku* 78(5): 557–61 Iwanami Shoten, Tokyo.

Cabinet Office, Japan (2008) 'Kyoto gitei-sho mokuhyo tassei keikaku' [Kyoto protocol achievement plan]. Available from: https://www.kantei.go.jp/jp/singi/ondanka/kakugi/050428keikaku.pdf [accessed 28 February 2022].

Carbon Markets Express (n.d.) 'JCM global partnership (JCM GP)' [website] <http://carbon-markets.env.go.jp/eng/jcmgp/> [accessed 11 February 2022].

Dauvergne, P. (2001) 'The rise of an environmental superpower? Evaluating Japanese environmental aid to Southeast Asia', in S.J. Maswood (ed.), *Japan and East Asian Regionalism*, pp. 52–68, Routledge, Oxford.

Evans, P.C. (1999) 'Japan's green aid plan: The limits of state-led technology transfer', *Asian Survey* 39: 825–44 <https://doi.org/10.2307/3021141>.

Global Environment Centre Foundation (n.d.) 'Basic concept of the JCM' [website] <https://gec.jp/jcm/about/> [accessed 18 February 2022].

Global Environment Centre Foundation (n.d.) 'Outline of GHG mitigation activity' [website] <https://gec.jp/jcm/projects/15pro_cam_01/> [accessed 18 February 2022].

Global Environment Centre Foundation (n.d.) 'Progress of the JCM in each partner country' [website] <https://gec.jp/jcm/about/> [accessed 18 February 2022].

Japan International Cooperation Agency (JICA) (2001) *The Second Study on Development Assistance for the Environment (Summary): Practical Approaches towards the Environmental Challenges*, Institute for International Cooperation. Available from: https://www. jica.go.jp/jica-ri/IFIC_and_JBICI-Studies/english/publications/ reports/study/topical/environment/pdf/environment.pdf [accessed 28 September 2021].

Kainou, K. (2021) 'Collapse of the CDM scheme under the Kyoto protocol and its spillover: Consequences of "carbon panic"', REITI Column, September 29 [website] <https://www.rieti.go.jp/en/ columns/a01_0659.html> [accessed 11 February 2022].

Kawakami, T. (2015) 'Nikokukan kurejitto seido (JCM) ni kannsuru kankyosho no torikumi' [MOE's initiatives for the Joint Crediting Mechanism]. Available from: http://gec.jp/jcm/jp/news/ gwsympo2015/1-1_MOE_Kawakami.pdf [accessed 15 October 2021].

Kim, S. (2012) 'Japan's "common but differentiated" approach to sustainable development and climate change in Africa', *Japanese Studies* 32(2): 255–74 <https://doi.org/10.1080/10371397.2012.708396>.

Konishi, M. (2011) 'Nikokukan kurejitto seido ni tsuite: Kikou hendo de okane wa dou ugoku? COP16 no kekka wo ukete' [On the Joint Crediting Mechanism: How will money move as climate changes? A reflection on the outcomes of COP-16] [PowerPoint slides] <https://www.wwf.or.jp/activities/upfiles/schdrbn02a.pdf> [accessed 25 February 2022].

Mawdsley, E. (2012) *From Recipients to Donors: Emerging Powers and the Changing Development Landscape*, Zed Books, London.

MinebeaMitsumi (2015) 'Minebea's plan unofficially selected by MOEJ as financing programme for JCM model project' [website] <https://www. minebeamitsumi.com/english/news/press/2015/1189640_7564. html> [accessed 10 March 2022].

MinebeaMitsumi JCM Team (2017) 'JCM in Cambodia: Introduction of high efficiency LED lighting utilizing wireless network' [PowerPoint slides] <https://archive.iges.or.jp/files/research/climate-energy/mm/PDF/20170301/8_akatsu.pdf> [accessed 25 February 2021].

Ministry of Environment Japan (MOE) (2016) 'The Joint Crediting Mechanism (JCM): Feasibility study through city-to-city collaboration'. Available from: https://www.env.go.jp/earth/coop/lowcarbon-asia/ english/project/data/jcm_pamphlet_03.pdf [accessed 16 February 2022].

MOE (2021) 'Recent developments of the Joint Crediting Mechanism (JCM)' [PowerPoint slides] <http://carbon-markets.env. go.jp/document/20210712_JCM_goj_eng.pdf> [accessed 20 August 2021].

Ministry of Foreign Affairs Japan (MOFA) (2020) 'Climate change: Joint Crediting Mechanism (JCM)' [website], March 30 <https://www. mofa.go.jp/ic/ch/page1we_000105.html#:~:text=The%20JCM%20 is%20a%20system,both%20partner%20countries%20and%20 Japan> [accessed 16 February 2022].

MOFA (n.d.) 'Official development assistance: 12. responding to global issues', [website] <https://www.mofa.go.jp/policy/oda/summary/1996/c_12.html> [accessed 9 February 2022].

Office of the DAC Chair (2004) 'ODA eligibility issues for expenditures under the Clean Development Mechanism (CDM)'. Available from: https://www.oecd.org/officialdocuments/publicdisplaydocumentp df/?cote=DAC/CHAIR(2004)4/FINAL&docLanguage=En [accessed 11 February 2022].

*Phnom Penh Post* (2021) 'Siem Reap on track for smart city status with Japanese help', *Phnom Penh Post*, 09 September [online] <https://www.phnompenhpost.com/national/siem-reap-track-smart-city-status-japanese-help> [accessed 15 October 2021].

UNFCCC (2001) 'The Marrakesh Accords & The Marrakesh Declaration' [website] <https://unfccc.int/cop7/documents/accords_draft.pdf> [accessed 5 November 2022].

UNFCCC (n.d.) 'Clean Development Mechanism' [website] <https://unfccc.int/process-and-meetings/the-kyoto-protocol/mechanisms-under-the-kyoto-protocol/the-clean-development-mechanism> [accessed 3 March 2022].

United Nations (1998) 'Kyoto Protocol to the United Nations Framework Convention on Climate Change'. Available from: https://unfccc.int/resource/docs/convkp/kpeng.pdf [accessed 3 March 2022].

WWF Japan (2010) 'Nikokukan kurejitto ni tsuite WWF ga motsu kenen' [WWF's concerns about the Joint Crediting Mechanism] [website] <https://www.wwf.or.jp/activities/opinion/2861.html> [accessed 10 March 2022].

# CHAPTER 7

# Oil industry structures and their effects on aid policies in East Asian countries

*Isamu Okada*\*

## Introduction

The demand for natural resources often stands out as a crucial factor in aid policies, closely related to other economic interests of East Asian donors. Since oil and other resources are unique strategic commodities of national interest in the globalized political economy, it is inevitable that the diplomatic policies of major donors – highly industrialized countries – would be in line with their strategies to secure their own resource supply. The recent increase of Chinese aid in Africa, Central Asia, and the South Pacific has augmented scrambling tones in international cooperation debates (Melber, 2009; Brant, 2013; McCarthy, 2013; Alvez, 2015). A similar discussion regarding Japanese aid, albeit it with different timelines and scales, took place in the late 20th century (Yasutomo, 1986).

Previous studies have addressed the similarities and differences in the resource–aid nexus for East Asian aid (Reilly, 2012; Barclay and Smith, 2013; Stallings and Kim, 2016, 2017). However, the difference between the countries has only rarely been focused on in the literature, as will be discussed later. This chapter aims to fill this gap, examining whether East Asian donors, namely Japan, South Korea, and China, have allocated aid money in relation to their resource supply strategies and when and why their strategies diverged.

If we take a closer look, Chinese aid in sub-Saharan Africa and other developing countries has little resemblance to that of Japan and South Korea. This paper suggests that the reason for this variation cannot be found in the countries' respective oil demand in the global market but in how each country's oil industry was structured historically. Japan, South Korea, and China are by and large considered to be developmental states, which built their heavy industries under state stewardship. As the resource politics literature suggests, the countries *with* oil endowments, such as China, Indonesia, and Malaysia, founded national oil companies (NOCs) no later than the 1970s. Moreover, they positioned their NOCs at the centre of developmental state making, giving them a certain level of prestige – although not autonomous from political elites.

Industrialized states *without* oil endowments, on the other hand, have a variety of options. France, Italy, and South Korea, for example, built their own NOCs. The UK and the US meanwhile left the industry under the control of private companies, provided that they had the capacity to satisfy national oil demands. Japan represents an intermediate case, with a handful of private companies operating with connections to line ministries. Consequently, the harmonization of national oil supply strategies and foreign aid policies has been dependent on the depth of state intervention in the resource sector.

This chapter will look at these issues in relation to the historical construction of oil sectors in East Asian countries and how it has specifically affected their distinctive oil–aid nexus over the past few decades.

This chapter is divided into five sections. Following this introduction, I will provide a review of the literature about economic factors affecting the aid policy of East Asian donors. The next section presents empirical facts with a regression analysis which tests the covariation between the resource potential of recipient countries and the foreign aid flows from China, South Korea, and Japan respectively. I then narrate the contrasting paths of oil industry development in Japan and China, illustrating structurally divergent trends in their oil industries and foreign aid policies. The last section concludes.

## East Asian donors and national economic interests revisited

Government decisions regarding international cooperation are rarely delinked from national interests anywhere in the world (Gilpin, 1987; Lancaster, 2006), but making foreign aid policies with these interests at the core appears to be most emblematic for East Asian donors. East Asian donors are arguably distinctive from Western countries in their similar pursuit of national economic interests by promoting private investment, market access, infrastructure building, and securing oil and mineral supplies for their industries (Sato and Shimomura, 2013; Watson, 2014; Stallings and Kim, 2017). In Japan, a strong bureaucratic apparatus guided the early industrialization in the 19th century and has accelerated growth since the 1950s (Johnson, 1982). Limited access to raw materials for achieving the goals of its economic model was one of the key determining factors of Japanese aid in the post-war era, as Sato (2013) has traced from historical records (see also Lancaster, 2010;

Kato et al., 2016). The developmental state model in which the state intervenes proactively in the economy is also widely acknowledged in South Korea and other Asian countries, including communist regimes such as China (Evans, 1995; Kohli, 2004; Nem Singh and Chen, 2017). According to the research, the origin of this similarity between Asian donors may well be attributed to having modelled policies based on Japan, which has been a leading aid donor to other countries in East and Southeast Asia (Sato and Shimomura, 2013; Reilly, 2012; Stallings and Kim, 2017). It is worth remembering, however, that the unique historical experiences in each country have also contributed to distinctive features among the countries (Kim et al., 2013).

While the structural similarities between Asian donors and the differences to conventional Western ones have been pointed out by many scholars (Sato and Shimomura, 2013; Stallings and Kim, 2017), few studies have dug deeper into the variation among East Asian countries. The variation is especially evident between the Chinese presence in the developing world and that of Japan and South Korea in the last two decades. A part of the growing literature stresses the characteristics of Chinese capital inflows, such as its large volume, squared economic interests, and lack of discrimination between political regime types, which is often viewed as overt economic greed, providing fewer benefits to the poorest people (Bräutigam, 2010; Brant, 2013). As Melber (2009: 69) notes, 'the Chinese gospel of non-interventionism is warmly welcomed by the autocratic leaders and oligarchies that continue to rule the roost in the majority of African countries, especially those in possession of vast natural resources'.

In contrast, the degree to which Japanese and South Korean ODA policies are contingent on their resource demands is more uncertain. Japan, as the world's third-largest oil consumer behind the US and China, has had a long-lasting demand for oil. This former frontrunner 'developmental state' has continuously promoted trade advantages for its private companies, albeit not always successfully (Koike et al., 2008). South Korea, similar to Japan, also has a strong demand for resources and a developmental state background, and has increased its aid volume since the 2000s. Most consider it closer to Japan than to China (Kondoh et al., 2010; Stallings and Kim, 2017).

The distinction can be seen in the Organisation for Economic Co-operation and Development (OECD) Development Assistance Committee (DAC), of which Japan and South Korea are both members, while China is not. Kondoh (2015) for example, argues that there has been a convergence to the DAC aid model among emerging donors. However, the extent to which DAC membership constrains aid patterns has also been debated. Stallings and Kim (2017), for example, stress several facts to challenge the reliability of this delineation, such as Japan and other DAC members frequently disregarding DAC norms, substantial variation among DAC donors, and divergence among non-DAC donors in assimilating or dissimilating the DAC aid model. I argue that whether or not a country is a DAC member does not fully explain overall aid patterns, and these patterns can be the result, not the cause, of each country's historical development.

The notable difference between China and the other two East Asian donors is, I argue, attributable to their methods of searching for oil and other hydrocarbons. More precisely, the relationship between the central government and upstream operators – state-owned or private corporations that explore, extract, and produce fuel resources – matters. Succinctly, it is a question of industrial structure and how closely economic and political decision-making is coordinated. The Chinese NOCs are giant operators closely linked to the Beijing government and capable of directing colossal capital to new terrains of strategic resource supply. Japanese oil companies and trading houses (*sogo shôsha*), on the other hand, are private, and while they also have close contacts to the central government, they also need to follow good practices in corporate governance in a globalized market economy. South Korean NOCs are influential in supplying energy resources to the domestic market, but for the same reason as Japan, it is questionable whether its aid policy is always streamlined along the particular objective of securing resources.

Among the burgeoning literature on the Chinese pursuit of oil (Christoffersen, 2016; Jiang and Sinton, 2011; Tang, 2006; Zweig and Bi, 2005), Zhao (2008: 207) has stressed the Chinese political leaders' 'neo-mercantilist thinking that relies on bilateral diplomatic contact with oil-producing countries to beef up energy security by the use of national resource and state-owned enterprise investments in overseas energy assets'. This simplistic assumption, however, is not always shared by others. Chen (2008), for example, opts for more careful interpretation, which recognizes the interests and strategies of Chinese NOCs as being independent from the government's, although, at the same time, both sides share the same objective of securing energy resources. A study on Chinese oil engagement in Kazakhstan concludes that 'the structure of the Chinese political system and informal and formal institutional controls suggest that the CCP [Chinese Communist Party] is able to compel the Chinese big-three oil companies to operate according to its "guiding principles"' (McCarthy 2013: 279). The ambiguity over the controllability of NOCs by the Chinese politburo, mainly after the institutional reforms in the 1980s (further discussed in the section on the development of the oil industry, below), is debatable. Still, the

Chinese government has certainly prompted its NOCs to expand foreign operations while backing them up with targeted aid-giving diplomacy to producer countries (McCarthy, 2013; Alvez, 2015).

As mentioned above, Japan and South Korea's models of state intervention and unification of objectives deviate from China's. Some scholars have argued that Japan pioneered the unique characteristics of the Asian model (Sato and Shimomura, 2013; Stallings and Kim, 2017). Although this Asian forerunner shifted from 'an economic model to a broader approach' around the 1990s, scepticism abounds as to whether the rhetorical focus on 'human security' actually accompanies substantial changes (Stallings and Kim, 2016: 40). Arase (1994) reveals the gradually obfuscated but persistent influence of the Ministry of International Trade and Industry (MITI) in diplomatic policy-making and the informal inclusion of private business through a secondment (*syukko*), their membership in advisory bodies (*Shingikai* or *Kenkyukai*), and contact with governing party politicians. Further reforms in aid policies from the late 2000s may, as discussed in the section 'Building the Japanese upstream oil sector', below, suggest the return of economic clout. However, Japanese aid and economic policies are also arguably a hybrid approach emblematic of the government providing indirect guidance to private actors. This public–private relationship is unlikely to have any equivalent impacts compared to the intimate relationship between NOCs and the central government in China because corporate decision-making in Japan primarily derives from the profit motive rather than achieving national political goals.

As for the case of South Korea, some researchers suggest that 'resource diplomacy' is a critical factor in shaping the country's aid policies, coalescing around Korean foreign direct investments (FDIs) targeting raw materials (Kalinowski and Cho, 2012). This is evident both in the government's diplomacy efforts and the fortified role of NOCs, such as the Korea National Oil Corporation and Korea Gas Corporation in overseas projects. Kim and Gray (2016), however, view this differently. They argue that 'the multiple and often conflicting objectives of ODA serve to problematize notions of any simple mechanistic connection between the substantive nature of Seoul's ODA programme to Africa and the "national economic interest"' (Kim and Gray, 2016: 650).

I posit that resource policy constitutes aid policy, particularly in terms of how the upstream oil industry is structured in a donor country. In a broader sense, aid policies are shaped through a process involving a diverse array of interests competing for influence. In order to better understand the origin of aid policies, it is helpful to identify the influential actors in policy-making and any systematic pattern created by their power. While the supply of hydrocarbon resources has usually played a certain role in the process, the strength of the resource sector depends more on the organizational unity within the industry and the political connections between corporate executives, line ministries, and politicians. When negotiating with state authorities, a market unified under a few sector organizations is stronger than one with multiple fragmented players. If the unified sector organizations are state-owned enterprises (SOEs) – although corporate structure may vary across cases – the institutional coordination between business and the government is smoother.

I contend that this perspective merits more attention. Still, it is unrealistic to assume that the historical relationship between the government and upstream oil operators is the sole factor regarding intra-Asian differences. There are a range of alternative explanations, including population size, the timing of industrialization, political regime type, and foreign policy objectives. I consider the first two to be not significant. I believe the latter two complement my hypothesis.

The first explanation is population size. While this may influence both the scale of oil demands and energy security strategy, two other factors, a significant deficit in production-consumption margin and consolidating a full-fledged developmental state, are supposed to have a more direct impact. Before it became one of the world's strongest economies in the 1990s, China was a net producer of oil. Therefore, it was less involved in the global pursuit of oil. China's current hunger for oil is thus a product of its rapid industrialization, accelerating oil shortfalls in the domestic market, and whether the state is willing to mobilize its institutional apparatus to search for a solution.

The timing of industrialization, on the other hand, might initially appear to have an influence on the intra-Asian variation. Observing the different approaches to Myanmar, Reilly (2013: 142) notes: '(t)he China-Japan comparison is, however, particularly interesting for its timing – Japan began to shift away from explicitly linking its development assistance to resource extraction just as China adopted this approach'. Japan accumulated partnerships, technologies, and supply networks in the second half of the 20th century, while China faced this task several decades later. Nonetheless, the ramifications of the relationship between the government and upstream oil operators, which directly impacts the resource–aid nexus, take a long time to appear. As will be shown below, the difference between Japan's and China's national energy strategies is a path-dependent process that originated before they became industrialized. The origin, I believe, has more to do with the intrinsic logic of oil-producing and non-oil producing countries rather than when energy resources are most needed.

The third explanation is political regime type. The political system is irrelevant in terms of energy policy, but relevant to aid policies. Whether a country takes a state-led or market-led approach for the upstream oil industry is independent of regime type. We can find predominantly NOCs in numerous countries, ranging from Indonesia to Norway. Regarding aid and diplomatic policies, democratic donors may allow more pluralistic policy-making involving civil society actors and take public opinion more into consideration than non-democratic donors. I believe this difference, however, only complements my hypothesis that focuses in particular on the influence of the oil industry among other stakeholders.

Diplomatic objectives are likely to influence both aid policy and energy policy, and subsequently variations in the resource–aid nexus. As mentioned above, Japan and South Korea are now DAC donors, obliging them to follow specific guidelines. Other diplomatic objectives range from a country's position in global politics and other national goals. Despite their slight initial differences, Japan, South Korea, and China all had to find a way to secure their energy resource supply, deploying their economic clout to win new partnerships. East Asian donors had to choose a proper position and role in the global power game at each decision-making step in that process. Japanese ODA for African countries from 1979 to 1998, for example, was significantly impacted by US strategic interests – measured by the number of US troops deployed and whether the country bordered on a communist regime (Tuman and Ayoub, 2004).[1] Others have also claimed that the aid policies of China, South Korea, Thailand, and India are contingent on the donor's own national plans (Kondoh et al. 2010). I have no objection to the notion that national goals and diplomatic objectives shape aid patterns in general. This chapter suggests that resource security is one such objective, defining some crucial aspects of aid policies.

### Empirical facts on resource–aid linkage

Beyond scholarly arguments, how empirically true is the connection between resource demand and foreign aid flows? Is there a difference between the ways East Asian donors select their aid recipients? This section explores empirical facts on the resource–aid nexus and intra-Asian variation.

Previous studies have widely confirmed a positive correlation between aid and FDI inflows in some cases (Harms and Lutz, 2006; Kimura and Todo, 2010; Anyanwu, 2012).[2] While Karakaplan et al. (2005) and Harms and Lutz (2006) report mixed results in terms of the worldwide average effect of aid on FDI inflows, Kimura and Todo (2010) find the 'vanguard effects' of a country's aid preceding the same country's flow of FDI to the recipient in the case of Japanese aid specifically targeting infrastructure. Using the 1991–2011 Korean ODA data for African countries, Yoon and Moon (2014) confirmed that oil exporters and least developed countries tend to receive more ODA from South Korea.

In the following analysis, I utilize net ODA flow data from the OECD for Japan and South Korea and AidData's Global Chinese Official Finance (GCOF) dataset for China (OECD, 2021; AidData, 2021). While the time-series ODA data for Japan and South Korea is readily available via the OECD database, the Chinese data is not. Due to the different data sources, the following results are not strictly comparable. The GCOF dataset includes all ODA-like and other official finance data for China collected from news media sources, while net ODA flow data in the OECD statistics are based on each DAC member country's self-reported information which is subject to the ODA criteria within the DAC criteria. Although this is suboptimal, I believe we can still approximate global oil–aid covariates (or lack thereof). Because of the limited range of the GCOF dataset and the duration of the last commodity boom, the time scope for the analysis used in this study is 2000–2014.

Figure 7.1 shows the aid trends for China, South Korea, Japan, and all DAC donors (including Japan and South Korea) to all regions in the developing world (see Appendix A for the list of recipient countries) between 2000 and 2014. China, Japan, and South Korea all exhibited increasing trends in aid disbursement during this period, while the total for all DAC donors decreased from 2008 onwards.

Table 7.1 summarizes the total aid flow for the same donors differentiated by the recipient countries in regard to whether they had made oil, natural gas, or coal exports in the previous years. Export dummy – not export volume – is used for the categorization because our interest here is the potential resource supply to donor countries both at present and in the future.[3] Table 7.1 shows clearly that all donors provided more aid to resource exporting countries on average. This examination, however, is insufficient; aggregated data containing only two variables crossed does not provide us with the true covariation because the effects of other variables cannot be controlled for. For a more robust estimation, a multiple regression analysis must be carried out.

Table 7.2 reports the result of the regression analysis (see Appendix B for the specific analytical design). The regressions were first run using each donor's aid flow (dependent variable) to all recipient countries worldwide and then to African countries. The independent variables are *LDC* (whether a recipient country belongs to the least developed

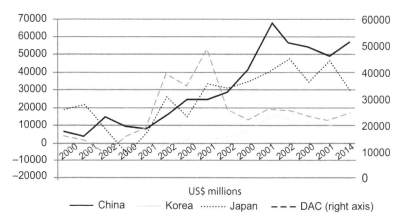

**Figure 7.1** Aid flow in 2014 US$ millions for East Asian donors and the total of all DAC donors
Note: see Appendix A for the list of recipient countries. The aid flow volume counts both ODA-like and other official financial supports for the Chinese data, net ODA flow for the rest.
*Source*: The author's elaboration based on GCOF dataset for China and OECD data for all other countries.

**Table 7.1** Aid flow to resource exporters and non-exporters

|  | Aid flow (2014 US$ millions) per unit (country/year) | | | |
| --- | --- | --- | --- | --- |
| *Resource export* | *China* | *Japan* | *South Korea* | *DAC* |
| No | 109.3 | 80.1 | 14.0 | 648.3 |
| Yes | 350.7 | 308.7 | 69.3 | 3017.3 |

*Note and source*: See Figure 7.1.

countries), *Resource* (whether a recipient country reported oil, natural gas, or coal exports), *GDP per capita*, *GDP growth*, *Export* (donor-specific export value from China, Japan, and South Korea to a recipient country, or total import value of a recipient country for DAC data), *FH score* (the level of political rights in a recipient country according to Freedom House), *Terror score* (the level of state-sanctioned terror), and *Africa* (whether a recipient country is located on the African continent; see Appendix A). All independent variables are lagged by a year. Year dummy variables are included in all models but not shown in the results. After the whole world samples, I reran similar regressions for African samples, assuming that the region has been widely debated in previous literature and equally distanced from the three East Asian donors (which is probably not the case in Southeast Asian or Central Asian recipients, for example).[4]

**Table 7.2** Marginal effects on aid flows from tobit regression analysis

| Model | (A) China (All countries) | (B) China (African countries) | (C) Japan (All countries) | (D) Japan (African countries) | (E) South Korea (All countries) | (F) South Korea (African countries) |
|---|---|---|---|---|---|---|
| LDC | 0.009387 (0.040563) | 0.022432 (0.059486) | 0.16636 (0.038596)*** | 0.063130 (0.042902) | 0.077160 (0.017759)*** | 0.072322 (0.015342)*** |
| Resource | 0.067729 (0.036520)* | 0.15314 (0.054473)*** | -0.11582 (0.034307)*** | -0.095952 (0.038947)** | -0.029717 (0.015651)* | -0.030197 (0.013481)** |
| GDP per capita | -0.000029 (0.000005)*** | 0.000003 (0.000009) | -0.000003 (0.000005) | 0.000009 (0.000006) | 0.000007 (0.000002)*** | 0.000022 (0.000002)*** |
| GDP growth | 0.005837 (0.002696)** | 0.005572 (0.003353)* | 0.000899 (0.002513) | -0.003376 (0.002329) | 0.000808 (0.001164) | -0.001550 (0.000854)* |
| Export | 0.043643 (0.023860)* | 0.008884 (0.041640) | 0.046252 (0.020465)** | 0.028007 (0.025651) | 0.077553 (0.009015)*** | 0.034613 (0.008496)*** |
| FH score | -0.019301 (0.009645)** | 0.035610 (0.016814)** | -0.009975 (0.009218) | 0.013817 (0.011843) | -0.015635 (0.004065)*** | -0.004747 (0.004099) |
| Terror score | 0.053184 (0.020621)*** | -0.036643 (0.034221) | 0.17758 (0.019451)*** | 0.087720 (0.024479)*** | 0.064981 (0.008638)*** | 0.011051 (0.008422) |
| Africa | 0.12900 (0.035014)*** | | -0.18195 (0.034534)*** | | -0.14983 (0.037434)*** | |
| Year dummies | YES | YES | YES | YES | YES | YES |
| n | 1,743 | 710 | 1,740 | 709 | 1,612 | 632 |
| Log-likelihood | -1970.056 | -816.4851 | -1914.12 | -586.0693 | -635.2593 | 38.55573 |

Note: * $p < 0.1$, ** $p < 0.05$, *** $p < 0.01$. See Appendix B for a detailed analytical design.

The results display a positive and significant covariation between resource export from recipient countries and aid flow from China (A, B) but negative ones in the cases of Japan and South Korea (C, D, E, and F). This confirms a strong oil–aid nexus only for China but not for the other donors.[5] Other findings suggest that Japan and South Korea provide more development assistance to the least developed countries. All East Asian donors offer more aid to countries that import their products. This verifies the trade interests of Japan and South Korea – but not resource interests – in their aid allocation. The political conditions in the recipient countries show a mixed result. Aid to recipient countries that carry out state-sanctioned terror shows a mostly similar trend across donors. In contrast, the level of political rights is taken less into consideration by China and South Korea worldwide, but is not consistent in African countries.

This finding reconfirms the argument in the previous section that China manifests demand for resources, while Japan and South Korea do not follow the trend, at least at the aggregate level in the period 2000–2014. Why did this variation develop? I will try to answer this in the next section by tracing the historical development of the oil industry in Japan and China.

## Origins: building an upstream oil sector in Japan and China

The development of upstream oil operators in China and Japan have taken starkly different paths over the years. China, which had oil reserves and production in the north-east and north-west by the 1970s, could nurture its NOCs gradually and then implement drastic reforms to renovate them in the 1980s and 1990s. It was not its recent accelerated economic growth that elicited the burgeoning state agencies to embark on a global quest for oil. Instead, the long-term developmental paths had paved the way for what emerged later as a powerful state complex in the upstream oil industry and its impact on aid policies. In contrast, Japan was not equipped with the state machinery to structure the upstream oil sector. The fact that Japan has very limited domestic oil production cannot be the only reason for this, given the fact that other non-oil producing countries, such as South Korea and Italy, did create their own NOCs, which are 'National-Flag' players. What was evident in Japan is path dependency. Early state intervention to protect domestic oil refineries in the downstream disincentivized them from seeking profit in the upstream sector and fragmented the industrial composition, thus setting back the founding of a 'National-Flag Oil Company' to a later stage.

### Building the Chinese upstream oil sector

China oil reserves and production are the largest recorded in the Asia-Pacific region since the mid-1970s (BP, 2021). In addition, its natural gas reserves and production have also been among the highest in Asian countries since 2012. However, Chinese hydrocarbon consumption has outpaced domestic production, with the country becoming a net oil importer in 1993. This transition from an oil producer to a net importer obfuscates the more complex development of the Chinese oil industry. At the time of the founding of the People's Republic of China in 1949, there was small-scale oil production in Yumen in the Gansu province. The country relied heavily on the Soviet Union for oil imports and its technology. Later in the 1960s, the discovery of larger oil fields in Daqing and Shengli in the Heilongjiang province helped the country achieve self-sufficiency amid the diplomatic rupture with the Soviet Union. This initial development of the oil industry, with China framing itself as a self-reliant producing country, consolidated a prototype of Chinese NOCs which, in later years, evolved into three giant oil conglomerates and their closely intertwined relationship with the Chinese Communist Party (CCP) and the state.

As discussed above, oil production was boosted and provided a net surplus from the 1970s until 1993. In this period, however, the Chinese oil industry was plagued with several problems. Firstly, the oil reserves did not increase sufficiently to minimize the risk of oil scarcity in the future. Secondly, the geographical separation between oil-producing regions in the north and the rapidly industrialized areas in the south demanded strategic planning to shift towards offshore oil exploration and oil imports for the southern area. Thirdly, by the 1960s, limited technology, constrained by China's self-reliant approach, while also influenced by other domestic political factors at that time, became an impediment to efficient oil production.

Finally, the oil shock at the end of the 1970s and the economic reforms after the Cultural Revolution ushered in a drastic reform of the Chinese economy, including the oil sector. The above-mentioned structural problems pushed new CCP leaders to introduce progressive pro-efficiency reforms in the Chinese oil sector starting in the early 1980s (Jiang, 2011). The first reform initiated the gradual separation between the planned economy and pro-market corporate governance. The reform in the 1980s created three major NOCs by dissolving the Ministry of Petroleum and Industry, which had been the sole national oil operator at the time. All offshore operations were reorganized under the China National Offshore Oil Corporation (CNOOC) in 1983. Then in the same year, the downstream refineries and petrochemical sector were transferred to the China Petrochemical Corporation (SINOPEC).

All upstream (exploration and exploitation) assets and operations were transformed into the China National Petroleum Corporation (CNPC) in 1988. This first reform established a contract responsibility system that enabled NOCs to make autonomous decisions on day-to-day activities such as the procurement of services and labour employment (Andrews-Speed, 2015). The reforms also aspired to attract foreign investors to boost technology transfer and open new frontiers in exploration, production, and refining.

However, the objectives of the first reform did not prove to be as successful as expected, as Chinese NOCs – particularly the CNPC – inherited such unproductive assets as schools and hospitals (Andrews-Speed, 2015). In order to address this problem, the second reform created subsidiary operators by splitting the core productive asset of the NOCs from the rest, namely PetroChina from CNPC, Sinopec Shanghai Petrochemical Ltd from SINOPEC, and CNOOC Ltd from CNOOC. Moreover, the CNPC and SINOPEC swapped the upstream and downstream assets to integrate the whole function by geographically delineating their main operational fields to the north for CNPC and the south for SINOPEC. Then the three NOCs were listed publicly in the private stock markets abroad, although the party-state never relinquished its majority share in the state-dominant holding companies.

The NOC reform in the 1990s, which manifested the party-state objective of detaching corporate governance from direct state command-and-control to encourage the internationalization of NOCs, spurred a debate on the characteristic of Chinese NOC governance and essentially the degree of effective autonomy from state control (Liu, 2009; Naughton, 2010; Jiang and Sinton, 2011; Jiang, 2011; Kong, 2011; Taylor, 2012, 2014; Andrews-Speed, 2015). Although some details are debatable, most researchers argue that state dominance undermines the market logic on two fronts (Jiang, 2011; Taylor, 2012). On the one hand, state ownership of NOCs is maintained by rule as the state retains the majority share of stocks in both holding companies and the subsidiaries. As the majority shareholder, the State-Owned Assets Supervision and Administration Commission (SASAC) of the State Council, created in 2003, owns the NOCs. It regulates its policies according to the general rule of SOEs in China, including their adherence to the Management Law of State-owned Assets, which stipulates the responsibility of the SOEs to promote and protect national interests.

On the other hand, the leadership rotation between NOCs, the CCP, and other government agencies works effectively to channel multiple state apparatuses towards common goals (Jiang, 2011; Taylor, 2012). The Organization Department of the Communist Party (CCP), not the SASAC, appoint the NOC's chief executives. The top executives hold a vice minister's rank and high-ranking membership in the CCP central committee (Jiang and Sinton, 2011). This leadership rotation, or overlapping executives, who share multiple titles in different entities, has been observed between the NOCs and the CCP politburo, the holding companies and subsidiaries, and even between rival NOCs (Taylor, 2012, 2014). Hence, the NOCs have delegated discretionary power in investment projects while maintaining close coordination with other state agencies. In the complex web of relationships among the state commanders, '(a)ttempts to align commercial interests overseas with government policy for diplomacy and trade are hardly new, and hardly restricted' (Jiang and Sinton, 2011: 27).

With the gradually upgraded balance between pro-efficiency corporate logic and state control, Chinese NOCs have established a strategic partnership with NOCs from other countries and international oil companies to acquire technologies and operational know-how and secure investment returns in politically unstable host countries (Jiang and Sinton, 2011). Chinese NOCs also signed market-for-resources deals with international oil companies that wish to gain access to the Chinese market. Three NOCs and the Chinese government together intensified packaged loan-for-oil or loan-for-gas schemes between 2009 and 2013. By design, those schemes first disburse loans to the host country from the China Development Bank or the China Export-Import Bank and later leave Chinese NOCs to repay the debt through the profit earned by oil production at market price (Jiang and Sinton, 2011). The Belt and Road Initiative, which was launched by President Xi Jinping in 2013 and recently has become a foreign policy blueprint, targets the countries in Central Asia, the Middle East, and Southeast Asia which possess close relationships in terms of energy security with China (Zhao et al., 2019).

Chinese aid policy analysts concur that aid became part of the country's ongoing global strategy (Kondoh et al., 2010). The primary decision-makers of Chinese foreign aid policies, high-level CCP leaders, the State Council, and the Ministry of Commerce, the China Eximbank, and – to a lesser degree – the Ministry of Foreign Affairs (Varrall, 2013), are all closely interlinked with NOCs. The refortified state control mechanisms align NOCs to partake in the devising of national strategies in tandem with other state agencies. However this does not preclude pro-market logic in the day-to-day operation or in a few cases where corporate interests come to the fore (Liu, 2009; Taylor, 2014; Andrews-Speed, 2015).

Just as the Japanese oil sector experienced reforms at the turn of the century, its Chinese counterpart faced a structural shift in corporate governance to enhance profitability in the globalized market. The historical contexts and following directions, however, were dissimilar. The lasting hope of crafting a National-Flag Oil Company in Japan – at least in the minds of some MITI officials and a few intellectuals of the field – weakened in the structural fragmentation of oil companies and inefficient government investment in the unsuccessful upstream sector. On the contrary, Chinese NOCs, historically founded on a self-reliant state model for domestic oil fields, and only recently deregulated to partial corporatization and partnerships with foreign capital, follow a new corporate model with continuing state control.

### Building the Japanese upstream oil sector

Japan is the only country in East Asia without a NOC or even a private oil company that plays a dominant and responsible role in securing energy supply. This is closely related to its developmental-state-like manoeuvre in the early 20th century, which, notwithstanding, favoured downstream business to the detriment of the upstream.[6] Kikkawa[7] (2011, 2012, 2013) indicates that the reason for the lack of a 'National-Flag Oil Company' in Japan can be traced back to the period before World War II. At that time, the government introduced a licensing system to settle a cartel agreement among domestic distributors and US-based transnational companies to benefit downstream distributors – not upstream operators. This pre-war arrangement had advantages for both the state and companies. The state regarded the controlled crude oil import as indispensable for fostering domestic distributors, stabilizing the domestic price of refined oil, and maintaining the external balance of its foreign currency. Most private companies, including transnationals, welcomed or reluctantly accepted the state regulation because the rent margin obtained by limited competition was lucrative.

Kikkawa (2012) chronicles the development of the pre- and post-war oil industry in Japan. Until the beginning of the 20th century, two major oil producers, Standard Oil and Royal Dutch Shell, and some domestic distributors each won a share in imported oil products. By the 1930s, the Japanese government gradually increased the import tax on refined oil to incentivize the installation of refineries in Japan. In 1932, six major companies signed a cartel agreement to 'freeze' what they had obtained as market shares at that moment. Soon after, in 1934, the Japanese government introduced a licensing system for the refining and importing of oil. The US-based transnationals reluctantly accepted the increased state control to secure their market share and profit given the increasing threat of a market newcomer importing oil from the USSR to the Japanese market (Kikkawa, 2012).

The policies adopted during the post-war period underscored the continuation of the pre-war arrangement (Kikkawa, 2012). In consultation with oil transnationals, the occupying forces commanded the rehabilitation of oil refineries in Japan instead of banning crude oil imports, making partnerships between oil-importing transnationals and domestic refining and distributing companies inevitable. Furthermore, a new oil law in 1962 reinserted the licensing system of oil imports, refining, and distribution under the Ministry of Industry, Trade, and Investment (MITI). Most private stakeholders again supported the reinvigorated state direction to benefit from limited competition. The Japanese government succeeded in fostering domestic downstream operators, but the intervention also resulted in fragmentation and a lack of leading figures. As can be seen in Table 7.3, the Japanese oil market had multiple downstream players, each maintaining a 10–15 per cent market share over most of the 20th century.

Several works have addressed the features that distinguish Japan from other developmental states in East Asia. These include the close but indirect engagement of the government in the economy. The upstream oil industry is composed of a line ministry as a rule-setter, state funding agencies such as the Japan Bank for International Cooperation and Japan Oil, Gas and Metals National Corporation (JOGMEC) as creditors, and private trading companies (*shôsha*) as operators in the market (Thorarinsson, 2018). JOGMEC was established in 2004, integrating the former Japan National Oil Corporation (JNOC), founded in 1967, and the former Metal Mining Agency of Japan. Neither JOGMEC nor JNOC undertook the ownership or operation of production projects but mainly supplied financial and technical assistance to private companies. A comparative study by Armstrong et al. (2016) judged this Japanese model advantageous to the Korean one since the operators/ producers in the Japanese model are private enterprises that retain market logic such as cost efficiency and transparency. In contrast, South Korea holds a NOC, Korea Petroleum Development Corporation, founded in 1979 and later renamed Korean National Oil Corporation, as leading operator. Thus, in the Korean case, rule-setting, credit-making, and operation are integrated under the state command, which sometimes loosens checks and balances in terms of cost-efficiency for project finance.

However, the Japanese model has not proven successful in the oil sector because private counterparts in the industrial sector lack the preconditions to take advantage of governmental assistance.

**Table 7.3** Market share of gasoline distributors

| | 1910 (%) | 1931 (%) | 1932 (%) | Partnership by 1952 | 1950 (%) | 1955 (%) | 1960 (%) | 1965 (%) | 1970 (%) | 1975 (%) | 1980 (%) | 1985 (%) | 1990 (%) |
|---|---|---|---|---|---|---|---|---|---|---|---|---|---|
| **Socony**[a] | 43 | 22.7 | 21.2 | **Tōa Nenryo & Stanvac**[e] **Exxon Mobil by 1999** | 23.4 | 22.9 | 18.3 | 18.3 | 17.2 | 17.2 | 16.6 | 17.4 | 16.0 |
| **Rising Sun (Shell)** | 22 | 34.5 | 32.2 | **Showa Oil & Shell** | 19.5 | 16.2 | 15.6 | 12.5 | 12.1 | 12.0 | 11.6 | 11.6 | 11.1 |
| **Nippon Oil** | 14 | 25.7 | 23.9 | **Nippon Oil & Caltex**[f] | 30.6 | 22.9 | 19.9 | 18.9 | 17.4 | 17.1 | 18.6 | 17.1 | 16.9 |
| **Houden Oil**[b] | 10 | | | | | | | | | | | | |
| **Ogura Oil**[c] | | 11.3 | 12.5 | | | | | | | | | | |
| **Mitsubishi Corp. & Oil**[d] | | 2.0 | 6.8 | **Mitsubishi Oil & Tide Water** | 6.5 | 10.3 | 9.4 | 8.4 | 8.4 | 7.8 | 7.6 | 7.5 | 8.3 |
| | | | | **Idemitsu Oil** | 8.6 | 10.7 | 14.3 | 16.7 | 14.3 | 14.0 | 14.5 | 15.9 | 14.4 |
| | | | | **Maruzen Oil & Union** | 6.5 | 9.4 | 10.7 | 8.2 | 8.5 | 8.7 | 7.6 | 13.4 | 13.2 |
| | | | | **Kyodo Oil** | | | | 10.5 | 12.4 | 13.8 | 13.5 | 12.4 | 13.4 |
| **Others** | | 3.8 | 3.4 | **Others** | 3.4 | 2.5 | 7.2 | 1.9 | 1.0 | 4.4 | 4.1 | 4.7 | 6.7 |

Notes: [a] Standard Oil Company of New York later merged with Vacuum Oil in 1931. [b] Merged with Nippon Oil in 1921. [c] Merged with Nippon Oil in 1941. [d] Co-invested by Associate Oil Company. [e] Standard Vacuum Oil Company. [f] California Texas Oil Company, Chevron group.
*Source:* The author's elaboration based on Kikkawa, 2012: 18–21, 27, 69, 204

As mentioned earlier, the MITI orchestrated the Japanese oil industry prioritization of the downstream sector as early as the 1930s. The subsequent history witnessed the tenacious fragmentation of both the downstream and upstream sectors, mainly due to the early configuration.[8] Consequently, the fragmented structure discouraged private operators from taking greater responsibility beyond earning profits for their companies since no single player was large enough to claim national representation. Also, the weak influence of corporate interests in government policy-making persisted.

From the 1960s to the 1990s, JNOC provided generous public finance to Japanese private upstream operators in their operations abroad. This financing, however, faced strong criticism by the end of the 20th century (Koike et al., 2008; Thorarinsson, 2018). The amount of public money provided did not meet MITI objectives of increasing overseas equity shares owned by Japanese companies.[9] Furthermore, several politicians reflected the mood among the Japanese public during an economic recession and criticized the inefficiencies of public financing of private companies in the oil sector. Horiuchi Mitsuo, a politician in the Liberal Democratic Party and a former Minister of MITI, attributed the widespread financial mismanagement of JNOC to the personal interests of MITI bureaucrats who received luxury executive positions in oil companies upon retirement (Horiuchi, 2000). These critiques heralded a series of public sector reforms under the Koizumi administration of the early 2000s. In the end, the reform rationalized JNOC, restructuring it to JOGMEC with stricter conditions imposed on financing upstream oil projects operated by private companies.

The disharmony between politicians, bureaucrats, and private oil companies resulted in a weak linkage between resource interests and aid policies by the end of the 20th century. Anecdotes support this diagnosis. For instance, the Arabian Oil Company, a Japanese investment with a large share of the foreign oil supply to the domestic market, failed to sign a new concession agreement with the Saudi Arabian government in 2000 (Kandil, 2006). Eventually, the company could not convince the Japanese government to endorse an infrastructure project using its cooperation scheme, the term of the new deal proposed by the counterpart.

This failure provoked criticism from experts who urged the Japanese government to increase its intervention in aligning the upstream oil industry and orchestrating the unification of the fragmented sector under a 'National-Flag Oil Company' (Fuchida, 2002; Kikkawa, 2011, 2013). The public sector reform in the late 1990s and the early 2000s resonated with this sentiment to the extent that government agencies need restructuring, but it never meant an increase in the *direct* intervention of the state. In a nutshell, Japan never created state apparatuses directly participating in the oil sector, nor did its indirect approach nurture strong domestic players. Paradoxically, a reason for this shortcoming was the path dependence from its early developmental intervention, which tried to foster the downstream sector in a non-oil producer country. This is in remarkable contrast to China, where NOCs have sustained a predominant market share, with explicit and implicit backing from the government, and greater discretion in using public money.

The oil reform in Japan coincided with ODA reforms. Japanese aid volume hit its peak in the 1990s, reflecting economic recession and budgetary constraints. In the meantime, Japan adopted a Development Cooperation Charter in 1992 and revised it in 2003, which redirected its aid policies toward tackling global problems, environmental conservation, basic human needs, human resources development, infrastructure improvement, and supporting structural adjustment (MOFA, 1999). These shifts strengthened inter-ministerial coordination in Japan's ODA policy-making, involving multiple sectors beyond the economic interests of the traditional developmentalist image (Sato, 2016). Nonetheless, the aid reform in quality and quantity did not silence the MITI – merged with other agencies to create the Ministry of Economy, Trade and Investment in 2001. Scholars have noted the cohabitation of 'people-centred' foreign aid with economic interests since the 1990s (Katada, 2002). The pursuit of resources appeared as a slogan in the Development Cooperation White Papers from 2007 onward. The newest Development Cooperation Charter established in 2015 mentioned 'national interests' (*kokueki*) as a policy objective.[10]

While recent changes and forthcoming trends need further studies, we hardly find any sign of swift change in the oil–aid nexus. The international movement towards a green economy and the Japanese government's initiative for a decarbonized society further limit any chance of massively reinvesting in hydrocarbon projects. Regardless of the recent trends, the historical path dependence indicates the indirect state intervention to be the norm and the fragmented industrial structure to be an insurmountable hurdle in the short run.

## Conclusions

This chapter has two messages. First, Japan and South Korea do not share China's close linkage between the quest for oil and other strategic natural resources and foreign aid. Statistical tests confirm the resource factor as a significant and positive determinant in China but not in Japan and South Korea. Although data access is an apparent limitation, we have no clear evidence to show the opposite.

Second, looking at historical processes in China and Japan, the distinctive pathways that built upstream oil industries distinctively in the two countries vividly demonstrate how the oil industry agents stayed in a policy-making circle in China but not in Japan. On the one hand, China has built its NOCs through self-reliance and gradual reforms, upgrading its corporate power in the global market but never losing the party-state's solid grip. On the other hand, some opinion leaders and MITI bureaucrats in Japan aspired to build a 'National-Flag Oil Company', but the dream vanished by the end of the 20th century. At the same time, Japanese foreign aid policies became further detached from oil interests, leaving the oil industry mainly in the hands of market logic.[11] This conclusion doesn't preclude the chance of MITI guiding aid policy. But the political decision has not always been in favour of oil interests, as was shown in the case of the Arabian Oil Company, nor is the industrial structure properly equipped to produce effective outcomes.

It is notable that path dependency from MITI's pre-war intervention in the downstream oil industry undergirded an oligopoly of medium to small enterprises and hence paved the way for the everlasting weakness of the upstream sector in Japan. In other words, the Japanese developmental state did foster the downstream oil industry akin to non-oil producer countries, but, at the same time, also deprived itself of future power resources which could have taken on more challenging international ventures. I contest that it was not the timing but the sequence of state intervention that determined the shaping of distinctive business–government relationships. I do not attribute the cross-country differences to political regime types since both democratic and non-democratic regimes build NOCs.

I neither claim that the oil industry structure determines all aspects of foreign aid policies nor insist that it works in the same way across countries. The diplomatic objectives of each country do matter in their aid policy designs. Increasingly, severe financial constraints and the watchful eyes of Japanese taxpayers may also complement the explanation for the weak links between foreign aid and corporate interests from the energy sector. Regardless, this chapter's comparative study reveals a remarkable difference among East Asian donors, embedded in a structural origin, reinforced over several decades, and unlikely to change in the near future.

## Appendices

### Appendix A

The following recipient countries were included in the dataset (n = 131). The underlined countries were included in the Africa dataset (n = 50).

Afghanistan, Albania, <u>Algeria</u>, <u>Angola</u>, Argentina, Armenia, Azerbaijan, Bahrain, Bangladesh, Barbados, Belarus, Belize, <u>Benin</u>, Bhutan, Bolivia, Bosnia and Herzegovina, <u>Botswana</u>, Brazil, <u>Burkina Faso</u>, <u>Burundi</u>, <u>Cabo Verde</u>, Cambodia, <u>Cameroon</u>, <u>Central African Republic</u>, <u>Chad</u>, Chile, Colombia, <u>Congo</u>, Costa Rica, <u>Côte d'Ivoire</u>, Croatia, Cuba, <u>Democratic Republic of the Congo</u>, <u>Djibouti</u>, Dominica, Dominican Republic, Ecuador, <u>Egypt</u>, El Salvador, <u>Equatorial Guinea</u>, <u>Eritrea</u>, <u>Eswatini</u>, <u>Ethiopia</u>, Fiji, <u>Gabon</u>, <u>Gambia</u>, Georgia, <u>Ghana</u>, Grenada, Guatemala, <u>Guinea</u>, <u>Guinea-Bissau</u>, Guyana, Haiti, Honduras, India, Indonesia, Iran, Iraq, Jamaica, Jordan, Kazakhstan, <u>Kenya</u>, Kiribati, Kyrgyzstan, Laos, Lebanon, <u>Lesotho</u>, <u>Liberia</u>, <u>Libya</u>, <u>Madagascar</u>, <u>Malawi</u>, Malaysia, Maldives, <u>Mali</u>, Marshall Islands, <u>Mauritania</u>, <u>Mauritius</u>, Mexico, Micronesia, Moldova, Mongolia, <u>Morocco</u>, <u>Mozambique</u>, Myanmar, <u>Namibia</u>, Nauru, Nepal, Nicaragua, <u>Niger</u>, <u>Nigeria</u>, Oman, Pakistan, Palau, Panama, Papua New Guinea, Paraguay, Peru, Philippines, <u>Rwanda</u>, Samoa, <u>Senegal</u>, <u>Seychelles</u>, <u>Sierra Leone</u>, Solomon Islands, <u>South Africa</u>, Sri Lanka, <u>Sudan</u>, Suriname, Syria, Tajikistan, <u>Tanzania</u>, Thailand, Timor-Leste, <u>Togo</u>, Tonga, Trinidad and Tobago, <u>Tunisia</u>, Türkiye, Turkmenistan, Tuvalu, <u>Uganda</u>, Ukraine, Uruguay, Uzbekistan, Vanuatu, Venezuela, Viet Nam, Yemen, <u>Zambia</u>, <u>Zimbabwe</u>

### Appendix B

The analytical design used in this chapter is as follows:

*Dependent variable*
Aid flow per population to a recipient country in a year. The data covers the period 2000–2014. For Chinese aid flow, the GCOF dataset was used (https://www.aiddata.org/data/chinese-global-official-finance-dataset). For the rest, OECD ODA data (https://data.oecd.org/oda/net-oda.htm).

*Independent variables*

1. *LDC*: Least developed countries. A dummy variable categorizing country/year based on the UN DESA report. (Source: United Nations Committee for Development Policy Secretariat. Triennial

review dataset 2000–2018.) Some country years are missing in original datasets.

2. *Resource*: A dummy variable describing whether a recipient country had any oil, natural gas, and coal exports in the previous year (Source: US Energy Information Administration).

3. *GDP per capita*: the real GDP per capita of a recipient country using the value of 2014 US$ in the previous year (Source: World Bank, World Development Indicators).

4. *GDP growth*: the annual GDP growth rate of a recipient country as a percentage in the previous year (Source: World Bank, World Development Indicators).

5. *Export*: a logarithm of export values from the indicated donor used for the analyses of China, Japan, and South Korea. All are in nominal US$ and lagged by one year (Source: Barbieri and Keshk 2016).

6. *FH score*: the political rights score of a recipient country in the previous year based on Freedom House. These are scaled inversely in which 7 represents the most free, and 1 the least free according to the original criteria (Source: Freedom House).

7. *Terror score*: the levels of state-sanctioned terror, such as tortures and killings, gauged for average from the indicators of Transparency International, the US Department of State, and Human Rights Watch. The scores are rescaled and range from 1 to 5, with 1 representing the highest level of terror (Source: Gibney et al., 2019).

*Control variable*
Year dummies

*Regression model*
Tobit regression analysis. I used a zero censored model (lower end) for all analyses since all negative values in net ODA flows of Japan and South Korea are set at zero, and the information about credit repayment in Chinese data is unavailable.

## Notes

* Professor of Political Science at the Graduate School of International Development, Nagoya University, Japan. isamuokada@gsid.nagoya-u.ac.jp
1. A later study found that US interest had no meaningful effect on the different dataset with an expanded time scope (Tuman et al., 2009).

2. It is crucial to refer to the time scope for each study since global trends vary over time.
3. Some literature (Yoon and Moon, 2014) uses export volume (continuous variable) while others use export dummy (Tuman et al., 2009). I consider the latter works better in avoiding confusing results because foreign aid might target *less* those countries with a large volume of exports, which means consumer markets of those exporters are already fixed. The precise data to gauge the prospective capacity of resource export in the near future for each year/territory is hardly available.
4. Scholars have focused on Africa and sometimes claimed that the limited experience of Asian donors in the region changed their aid pattern per region (see, for example, Stallings and Kim, 2017).
5. The regression result for the aggregate data of all DAC donors reports a similar result to that of Japan and South Korea (not presented here).
6. Japan produces oil on a minor scale, which begot Nippon Oil in the Meiji era.
7. Kikkawa Takeo is an economist who also served as a member of government committees on various occasions.
8. While the ebb and flow of international prices are inevitable in the hydrocarbon sector, most companies try to integrate the upstream and downstream to offset the temporal loss of one side with the profit from the other. Accordingly, the two parts usually develop in tandem.
9. By 1993, only 13.7 per cent of imported oil was produced from oil fields owned by Japanese capitals, while the MITI had announced 30 per cent as its objective (Kikkawa, 2011).
10. I am grateful to Sanae Ito for suggesting this point.
11. This does not oppose strong state control in others, such as the nuclear power sector.

## References

AidData (2021) 'AidData's Global Chinese Development Finance Dataset, Version 2.0' [website] <https://www.aiddata.org/data/aiddatas-global-chinese-development-finance-dataset-version-2-0> [accessed 27 July 2021].

Alvez, A.C. (2015) 'China and Brazil in sub-Saharan African fossil fuels: a comparative analysis', in S. Scholvin (ed.), *A New Scramble for Africa? The Rush for Energy Resources in Sub-Saharan Africa*, Ashgate, Farnham.

Andrews-Speed, P. (2015) *China's Oil and Gas Industry: Stranded Between the Plan and the Market*, Palgrave Macmillan, Basingstoke.

Anyanwu, J.C. (2012) 'Why does foreign direct investment go where it goes? New evidence from African countries', *Annals of Economics and Finance* 13(2): 425–62.

Arase, D. (1994) 'Public-private sector interest coordination in Japan's ODA', *Pacific Affairs* 67(2): 171–99 <https://doi.org/10.2307/2759416>.

Armstrong, M., D'Arrigo, R., Petter, C. and Galli, A. (2016) 'How resource-poor countries in Asia are securing stable long-term reserves: comparing Japan's and South Korea's approaches', *Resources Policy* 47: 51–60 <https://doi.org/10.1016/j.resourpol.2015.12.001>.

Barbieri, K. and Keshk, O.M.G. (2016) 'Correlates of war project trade data set codebook', Version 4.0 [website] <http://correlatesofwar.org> [accessed 27 July 2021].

Barclay, K. and Smith, G. (2013) 'Introduction: the international politics of resources', *Asian Studies Review* 37(2): 125–40 <https://doi.org/10.1080/10357823.2013.794512>.

BP (2021) 'Statistical review of world energy' [website] <https://www.bp.com/en/global/corporate/energy-economics/statistical-review-of-world-energy.html> [accessed 27 July 2021].

Brant, P. (2013) 'Chinese aid in the South Pacific: linked to resources?' *Asian Studies Review* 37(2): 158–77 <https://doi.org/10.1080/10357823.2013.767311>.

Bräutigam, D. (2010) *China, Africa and the International Aid Architecture*, Working Paper Series No.107, African Development Bank, Tunis.

Chen, S. (2008) 'Motivations behind China's foreign oil quest: a perspective from the Chinese Government and the oil companies', *Journal of Chinese Political Science* 13(1): 79–104 <https://doi.org/10.1007/s11366-008-9017-7>.

Christoffersen, G. (2016) 'The role of China in global energy governance', *China Perspectives* 2016(2): 15–24 <https://doi.org/10.4000/chinaperspectives.6968>.

Evans, P. (1995) *Embedded Autonomy: States and Industrial Transformation*, Princeton University Press, Princeton, NJ.

Fuchida, T. (2002) 'Sugata mienai sekiyu kodan haishigo no sekiyu kaihatsu: Aratana kanmin kyocho taisei no kouchiku ga hitsuyou' [Missing insights in the oil development after the dissolution of the JNOC: A new public-private partnership regime is needed] *Energi* 35(4): 50–54.

Gibney, M., Cornett, L., Wood, R., Haschke, P., Arnon, D., Pisanò, A., Barrett, G. and Park, B. (2019) 'The political terror scale 1976–2018' [website] <http://www.politicalterrorscale.org> [accessed 27 July 2021].

Gilpin, R. (1987) *The Political Economy of International Relations*, Princeton University Press, Princeton, NJ.

Harms, P. and Lutz, M. (2006) 'Aid, governance, and foreign direct investment: some puzzling findings for the 1990s', *Economic Journal* 116(513): 773–90 <https://doi.org/10.1111/j.1468-0297.2006.01111.x>.

Horiuchi, M. (2000) 'Arabia Sekiyu mondai ha hyouzan no ikkakuda: Sekiyu koudan ha kaisan shiro' [The problem of Arabian Oil

Company is the tip of an iceberg: The JNOC should be dissolved], *Bungeishunju*, May 2000.

Jiang, B. (2011) 'China National Petroleum Corporation (CNPC): a balancing act between enterprise and government', in D.G. Victor, D.R. Hults, and M.C. Thurber (eds), *Oil and Governance: State-Owned Enterprises and the World Energy Supply*, Cambridge University Press, Cambridge.

Jiang, J. and Sinton, J. (2011) *Overseas Investments by Chinese National Oil Companies: Assessing the Drivers and Impacts*, IEA Information Paper 2011(3), OECD Publishing <https://doi.org/10.1787/5kgglrwdrvvd-en>.

Johnson, C. (1982) *MITI and the Japanese Miracle*, Stanford University Press, Stanford, CA.

Kalinowski, T. and Cho, H. (2012) 'Korea's search for a global role between hard economic interests and soft power', *European Journal of Development Research* 24(2): 242–60 <https://doi.org/10.1057/ejdr.2012.7>.

Kandil, A. (2006) 'The political economy of international cooperation between Japan and Saudi Arabia', *Annals of Japan Association for Middle East Studies* 22(1): 21–61 <https://doi.org/10.24498/ajames.22.1_21>.

Karakaplan, U., Neyapti, B. and Sayek, S. (2005) *Aid and Foreign Direct Investment: International Evidence*, Discussion Paper No. 2005/12, Turkish Economic Association, Ankara.

Katada, S.N. (2002) 'Japan's two track aid approach', *Asian Survey* 42(2): 320–42 <https://doi.org/10.1525/as.2002.42.2.320>.

Kato, H., Page, J. and Shimomura, Y. (2016) *Japan's Development Assistance: Foreign Aid and the Post-2015 Agenda*, Palgrave Macmillan, London.

Kikkawa, T. (2011) *Shigen Energy Seisaku* [Resource and Energy Policy], RIETI, Tokyo.

Kikkawa, T. (2012) *Nihon Sekiyu Sangyô no Kyousouryoku* [The Competitiveness of Japanese Oil Industry], Nagoya University Press, Nagoya.

Kikkawa, T. (2013) *Nihon no Energy Mondai* [The Problems of Japanese Energy], NTT shuppan, Tokyo.

Kim, E-M., Kim, P.H. and Kim, J. (2013) 'From development to development cooperation: foreign aid, country ownership, and the developmental state in South Korea', *The Pacific Review* 26(3): 313–36 <https://doi.org/10.1080/09512748.2012.759263>.

Kim, S. and Gray, K. (2016) 'Overseas development aid as spatial fix? Examining South Korea's Africa policy', *Third World Quarterly* 37(4): 649–64 <https://doi.org/10.1080/01436597.2015.1108162>.

Kimura, H. and Toko, Y. (2010) 'Is foreign aid a vanguard of foreign direct investment? A gravity-equation approach', *World Development* 38(4): 482–97 <https://doi.org/10.1016/j.worlddev.2009.10.005>.

Kohli, A. (2004) *State-Directed Development: Political Power and Industrialization in the Global Periphery*, Cambridge University Press, New York.

Koike, M., Mogi, G. and Albedaiwi, W.H. (2008) 'Overseas oil-development policy of resource-poor countries: a case study from Japan', *Energy Policy* 36(5): 1764–75 <https://doi.org/10.1016/j.enpol.2008.01.037>.

Kondoh, H. (2015) *Convergence of Aid Models in Emerging Donors? Learning Processes, Norms and Identities, and Recipients*. JICA-RI Working Paper 106, JICA Research Institute, Tokyo.

Kondoh, H., Kobayashi, T., Shiga, H. and Sato, J. (2010) *Diversity and Transformation of Aid Patterns in Asia's 'Emerging Donors'*, JICA-RI Working Paper 21, JICA Research Institute, Tokyo.

Kong, B. (2011) 'Governing China's energy in the context of global governance', *Global Policy* 2(special issue): 51–65 <https://doi.org/10.1111/j.1758-5899.2011.00124.x>.

Lancaster, C. (2006) *Foreign Aid: Diplomacy, Development, Domestic Politics*, University of Chicago Press, Chicago.

Lancaster, C. (2010) 'Japan's ODA: naiatsu and gaiatsu', in D. Leheny and K. Warren (eds), *Japanese Aid and the Construction of Global Development*, Routledge, New York.

Liu, Y. (2009) 'A comparison of China's state-owned enterprises and their counterparts in the United States: performance and regulatory policy', *Public Administration Review* 69(supplement to vol. 69): 46–52 <https://doi.org/10.1111/j.1540-6210.2009.02088.x>.

McCarthy, J. (2013) 'Crude "oil mercantilism"? Chinese oil engagement in Kazakhstan', *Pacific Affairs* 86(2): 257–80 <https://doi.org/10.5509/2013862257>.

Melber, H. (2009) 'Global trade regimes and multi-polarity: The US and Chinese scramble for African resources and markets', in S. Roger and H. Melber (eds) *A New Scramble for Africa? Imperialism, Investment and Development*, pp. 56–82, University of KwaZulu-Natal Press, South Africa.

Ministry of Foreign Affairs of Japan (MOFA) (1999) 'Japan's Official Development Assistance Charter' [website] <https://www.mofa.go.jp/policy/oda/summary/1999/ref1.html> [accessed 27 July 2021].

Naughton, B. (2010) 'China's distinctive system: can it be a model for others?', *Journal of Contemporary China* 19(65): 437–60 <https://doi.org/10.1080/10670561003666079>.

Nem Singh, J. and Chen, G.C. (2017) 'State-owned enterprises and the political economy of state-state relations in the developing world', *Third World Quarterly* 39(6): 1077–97 <https://doi.org/10.1080/01436597.2017.1333888>.

Organisation for Economic Co-operation and Development (OECD) (2021) 'Net ODA' [website] <https://data.oecd.org/oda/net-oda.htm> [accessed 27 July 2021].

Reilly, J. (2012) 'A northeast Asian model of ODA? Comparing Chinese, Japanese and Korean official development assistance', in C.M. Dent and J. Dosch (eds), *The Asia-Pacific, Regionalism, And the Global System*, pp. 216–35, Edward Elgar, Northampton.

Reilly, J. (2013) 'China and Japan in Myanmar: aid, natural resources and influence', *Asian Studies Review* 37(2): 141–57 <https://doi.org/1 0.1080/10357823.2013.767310>.

Sato, J. (2013) 'Domestic functions of economic cooperation: Japan's evolution as a donor in the 1950s', in J. Sato and Y. Shimomura (eds), *The Rise of Asian Donors: Japan's Impact on the Evolution of Emerging Donors*, pp. 11–28, Routledge, London.

Sato, J. (2016) 'The benefits of unification failure: re-examining the evolution of economic cooperation in Japan', in H. Kato, J. Page, and Y. Shimomura (eds.), *Japan's Development Assistance: Foreign Aid and the Post-2015 Agenda*, pp. 88–102, Palgrave Macmillan, London.

Sato, J. and Shimomura, Y. (2013) *The Rise of Asian Donors: Japan's Impact on the Evolution of Emerging Donors*, Routledge, London.

Stallings, B. and Kim, E-M. (2016) 'Japan, Korea, and China: styles of ODA in East Asia', in H. Kato, J. Page, and Y. Shimomura (eds), *Japan's Development Assistance: Foreign Aid and the Post-2015 Agenda*, pp. 120–34, Palgrave Macmillan, London.

Stallings, B. and Kim, E-M. (2017) *Promoting Development: The Political Economy of East Asian Foreign Aid*, Palgrave, Singapore.

Tang, J. (2006) *With the Grain or against the Grain? Energy Security and Chinese Foreign Policy in the Hu Jintao Era*, Brookings Institution Working Paper 2372, Research Collection School of Social Sciences.

Taylor, M. (2012) 'China's oil industry: "corporate governance with Chinese characteristics"', in Xu Yi-Chong (ed.), *The Political Economy of State-owned Enterprises in China and India*, pp. 69–93, Palgrave Macmillan, Basingstoke.

Taylor, M. (2014) *The Chinese State, Oil and Energy Security*, Palgrave Macmillan, Basingstoke.

Thorarinsson, L. (2018) *A Review of the Evolution of the Japanese Oil Industry, Oil Policy and its Relationship with the Middle East*, Paper 76, Oxford Institute for Energy Studies, Oxford.

Tuman, J.P. and Ayoub, A.S. (2004) 'The determinants of Japanese official development assistance in Africa: a pooled time series analysis', *International Interactions* 30: 45–57 <https://doi.org/10.1080/725289042>.

Tuman, J.P., Strand, J.R. and Emmert, C.F. (2009) 'The disbursement pattern of Japanese foreign aid: a reappraisal', *Journal of East Asian Studies* 9: 219–48 <https://doi.org/10.1017/S159824080000299X>.

Varrall, M. (2013) 'Chinese views on China's role in international development assistance', *Pacific Affairs* 86(2): 233–55 <https://doi.org/10.5509/2013862233>.

Watson, I. (2014) *Foreign Aid and Emerging Powers: Asian Perspectives on Official Development Assistance*, Routledge, London.

Yasutomo, D.T. (1986) *The Manner of Giving: Strategic Aid and Japanese Foreign Policy*, Lexington Books, Lexington, MA.

Yoon, M.Y. and Moon, C. (2014) 'Korean bilateral official development assistance to Africa under Korea's initiative for Africa's development', *Journal of East Asian Studies* 14(2): 279–301 <https://doi.org/10.1017/S1598240800008936>.

Zhao, S. (2008) 'China's global search for energy security: cooperation and competition in Asia-Pacific', *Journal of Contemporary China* 17(55): 207–27 <https://doi.org/10.1080/10670560701809460>.

Zhao, Y., Liu, X., Wang, S. and Ge, Y. (2019) 'Energy relations between China and the countries along the Belt and Road: an analysis of the distribution of energy resources and interdependent relationships', *Renewable and Sustainable Energy Reviews* 107: 133–44 <https://doi.org/10.1016/j.rser.2019.03.007>.

Zweig, D. and Bi, J. (2005) 'China's global hunt for energy', *Foreign Affairs* 84(5): 25–38 <https://doi.org/10.2307/20031703>.

# CHAPTER 8

# Sharing Korea's developmental experience with developing countries: the case of the Knowledge Sharing Program (KSP)

*Kyungyon Moon**

## Introduction

Korea is considered a representative case of a country that has rapidly transformed itself into a developed country. This rapid change was achieved by adopting a state-centred development strategy in a broad range of economic and social areas. This distinguishes Korea's experience from other advanced countries which developed over a long period of time. This development experience is often praised by developing countries in the post-World War II era for the 'timeliness' and 'applicability' of its experience, technologies, and policies.

In this context, the Korean government initiated the Knowledge Sharing Program (KSP) in 2004, as a type of technical cooperation to transfer the country's economic experience and knowledge to the developing world. The programme is not intended to simply transfer Korea's experience and knowledge on a one-to-one basis, but to serve as a development cooperation model which aims to recommend policies customized to the local circumstances and needs of the specific countries. Korea highlights the initiative's purpose as supporting sustainable economic and social developments in developing countries (KSP website, 2021).[1]

The KSP was first launched in Vietnam and Uzbekistan in 2004, providing sectoral policy recommendation for a one-year period. It has since turned into a brand entitled 'Shaping the Future with Korea', offering economy-wide policy consulting for a period of three years based on the partner country's mid- to long-term economic development plans. The KSP, which started with the above-mentioned two countries, originally consisted of two projects with 11 subjects on specific development strategies as well as general economic policies. As of 2020, it is operating in 76 countries, implementing 50 projects, and covering 107 subjects. The programme is now positioned as Korea's flagship cooperative programme (KSP website, 2022).

The Korean government originally set its national goal of economic development based on the principles of private property and a market economy, mobilizing and controlling diverse resources. This led to rapid economic growth and helped the country successfully transition into a developed country. The KSP, implemented in the form of aid to developing countries, incorporates Korea's unique experience and knowledge, now in the role of a donor country. This chapter will introduce the KSP, first, in order to analyse the governance structure influencing the major elements of the programme. The next section explores its policies, policy execution structure, history, related laws and systems, main actors and principles. Then, in order to understand the KSP's current work, we will break down the areas of knowledge transfer according to major implementing agencies and analyse the characteristics of each project. Finally, we will provide a general evaluation of the programme's impacts on economic and social development in partner countries and examine how this aid programme – in passing on Korea's characteristics as a developed country to the developing world – has impacted the economic and social progress in the partner countries.

## KSP aid architecture: respecting sectoral expertise

### Legal basis and history of the KSP

Korea has a relatively short history as an emerging donor. The Act on the Economic Development Cooperation Fund (EDCF) was adopted as a legal basis for aid loans in 1986. The Ministry of Economy and Finance (MOEF) is responsible for policy coordination and the Export-Import Bank of Korea (KEXIM) for implementation. For grant aid, however, the Ministry of Foreign Affairs was designated for policy coordination, and the Korea International Cooperation Agency (KOICA) was established for implementation purposes in 1991. A dual structure was thus built into the official development assistance (ODA). Despite the fact that the KSP is a grant, and not a loan type aid, it is nonetheless managed by the MOEF and KEXIM, which are in charge of ODA loans. This unusual case was only possible because the MOEF had played a leading role throughout Korea's economic development process. This ministry was given an exception to operate the KSP with the purpose of transferring the country's development experience to the developing world.

In order to operate the KSP in a stable and efficient manner, the Korean government enacted the Ordinance of the MOEF No. 101 on 4 May 2012, which formulated regulations on the procedures for sharing Korea's economic development experience. The first project under the programme, however, dates back to 2004, meaning the KSP did not have a legal basis for eight years. The motivation for institutionalizing the programme via related laws can be explained by Korea's obtaining membership in the Organisation for Economic Co-operation and Development's Development Assistance Committee (OECD/DAC) at the end of 2009. The legal basis for ODA loans was adopted in 1986, and the KOICA, established under the Korea International Cooperation Agency Act, operates ODA grants. When Korea joined the OECD/DAC, a club of donor countries, the country needed to enact a framework for international development cooperation which would serve as the supreme law governing both ODA loans and grants. Thus, the Framework Act on International Development Cooperation was enacted on 26 July 2010. Accordingly, the MOEF started to develop a legal basis for the KSP and finally established the regulations on sharing Korea's economic development experience, as mentioned above, in May 2012.

As shown in Figure 8.1, the KSP that started in 2004 first targeted Vietnam, the top recipient of Korean aid at the time, and Uzbekistan, which was then in the process of transitioning from a socialist economy to a market economy. The first Dissemination Seminar was organized in 2006 based on the results from this two-year pilot project. The KSP then started a separate round of the programme targeting upper-middle and high-income countries in 2007, which shows the

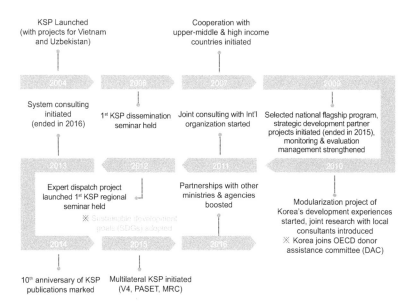

**Figure 8.1** Key historical events of KSP
*Source*: KSP, n.d., 'History'

programme is not only focused on the DAC list of ODA recipients. Although its operations in the listed countries is considered ODA, the programme also benefits those non-recipient countries interested in gaining Korea's development experience and know-how.

In 2009, the fifth year after the launch, the programme tried a range of projects. That year, under the strategic development partnership with priority countries, the programme initiated a project to provide technical advice on establishing a multi-year economic development strategy, which went beyond simple knowledge transfer and technical support. The project continued for six years. In 2010, another project was carried out to modularize Korea's development experience in a systematic manner for the first time. It was aimed to modularize Korea's sector-specific knowledge and experience into universal knowledge and allow the partner countries to adapt the processed knowledge to the local context. In the same year, the KSP introduced a joint research project with local consultants in the partner countries. In 2011, a multi-lateral project was launched together with international organizations to provide joint consulting on the development in such countries. As of 2021, three types of KSP have been formulated, which continue to the present: 'Policy Consulting' as a bilateral KSP, 'Joint Consulting with International Organizations' as a multilateral KSP, and 'Korea's Development Experience Case Study' which is a modularization project based on the country's development path.

In 2012, the KSP adopted a field-oriented approach for project development. This new approach aimed to enhance the effectiveness of development cooperation projects by deploying experts to the project fields. In 2016, it was up-scaled to inter-ministerial/departmental/agency projects, where involved entities could transfer their experience and accumulated know-how in the development process to the developing world through the KSP channels. This enabled the MOEF, the principal implementer, to pass on Korea's acquired experience and knowledge in a broad range of areas beyond its own fields of economy, financing, and public finance, spanning social development arenas including agriculture, education, and environment. Today it is positioned as, Korea's flagship ODA programme. As cooperations with other ministries/departments as well as affiliated organizations to the MOEF expanded, the MOEF revised the programme guidelines on the sharing of economic development experience in the MOEF Guidelines No. 455 on 2 October 2019. The revised guidelines provide guidance on the KSP implementation systems and operations, including detailed instructions on the KSP steering committee, expert appointment committees for selecting senior advisors, codes of conduct, and project operation manuals. It is a set of measures to enhance transparency and systematicity in the operation.

## KSP governance

The KSP is an ODA grant project implemented by the MOEF, the top policy decision-making body. According to the project regulations for sharing economic development experience, which serves as the legal ground for the KSP, the programme should have a coordinating organization. The Center for International Development (CID), affiliated with the Korea Development Institute (KDI), is in charge of supervising and implementing the programme. The KDI, a state-run economic policy research institute, plays a key role in Korea's economic development. Among the three types of projects, the CID is responsible for managing policy consultation projects for developing countries, as well as supervising and implementing the KSP. The CID directly provides technical and policy consultancy on the countries' policies, and since 2016, shares Korea's development experience in a range of industrialization and technology areas separate from the macro and micro economy sector. It also supervises the implementation of KSP projects by other assigned ministries/departments and affiliated organizations. From 2004 to 2020, the CID completed more than 1,000 policy consultations and capacity building workshops in 66 countries (KSP website, 2022).

The KDI School of Public Policy and Management (hereafter referred to as 'KDI School'), a graduate school for international policy established in 1997, has carried out a project on the modularization of development experience since 2010. Despite a relatively short history, it serves as a college affiliated with the KDI, Korea's think-tank for policy-making mentioned above. It is a specialized graduate school that educates, researches, and distributes KDI's knowledge and experience on economic development. Accordingly, the KDI School is dedicated to the research project to modularize Korea's economic development. The project systematizes Korea's original policies, contributing to its economic and social development, institutional grounds, the government's support programmes, effective implementation systems, and evaluates the implications of policies. It processes the experience and knowledge into a form of KSP to share with the international community. The KDI School has researched and modularized 149 policy cases in eight areas, including economic policy, agriculture and fishery, industrial policy, administration, ICT, environment, territorial development, health care, human resource development, and the like, as shown in Figure 8.2. Any developing country interested in its report on modularized policy cases can download it on the KSP official website.

The Korea Export-Import Bank has been operating a joint consultation project in partnership with international organizations such as the Multilateral Development Bank since 2011. It is another form of

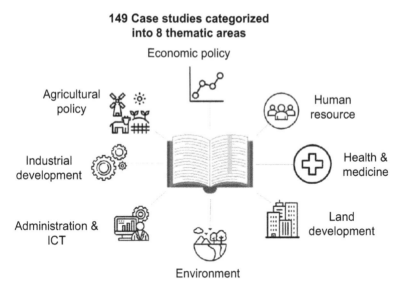

149 Case studies categorized
into 8 thematic areas

Economic policy

Agricultural
policy

Human
resource

Industrial
development

Health &
medicine

Administration &
ICT

Land
development

Environment

**Figure 8.2** Eight thematic areas of Korea's development experience case study
*Source*: Adapted from KSP, n.d. 'KSP Brochure': 11.

the KSP. This project aims to create synergies by building linkages between Korea's development experience and its partners' global networks. Korean experts and persons assigned by partner organizations jointly implement a development cooperation project in the partner country, focusing on more effective implementation. As part of this project, the KSP has worked on 134 joint consultation projects by 2020 with 11 partner organizations, including the World Bank, Asian Development Bank, Inter-American Development Bank, African Development Bank, European Bank for Reconstruction and Development, Development Bank of Latin America, Global Green Growth Institute, International Trade Centre, OECD, the UN Asian and Pacific Training Centre for Information and Communication Technology for Development, and Central American Bank for Economic Integration, as shown in Figure 8.3.

## The five principles of KSP

The KSP's pragmatism can be seen in its five official main principles (see Table 8.1). First, the programme can be defined as a donor initiative in terms of Korea sharing its economic development experience. The first principle of KSP, in fact, emphasizes a 'demand-driven' approach to identify and develop projects based on the

**Figure 8.3** KSP partner organizations
*Source*: Adapted from KSP, n.d., 'KSP Brochure': 21.

**Table 8.1** Five principles of KSP

| Principles | Guidelines |
| --- | --- |
| Demand driven | Develop a project based on the partners' needs |
| Comprehensive | Engage relevant policy areas and stakeholders to effectively resolve issues |
| Mutual learning | Share explicit, tacit knowledge based on mutual learning, not through a unilateral transfer of knowledge |
| Best matches | Make a comprehensive consideration of a partner's barriers to development and capability to execute a policy, based on which applicable policy alternatives are recommended |
| Capacity to act | Develop measures and build linkages so that shared knowledge can make real change, like improved policies and linkages with follow-up programmes |

*Source*: KSP, n.d., 'What is KSP'.

partners' actual needs. In line with this, the first step in developing a project is that the governmental ministry/department/public agency in the target country wishing to participate in a KSP project submits a project application to their coordinating ministry/department for controlling ODA. The body in charge of ODA programmes/projects then prioritizes the proposed projects and submits the list of projects and their applications along with an official letter to the Korean Embassy in the country. This then starts the process of discussing which of the proposed projects will be funded.

The second KSP principle, the 'comprehensive' principle, highlights the importance of engaging relevant policy areas and stakeholders to effectively resolve issues. In other words, the KSP seeks to share knowledge in a very broad range of areas, covering economic and other related fields, such as public finance, macro/financial policy, industrial/ trade policy, territorial/agricultural land development, environment, public health/welfare, science and technology, culture/sports/tourism, administration, human resource development, labour market, and so forth. The KSP adopts many means of involving various stakeholders, including the areas of target-specific policy advice, training for capacity building, and dispatching policy advisors.

Third, the KSP's 'mutual learning' principle is intended to share explicit knowledge based on exchange benefiting both sides instead of a unilateral transfer of knowledge. Through close partnerships and communication, the programme tries to present objective, novel perspectives on the partners' major policies. It is designed for Korean experts to offer an in-depth analysis of the partners' policies and for those involved in KSP projects to learn lessons from Korea's policy experience. This principle enables the KSP to offer a more objective, accurate diagnosis of the partner's policy issues.

The programme's fourth principle, 'best matches', based on Korea's own development process, involves taking a comprehensive look at a partner's barriers to development and ability to execute policy, based on which applicable policy alternatives are recommended. The KSP allows a team, including sector-specific Korean specialists, local authorities in charge, and private experts, to jointly identify solutions to the partner's issues. It provides a tailor-made policy solution selected from applicable alternatives that are compatible with the local policy environment based on various analyses and in-depth studies. The project system-atizes Korea's original policies which contributed to its economic and social development, institutional basis, government support programmes, effective implementation systems, and evaluation and implications of policy decisions. One of the basic principles is not to apply a policy to the local context as it is but to adapt that policy to the partner's circumstances. Sachs said that, 'Korea still has the memory of being a poor country and has the benefit of a wealthy country right now and that's an experience that I think Korea can share with its partner countries in Africa and in Asia, and should share' (KSP, n.d., 'What is KSP'), acknowledging that the programme is highly attuned to the needs of partners.

Finally, the 'capacity to act' principle guides the KSP to develop measures and build linkages in order to go beyond simple transfer of knowledge and make real change through shared knowledge, such as improved policies and linkages with follow-up programmes. The MOEF is equipped with organizational systems through which an issue or policy identified by the KSP can be translated into action as a programme or project. The MOEF operates the KSP, and as governing body of the EDCF, the ministry entrusts the Export-Import Bank of Korea to implement the EDCF for ODA loans. As the programme covers many different fields, there are cases that should be supported by grants. In this case, the Korean government underscores the coordination between ODA grants and loans. When forming a project, the Office for International Development Cooperation under the Office for Government Policy Coordination works to develop linkages among the KSP, ODA grants, and loans.

## Overview of the KSP

Since its inception in 2004, the KSP has implemented 583 projects together with multiple partners, including 87 countries and 11 international organizations. The programme is designed to systematically organize Korea's experience, know-how, and knowledge gained from different fields over its economic and social development history, analyse the current profiles of partner countries, and recommend policy alternatives customized to each partner. This prompts the programme to develop joint projects with other Korean specialized organizations based on their analyses, research, and experience of development processes and pathways. Sector-specific national think-tanks affiliated with the National Research Council for Economics, Humanities and Social Sciences, also play a key role in operating the programme. In this section, I will provide a detailed overview of the actors who have carried out KSP projects, including the types of projects and partner countries.

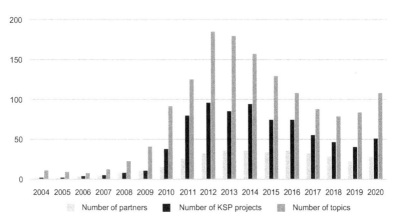

**Figure 8.4** Overview of KSP partner countries, programmes, and sectors
*Source:* KSP, n.d., 'KSP at a Glance'.

**Table 8.2** KSP projects implemented by each national research institute

| No. | Institute | Number of implemented KSP projects |
|-----|-----------|------------------------------------|
| 1 | Korea Development Institute (KDI) | 148 |
| 2 | Korea Institute for Industrial Economics & Trade (KIET) | 17 |
| 3 | Korea Research Institute for Human Settlements (KRIHS) | 16 |
| 4 | Korea Transport Institute (KTI) | 9 |
| 5 | KDI School | 8 |
| 6 | Science and Technology Policy Institute (STPI) | 4 |
| 7 | Korea Research Institute for Vocational Education & Training (KRIVET) | 4 |
| 8 | Korea Institute of Public Finance (KIPF) | 3 |
| 9 | Korea Institute of Public Administration (KIPA) | 3 |
| 10 | Korea Rural Economic Institute (KREI) | 2 |
| 11 | Korea Institute for International Economic Policy (KIIEP) | 1 |
| 12 | Korea Energy Economics Institute (KEEI) | 1 |
| 13 | Korea Information Society Development Institute (KISDI) | 1 |
| 14 | Korea Labour Institute (KLI) | 1 |
| 15 | Korea Maritime Institute (KMI) | 1 |

*Source*: Author's own work based on KSP website, www.ksp.go.kr (accessed 13 August 2021).

During the period from its launch in 2004 to the end of 2018, the KDI, as governing body of the KSP, has directly carried out 148 projects and led 219 projects implemented with other research institutes. Other national research institutes have also carried out projects as shown in Table 8.2. For example, the Korea Institute for Industrial Economics and Trade, with its expertise in industrial policy, the vital sector for economic development, implemented 17 KSP projects during this period. The Korea Research Institute for Human Settlements (KRIHS), with know-how in land development, carried out 16 projects; the Korea Transport Institute, the key think-tank in building national transport infrastructure, completed 9 projects; and the KDI School, as the leading agency for the modularization of Korea's economic development experience, has implemented 8 projects thus far.

**Table 8.3** KSP projects implemented by the KDI according to sector

| Number of projects[a] | Content |
|---|---|
| 101 | Industrial and trade policy (small-and-medium-enterprises policy, trade and export promotion, industrial complex, system transition and economic diversification, business enabling environment, direct investment, other policies) |
| 45 | Macro/financial policy (financial institutions and systems, financial stability, monetary and credit policies, exchange rates and international finance, other policies) |
| 42 | Finance (fiscal policy, public investment, PPP) |
| 23 | Economic development plan |
| 47 | Science and technology (R&D and innovation, ICT, other policies) |
| 34 | Human resource development (vocational competency development, education) |
| 24 | Territorial development (urban development, infrastructure investment, balanced regional development, other policies) |
| 26 | Administration (public sector management, e-Government, public corporations) |
| 17 | Rural development |
| 16 | Environment (environmental and natural resource management) |
| 11 | Labour market (labour market policy and business) |
| 6 | Public health and welfare (public health care, social security) |

Note: [a] The KDI has carried out a total of 148 KSP projects as of 2018, but as there are cases covering multiple areas, the sum here exceeds 148 projects.
*Source*: Author's own work based on KSP website, www.ksp.go.kr (accessed 13 August 2021).

The KDI, the most experienced agency in the KSP, was able to accumulate immense knowledge and know-how in knowledge-sharing, technical cooperation projects for the developing world through its 148 projects. The Center for International Development was established under the KDI in 2010 to offer improved organizational efficiency. As shown in Table 8.3, the KDI has worked mainly in the area of economics to transfer knowledge, specifically as follows: 101 projects in industrial and trade policy, 45 projects in macro/financial policy, 42 projects in fiscal policy, and 23 projects in economic development planning.

As mentioned above, the Korea Institute for Industrial Economics and Trade (KIET) has also been very active, completing 17 KSP projects in the economic sector. KIET has particularly targeted those countries undergoing system transitions, such as Russia, Cuba, and Vietnam, carrying out projects on economic diversification and system reform.

**Table 8.4** KSP projects implemented by the KIET

| Number of projects | Content | Partner countries |
|---|---|---|
| 17 | Industrial/trade policy (system transition and economic diversification, business enabling environment, trade and export promotion, industrial complex and cluster, small-and-medium-enterprises policy, direct investment) | Bangladesh, Russia, Peru, Pacific Islands, Cuba, Kenya, Bulgaria, United Arab Emirates, Ecuador, Thailand, Gabon, Vietnam |
| 1 | Economic development plan | Peru |
| 5 | Science and technology (ICT, R&D and innovation, other policies) | Bulgaria, Peru, Thailand, Gabon |
| 3 | Culture, sports, tourism | Russia, Pacific Islands, Gabon |
| 3 | Administration (e-government, public corporations, public sector) | Bulgaria, Ecuador, Peru |
| 2 | Human resource development (education, vocational competency development) | Peru |
| 2 | Environment (environmental and natural resource management) | United Arab Emirates, Thailand |
| 2 | Rural development | Russia, Gabon |
| 1 | Territorial development (balanced regional development) | Ecuador |

*Source*: Author's own work based on the KSP website, www.ksp.go.kr (accessed 13 August 2021).

In addition, it has conducted research on ODA trends and policy in the industrial sector as well as providing advisory consulting on economic development policy for developing countries. The institute has also carried out research on China's industrial and trade policy, Korea–China industrial cooperation strategy, North Korea's industries and corporations, and South–North Korea industrial cooperation strategy, as can be seen in Table 8.4.

As shown in Table 8.5, the KDI School has carried out a total of eight KSP projects, of which five projects are in the area of macro-financial policy. It has provided consulting for financial institutions and systems, financial stability, and monetary and credit policy.

**Table 8.5** KSP implemented by the KDI School

| Number of projects | Content | Partner countries |
|---|---|---|
| 5 | Macro/financial policy (financial institutions and systems, financial stability, monetary and credit policy) | Cambodia, Algeria, Indonesia, Uzbekistan, Vietnam |
| 3 | Fiscal (fiscal policy) | Cambodia, Turkey, Uzbekistan |
| 1 | Economic development plan | Vietnam |
| 3 | Administration (public corporations, public sector management) | Turkey, Indonesia, Vietnam |
| 2 | Human resource development (education, vocational competency development) | Turkey, Vietnam |
| 1 | Science and Technology (R&D and innovation) | Turkey |
| 1 | Labour market (labour market policy and business) | Mexico |
| 1 | Environment (environmental and natural resource management) | Vietnam |

Source: Author's own work based on KSP website, www.ksp.go.kr (accessed 13 August 2021).

The institute has also targeted countries in transition like Algeria, Uzbekistan, and Vietnam, where it has demonstrated that it has the necessary know-how to lead technical cooperation projects for such countries experiencing rapid change.

We will next turn our attention to the Korea Institute of Public Finance, which has carried out two macro-financial policy projects and one fiscal policy KSP project. The institute, in particular, conducted

**Table 8.6** KSP implemented by the Korea Institute of Public Finance

| Number of projects | Content | Partner countries |
|---|---|---|
| 2 | Macro/financial policy (financial institutions and systems, monetary and credit policy) | Moldova |
| 1 | Fiscal (fiscal policy) | Vietnam, Albania, Cambodia, the Philippines |

Source: Author's own work based on KSP website, www.ksp.go.kr (accessed 13 August 2021).

**Table 8.7** KSP projects implemented by KRIHS

| Number of projects | Content | Target countries |
|---|---|---|
| 14 | Territorial development (infrastructure investment, urban development, balanced regional development, other policies) | Paraguay, Argentina, Myanmar, Sri Lanka, Mongolia, Indonesia, Vietnam, Jamaica, Brazil, Uruguay, El Salvador, Thailand |
| 2 | Science and technology (ICT) | Mongolia, Sri Lanka, Indonesia, Jamaica |
| 1 | Environment (environmental and natural resource management) | Vietnam |
| 1 | Industrial/trade policy (industrial complex and cluster) | Myanmar |

*Source*: Author's own work based on KSP website, www.ksp.go.kr (accessed 13 August 2021).

a study on financing in transition economies and its implications for North Korea. Considering the special relations between South and North Korea, it also worked on South–North Korean economic cooperation and financial backers (e.g. Vietnam and China) for North Korea's economic development. By researching how transition economies finance themselves, it explored financing methods and necessary measures that can be taken by North Korea.

Another player in the KSP is the Korea Research Institute for Human Settlements (KRIHS), which has implemented 16 KSP projects, as can be seen in Table 8.7. Based on its own expertise, the KRIHS conducted consulting projects in specific economic-related areas rather than for the economy as a whole. The institute has actively engaged in multiple research projects focusing on development in developing economies and has also partnered with international organizations including the United Nations Development Programme, Asian Development Bank, and other international bodies involved in cooperation projects, such as KOICA. The institute's active role in international cooperation is evident from its membership in the council of the Network of Research, Training and Information Institutes on Human Settlements in Asia and the Pacific, newly established by the United Nations Economic and Social Commission for Asia and the Pacific. In addition, it takes part in invitational training programmes for participants from developing countries. The KRIHS also set up the Global Development Partnership Center to systematically support developing countries through training, consulting, and planning.

A number of other public think-tanks have also made contributions in a range of sectors via the KSP based on their specific areas of expertise. These include the following organizations:

- Korea Transport Institute in the areas of territorial development (9 projects) and science and technology policy (1 project);
- Science and Technology Policy Institute in science and technology (4 projects) and industrial and trade policy (1 project);
- Korea Research Institute for Vocational Education and Training in human resource development (2 projects) and the labour market, science and technology, and industrial and trade policy (1 project in each area);
- Korea Institute of Public Administration in e-government, including ICT (2 projects), electronic administration (1 project), public health and welfare (1 project), and fiscal policy (1 project);
- Korea Rural Economic Institute in rural development (2 projects), macro-financial policy (1 project), and culture/sports/tourism (1 project);
- Korea Institute for International Economic Policy in industrial and trade policy (1 project);
- Korea Energy Economics Institute in territorial development (1 project);
- Korea Information Society Development Institute in science and technology policy (1 project);
- Korea Labor Institute in human resource development (1 project); and
- Korea Maritime Institute in rural development (1 project).

This section shows the vast range of KSP projects conducted by the many involved Korean agencies, as shown in Table 8.8. The Korea Development Institute has played a leading role in the KSP's work for countries in transition. The Korea Institute for Industrial Economics and Trade (KIET) has provided consulting services on how to invigorate industries and investments in transition economies, while the KDI School has offered policy consultations for promoting financial and trade sectors. For Cambodia, the latter conducted a KSP on how to cover a fiscal deficit, which was a meaningful intervention in one of the very realistic challenges facing those in economic transition. The Korea Institute of Public Finance worked on the improvement of digital payment systems and the financial sector, which was a useful engagement in terms of recommending solutions to the real problems arising in transition economies.

**Table 8.8** KSP for countries in transition implemented by national research institutes

| Name of institute | Number of projects | Content | Partner country |
|---|---|---|---|
| Korea Development Institute (KDI) | 73 | Industry, economy, territorial development, etc. | Various |
| Korea Institute for Industrial Economics & Trade (KIET) | 7 | Fishery cluster in Kamchatka (industrial complex and others) | Russia |
| | | Trade promotion organization, investment promotion organization (trade, investment) | Cuba |
| | | Improving the investment environment in Kamchatka (investment) | Russia |
| | | Marine aquaculture industry in Sakhalin (investment) | Russia |
| | | Industrial complex development, knowledge economy, etc. | Bulgaria |
| | | Improving the investment environment in Khabarovsk | Russia |
| | | Eco-friendly industrial complex | Vietnam |
| Korea Research Institute for Human Settlements (KRIHS) | 7 | Establishment of database for transportation policy and investment planning | Mongolia |
| | | Support for PPP metro route planning in Ho Chi Minh City | Vietnam |

*(Continued)*

**Table 8.8** Continued

| Name of institute | Number of projects | Content | Partner country |
|---|---|---|---|
| | | Improvement of nuclear power-related laws, systems, and community support programmes for surrounding areas | Vietnam |
| | | Policy advice on industrial complex for economic cooperation | Myanmar |
| | | Policy advice on development of the Hong River Banks in Hanoi | Vietnam |
| | | Regional Development Plan for Yangon Southwest | Myanmar |
| | | Support for the establishment of policy for improving geographical information | Myanmar |
| KDI School | 4 | Low-carbon green growth policy development (environmental/industrial policy) | Vietnam |
| | | Covering fiscal deficit and others (fiscal policy) | Cambodia |
| | | Growing manufacturing industry for export promotion (economy, industry) | Uzbekistan |
| | | Open economy challenges and responses (finance, trade, etc.) | Vietnam |
| Korea Institute of Public Finance (KIPF) | 3 | Improvement of digital payment system (financial system) | Moldova |

*(Continued)*

**Table 8.8** Continued

| Name of institute | Number of projects | Content | Partner country |
|---|---|---|---|
| | | Introduction of Financial Management Information System (FMIS) (public finance) | Vietnam, Albania, Cambodia |
| Korea Transport Institute (KTI) | 3 | Implementation plan for high-speed railway construction (infrastructure) | Myanmar |
| | | Establishment of intelligent transportation system (infrastructure) | Mongolia |
| | | Improvement of railway logistics infrastructure for dry port development | Myanmar |
| Korea Research Institute for Vocational Education & Training (KRIVET) | 2 | Vocational competency development policy | Vietnam |
| | | Green jobs, vocational competency development | Vietnam |
| Korea Institute of Public Administration (KIPA) | 1 | Civil registration and vital statistics (e-government) | Laos, Myanmar |
| Korea Information Society Development Institute (KISDI) | 1 | ICT knowledge sharing (information technology) | Vietnam |
| Korea Rural Economic Institute (KREI) | 1 | Increasing the export of agricultural products (rural development) | Azerbaijan |

*Source*: Author's own work based on KSP website, www.ksp.go.kr (accessed 13 August 2021).

## Sustainable impact of the KSP

Korea was able to accumulate economic development experience and knowledge throughout its period of rapid development. The KSP is a policy consultancy programme which customizes Korea's experience and knowledge to each partner country's circumstances, leading to tangible results. Drawing on the recommendations from the KSP's consultations, the partners have improved or newly adopted relevant policies, institutions, and legislations. In order to put them in place, the programme helped set up a vital organization or infrastructure within the governmental body or financial agency and also established a specialized educational institution and a national research institute to nurture and strengthen the capacity of government officials and area-specific experts who will be responsible for helping achieve economic and social progress.

This is the most meaningful success of the KSP, in line with the values of the Sustainable Development Goal era that highlight 'sustainability'. Another unmistakable success of the KSP is that it has gone beyond simply knowledge transfer and cooperation. Based on the results of policy consultations, the KSP has, together with Korea's ODA bodies, raised funds for loans and grants to build infrastructure in partner countries, the bedrock of economic and social development. This was all possible due to the KSP's effort. The following section will look at the programme's successes in more detail.

Since first being implemented in Vietnam and Uzbekistan in 2004, these two countries have been the most active partners in the KSP During this time there have been many success stories. First, the KSP made a policy recommendation to build export financing systems, based on which the Vietnam Development Bank was established in May 2006. In 2009, the country was selected to participate in a pilot project to support priority partners, considering its high potential for economic cooperation with Korea. The KSP took part in drafting the 'Vietnam Socioeconomic Development Strategy 2011–20', where the KDI School could transfer its experience and know-how. Indonesia, the second most active partner in Asia, improved regulations on credit information and set up a national credit information system with the help of the KSP. In 2017, the programme also assisted in revising its laws and regulations to improve the government employees' pension service. In Myanmar, based on the KSP's consulting, the Myanmar Development Institute was set up as a state-run research institute to develop the country's economic development plans and policies. KOICA, Korea's ODA grants agency, also supported its establishment. The programme held a ground-breaking ceremony for the

Korea-Myanmar Industrial Complex implemented in partnership with the Korea Land & Housing Corporation. Finally, it also helped Cambodia draft the 'Cambodian Financial Sector Development Strategy 2011–20' and 'Industrial Development Policy 2015–25'.

Uzbekistan is the country with the second most KSP projects across the whole KSP network. The country accepted the KSP's policy recommendation to create a special economic zone for export promotion, and the Navoi Free Industrial Economic Zone was established in December 2008. Among Central Asian countries, Kazakhstan is the second most active KSP partner. The programme supported the process of drafting the 'Industrial-Innovative Development Plan of Kazakhstan 2010–14' and 'Kazakhstan Business Roadmap 2020'. It also provided policy consultations for Fund of Problem Loans organizational capacity building and efficient Non-Performing Loan resolution in Kazakhstan's banking sector (2015/2016) and for capacity building in the country's trade promotion organization (2015). In Russia, the KSP has focused on sharing essential knowledge and know-how for establishing and implementing the Far East Economic Zone and strategies for export-oriented economic development, one of the Russian government's special concerns. The following is a list of KSP consulting projects in Russia: 'Policy Recommendations for Developing Export Potential and Strengthening Export Support System of Khabarovsk Krai (2017/2018)'; 'Policy Consultation on Improvement of the Investment Environment of Kamchatskiy Krai and Khabarovsk Krai (2014/2015)' and 'Russia Russky Island Development Strategy and Investment Promotion Plan (2016/2017)'. Regarding the final project, Russky Island has approved the development strategy proposed by the KSP.

The KSP has also carried out a wide range of projects in Latin America. The programme, for example, assisted the Dominican Republic in establishing a mid- to long-term development strategy for export promotion. The result was the founding of the export-import bank, Banco Nacional de las Exportaciones, between 2011 and 2012. In addition, as part of the KSP's consulting service, the state-run Korea Electric Power Corporation carried out the 'Modernization Project of Electricity Distribution System' in the Dominican Republic. In Guatemala, the KDI School has been carrying out a capacity building project on public policy and management for Latin America since 2013 both in Korea and in the region. The aim of this project was to help set up a regional school for public policy development to provide high-quality education in public administration and policy development for young leaders in Latin America. Based on this work, the Regional School of Public Policy for Development (Escuela Regional de Politicas Publicas para el Desarrollo) was established in 2017. Chile initiated the 'ICD-based Health Monitoring Service Pilot for Chilean Chronic Illnesses' based on a KSP consulting project. The programme was also involved in improving the Honduras government's portal. In Colombia, financing for small- and medium-sized enterprises could be expanded through the reorganizational restructuring of Bancoldex (a state-owned commercial bank). Thanks to KSP consulting and funded by Korea's ODA loan, Nicaragua was able to implement a plan for broadband-based services (e-Government, e-Education, e-Health, small- and medium-sized enterprises, etc.). And finally, in Mexico, the programme assisted in establishing the Industry Academic Cooperation Center, the opening of the Colima Science and Technology Park, and establishing the 'City of Knowledge' plan in Hidalgo State.

The KSP has also been responsible for a series of projects in the Middle East. In Saudi Arabia, for example, policy consulting was involved in establishing the Saudi Development Institute in 2011, improving public education and lifelong learning based on a Korean model, and capacity building of government officials in terms of economic development from 2013 to 2015. For the United Arab Emirates, the KSP provided consulting services to strengthen policies for small- and medium-sized enterprises, build a patent information system, enhance patent-related services, and bolster the country's industrial investment capability. The programme was also able to achieve a number of results in Algeria, including the following: the adoption of electronic inter-bank funds transfer, which is now in operation, and the establishment of the National Investment Fund-Algerian Development Bank as a policy financing institution. The KSP also helped revise statutory laws in Algeria, another success story. While in Kuwait, the project for South Saad Al Abdullah City was developed between the Public Authority for Housing Welfare of Kuwait and the Korea Land & Housing Corporation based on a KSP's consultation.

## Discussion and conclusion

Korea is considered a representative model of a country that has transformed into a developed country by adopting a state-centred development strategy in many economic and social fields. Its unique experience in achieving rapid state-led growth can be compared to that of other advanced countries which have developed over a long period of time. Above all, Korea's development experience and know-how in economic and social sectors were enough to attract the interest of the developing world in that such experience and know-how were unique and achieved in a relatively recent time. For it is knowledge that quenches the needs of developing countries' economic development.

Since its inception in 2004, the KSP has carried out 583 policy consultation projects in 87 countries and set up partnerships with 11 international organizations. The programme has achieved much in the past 18 years. One achievement that should not be overlooked is that the KSP does not simply transfer Korea's knowledge and experience, but also recommends policies customized to the local circumstances and needs of partner countries as part of a development cooperation model. It is a meaningful intervention to use this programme in order to support sustainable economic and social developments in developing countries.

Korea set its national goal of economic development based on the principles of private property and market economy and was able to mobilize and control diverse resources, which led to rapid economic growth and the successful transformation to a developed country. This chapter presented the case of the KSP which turned Korea's unique experience and knowledge into grant aid as a donor country for developing economies. It has explored what the KSP has actually achieved by presenting Korea's economic development experience and knowledge, acquired during the period of rapid growth, as a form of policy consultation customized to the unique reality of each partner country.

Based on the KSP consultancy work, the partners have been able to improve or adopt new relevant policies, institutions, and legislations. In order to put them in place, the KSP helped set up vital organizations or infrastructures within governmental bodies or financial institutions and also established specialized educational and national research institutes to nurture and strengthen the capacity of government officials and area-specific experts to lead economic and social progress. This is the most meaningful KSP success story in the era of the UN's Sustainable Development Goals. Another unmistakable KSP success story is that it went beyond simply knowledge transfer and cooperation. Based on the results of consultations, the KSP was able, together with Korea's ODA bodies, to provide loans and grants to build infrastructure for the partners, the bedrock of economic and social development. This was only possible thanks to the KSP's effort.

It is anticipated that the KSP will continue to expand and grow with synergies created by its main actors. The Korean government pays special attention to KSP because of its high visibility and demands from the developing countries. The Ministry of Economy and Finance, a so-called 'Super Ministry' above other ministries, secures funding sources for its flagship programme. In the level of implementation, the KDI with its robust organizational capability and expertise are enough to deliver the experience and know-how of Korea as a developmental state to the developing countries.

Despite all of the programme's successes, there are also a number of limitations. First, its consulting focus is concentrated on economic development, whereas non-economic fields, like social development and environment, are less supported. Another challenge to be resolved is that the KSP mainly targets government officials of partner countries, instead of academia, civil society, and businesses. This may be a typically Korean characteristic of the programme in terms of transferring the country's experience of success, as Korea's economic development itself was government- and elite-led development. Non-government actors, however, such as academia, civil society, and business play a key role in a nation's development. Another challenge for the KSP will be to involve more non-government actors.

In addition, the KSP, as a representative model of Korean ODA, has been criticized for its donor-centred nature that unilaterally delivers the developing country model to developing countries (Lee, 2021). Lastly, Yoo, Park, and Jung argue that political and economic interests are important motivations affecting the decisions of KSP (Yoo et al., 2018). Such interests include the summit meeting with Korea and partner countries, the period of establishing diplomatic relations, and the size of foreign direct investment between Korea and the partner country. They revealed that the demand for KSP from the developing countries is less important (Yoo et al., 2018). It can be said that the criteria for selecting countries subject to these projects contradict the recommendation that aid is distributed based on the demands of developing countries emphasized by the international community. In this sense, further research is needed to objectify the KSP's achievements, limitations, and implications, based on a systematic evaluation of the KSP's results.

Finally, the KSP has been criticized for being used as a means to spread neoliberalism and promote the entry of the Korean *chaebol* (a large, family-owned business conglomerate in South Korea) into developing countries (Schwak, 2020). This evaluation is based on the fact that KSP emphasizes the importance of market economies and trade and deals with relatively many topics related to deregulation. However, contrary to the recommendation that neoliberalism should reduce the role of the government in the market, the KSP views the role of the government and bureaucrats in economic development as a very important factor and actually focuses on strengthening their capabilities. Regarding deregulation, the KSP is also active in policy suggestions to promote foreign direct investment, but emphasizes fostering private companies in developing countries and strengthening

R&D capabilities. These characteristics of KSP are contrary to Schwak's argument. Regarding the claim that KSP is used as a means to enter developing countries and thus strengthen Korea's economic development, we need a neutral evaluation of *chaebols*. For example, supporting domestic companies that can compete with multinational companies in advanced countries was an essential aspect of KSP. Since the name *chaebol* itself is often associated with negative factors, it is also necessary to critically discuss the claim that the KSP may be being used as a means to facilitate the *chaebol's* entry into developing countries. In fact, the Korean government has not established a strategy to link KSP with domestic companies' overseas expansion and a governance structure to implement it.

The international community has considered and described Korea as one of the typical developmental states. In this sense, this chapter introduced the KSP as a technical cooperation programme of the Korean government to transfer the country's economic development experience to developing countries. This chapter identifies the limitations of KSP that need a more comprehensive approach tackling socio-cultural and political sectors as well as the economic sector and a more inclusive manner in terms of programme delivery. However, it seems that the external evaluation of KSP from the partner countries, mainly the developing countries and international aid community, is positive on the impact and objectives of KSP. Also, we can easily expect that the Korean government will continue to expand the budget of KSP, number of partner countries for KSP, and subjects for KSP consulting. Regarding the limitations of KSP identified in this chapter, it is time for the Korean government to search for a more comprehensive, inclusive approach.

## Notes

* Kyungyon Moon is Associate Professor of the School of International Studies at Jeonbuk National University, South Korea, kymoon@jbnu.ac.kr
1. KSP website: https://www.ksp.go.kr/english/index

## References

Knowledge Sharing Program (KSP) (n.d.) 'What is KSP?' [online] <https://www.ksp.go.kr/english/pageView/ksp-is> [accessed 13 August 2021].
KSP (n.d.) 'KSP Brochure' [online] <https://www.ksp.go.kr/resources/contents/KSPBrochure_en.pdf> [accessed 17 July 2022].
KSP (n.d.) 'KSP at a glance' [online] <https://www.ksp.go.kr/english/pageView/ksp-at-a-glance> [accessed 17 July 2022].

KSP (n.d.) 'History' [online] <https://www.ksp.go.kr/english/page View/194> [accessed 17 July 2022].

Lee, T.J. (2021) 'Anthropological reflections on the culture of 'Korean-style' development aid: focusing on the Global Saemaeul ODA and the Knowledge Sharing Program', *Korean Cultural Anthropology* 54(3): 43–44 <https://doi.org/10.22913/KOANTHRO.2021.11.30.3.43>.

Schwak, J. (2020) 'Nothing new under the sun: South Korea's developmental promises and neoliberal illusions', *Third World Quarterly* 41(2): 302–20 <https://doi.org/10.1080/01436597.2019.1664898>.

Yoo, J.W., Park, G.W. and Jung, H.J. (2018) 'An empirical analysis of South Korea's KSP determinants of the policy consultation program', *National Strategy* 24: 123–52 <https://doi.org/10.35390/sejong.24.2.201805.005>.

# CHAPTER 9*

# Chinese social organizations in foreign aid: the dual logic of developmental state and country in transition

*Zhao Wang***

## Introduction

The People's Republic of China has been providing aid to other countries ever since it was established in 1949. Historically, China's foreign aid can be divided into four periods based on changes in its management and implementation system (see Figure 9.1): the Global Cold War and Geopolitics Period (1949–1978), the Shrinkage and Adjustment Period (1979–1994), the Grand Economic and Trade Period (1995–2018), and Adjustment Again with Uncertain Prospects (2018 up to now).

China's foreign aid during the first period from 1949 to 1978 was typical for socialist countries' aid programmes and can be seen as part of the Global Cold War (Westad, 2005). They were described as, for example, 'at the request of recipients' and 'promoting communist revolution all around the world'. Around 1979, China began to reduce its foreign aid budget and started receiving aid from capitalist countries such as Japan whose yen loans were thought to have a profound influence on China and its foreign aid policy after the 1990s (Brautigam, 2009). In 1992, China confirmed the reform direction of transitioning from a socialist planned economy to a market economy. The transition resulted in a policy of foreign aid serving the 'Grand Economic and Trade Strategy'.[1] Meanwhile, China's banking system reform was fully launched in 1994 when the 'Big Five' state-owned banks went through a restructuring process, assigning their non-market tasks to the three newly established policy banks: the China Development Bank, the Export-Import Bank of China (EXIM Bank), and the Agricultural Development Bank of China. Among them, the EXIM Bank began to provide 'concessional loan aid' in 1995 and further added its 'preferential export buyer's credit' business in 2001. The two types of loans are considered a constituent part of China's foreign aid as their concessional level meets the 25 per cent threshold of the ODA. The scale of these two types of loans has

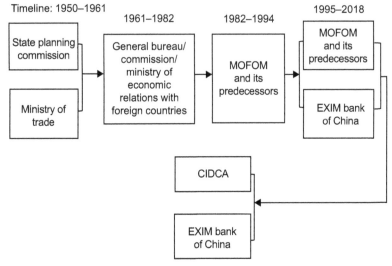

**Figure 9.1** How China's foreign aid management system has evolved (1949 to now)
Note: MOFCOM, Ministry of Commerce of the People's Republic of China; CIDCA, China International Development Cooperation Agency.
*Source:* Author

risen dramatically since the 21st century and has become an essential tool for China's energy supply security and overseas infrastructure investment. In summary, China has become an emerging donor that has attracted the international community's attention during the third period (1995–2018). On the one hand, this is because China's foreign aid scale has increased dramatically. On the other hand, China's foreign aid differs from that of the Organisation for Economic Co-operation and Development's Development Assistance Committee (OECD DAC) donors in many ways, such as in its emphasis on mutual benefit and economic win-win rather than mutual accountability.

Massive concessional loans mixed with other overseas investment and financing after 1995 have led to a misunderstanding that all of China's foreign aid is allocated to infrastructure and productive sectors. In reality, China continues to provide a significant share of grant and interest-free loan aid carried over from its first aid period (1949–1979). According to the State Council Information Office of China (2021a), China allocated ¥270.2 bn (approx. US$38.6 bn) in foreign aid between 2013 and 2018. This included ¥127.8 bn in grants, ¥11.3 bn in interest-free loans, and ¥131.1 bn in concessional loans, representing 47.30 per cent, 4.18 per cent, and 48.52 per cent of total aid, respectively. The grants mainly target poverty reduction, social welfare, public service, and humanitarian relief; the interest-free loans

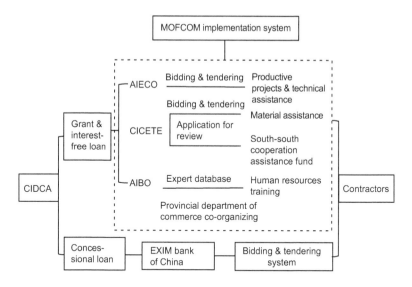

**Figure 9.2** The implementation system of China's foreign aid at present
Note: MOFCOM, Ministry of Commerce of the People's Republic of China; CIDCA, China International Development Cooperation Agency; AIECO, Agency for International Economic Cooperation; CICETE, China International Center for Economic and Technical Exchanges; AIBO, Academy for International Business Officials.
*Source:* Author

are mainly used to help recipient countries construct public facilities and launch agricultural projects; while the concessional loans primarily help recipients carry out manufacturing, resource, and energy, as well as infrastructure projects to increase economic benefits, or supply complete plants, machinery, and electrical products.

Civil society organizations (CSOs) have become much more central to the delivery of foreign aid over the last few decades (Suárez and Gugerty, 2016). The OECD DAC has identified CSOs as key development stakeholders for collaborations and exchanging information (OECD, 2018). How is China's foreign aid then implemented, especially in the social sector? Figure 9.2 shows China's current foreign aid implementation system. The China International Development Cooperation Agency (CIDCA), a newly established ministerial agency that replaced the Foreign Aid Department of the Ministry of Commerce (MOFCOM) in 2018, is in charge of formulating China's foreign aid strategy, supporting relevant legislation and institution building, and monitoring and evaluating aid projects. However, the aid implementation system has not changed since the government's structural reform.

MOFCOM's three agencies are still in charge of implementing aid: the Agency for International Economic Cooperation (AIECO) is responsible for productive projects and technical assistance; the China International Center for Economic and Technical Exchanges (CICETE) for managing material aid supply; and the Academy for International Business Officials (AIBO) for human resources training aid. MOFCOM's three agencies identify contractors for the grant and interest-free loans through a bidding and tender system, most of which are Chinese manufacturing firms. Not to mention the project contractors for the concessional loans from the EXIM Bank, which are mainly Chinese large engineering and machinery manufacturing firms. Compared to businesses, social organizations[2] play only a minimal role in China's foreign aid implementation.

In recent years, the most noteworthy change related to social organizations in China's foreign aid was the establishment of the South–South Cooperation Assistance Fund as part of the foreign aid budget in 2015, with an initial stock of $3 bn. After being assessed by the CICETE and approved by the CIDCA, this fund can be used for projects designed and carried out by social organizations. However, interviews with officials from these agencies have revealed that only projects involving mainstream international organizations like the United Nations have thus far been approved. To date, not a single fundraising application from a Chinese grassroots social organization has been approved.

Based on the background discussed above, this chapter examines the limited but complicated role that Chinese social organizations play in foreign aid activities. This chapter is organized as follows: the second section provides a literature review, followed by the third section explaining the analytical framework. This is followed by two sections presenting three case studies each, illustrating how Chinese social organizations internationalize and participate in foreign aid, respectively; and lastly, the conclusion.

## Literature review

In Western aid, CSOs play a vital role in formulating ODA policies and implementing medium- and long-term development projects abroad. In contrast, Chinese social organizations' internationalization presence, let alone their involvement, in foreign aid is still in its infancy (Li and Dong, 2018). Why are Chinese social organizations so poorly internationalized and involved in foreign aid affairs? This chapter aims to answer this question based on published research and a series of stakeholder interviews.

### Civil society theory and corporatism

Foreign aid policies are part of state decision-making, while social organizations are key and concrete actors in a society. Hence, it is necessary to begin by studying the literature on state–society relations to understand how social organizations are involved in foreign aid. The relationship between state and society is primarily analysed using the concepts of civil society theory and corporatism. And when specifically discussing Chinese issues, it is common to make use of the 'strong country–weak society' framework.

The civil society theory generally claims that China's political context suppresses social organizations' bottom-up growth and participation in state decision-making. Specifically, the theory suggests that Chinese social organizations' low participation in foreign aid results from their low level of development and restricted participation in national policies, compared with those of OECD countries.

Corporatism, according to the classic definition, is defined as a system of interest representation in which the constituent units are organized into a limited number of singular, compulsory, non-competitive, hierarchically ordered, and functionally differentiated categories, recognized or licensed (if not created) by the state and granted a deliberate monopoly within their respective categories in exchange for observing certain controls on their selection of leaders and articulation of demands and supports (Schmitter, 1979: 8). Corporatism is widely viewed as the most appropriate theory to explain China's social organization issues (Howell, 2012; Lai et al., 2015; Liu, 2019). Furthermore, the 'Government-organized non-governmental organizations (GONGOs) Dominate All' argument about social organizations in China's foreign aid is also based on corporatism. These writers claim that, under the strong state–weak civil society context, the Chinese government organizes non-governmental organizations from top to bottom and sponsors them to participate in foreign aid affairs to implement established national strategies such as public diplomacy, soft power, and closer people-to-people ties under the Belt and Road Initiative (BRI) (Punyaratabandhu and Swaspitchayaskun, 2018; Hasmath et al., 2019).

The two theories above can explain to some extent the static structure part: Chinese social organizations display a low level of development and participation in foreign aid, while Chinese GONGOs are heavily involved in foreign aid. However, there are some peculiarities about China's foreign aid, mainly evident in the following two perspectives. First, there is some exploratory attribute about aid at the state level. Considering that the CIDCA, the successor to the Foreign Aid Department of MOFCOM, was only established in 2018, one could argue that the Chinese government is still on the learning curve in terms of 'international development', a core concept that Westerners take for granted when conceiving foreign aid. International development norms now being internalized in China give rise to the possibility of expanding political space for social organizations participating in foreign aid. Second, when social organizations implement aid projects overseas, these are often full of hardships. That means it is more difficult for social organizations to participate in foreign aid projects than to provide domestic social services. For example, the recipient countries are often the least developed countries (LDCs), and community interactions where social organizations normally have advantages are often more challenging grassroots affairs. Therefore, social organizations in China's foreign aid do not only display one kind of vested interest distribution. Instead, the requirements for their professional capabilities and self-motivation must be extremely high. Taking these points into consideration, how can we explain the dynamic process of Chinese social organizations participating in foreign aid beyond the static structure?

### The state–society relationship based on the Developmental State Framework

The Developmental State Framework is another essential perspective for examining state–society relationships, especially in East Asia. Developmental state theory focuses on the 'state–market' relationship in its early stages, which refers to the state's selective intervention in the market through industrial policies, financial controls, and close political–business ties to accelerate national economic growth and industrialization (Johnson, 1982; Amsden, 1989; Wade, 1990). Some literature based on this theory (e.g. Hsu, 2018) has further extended the 'state–society' framework to explain the shift in East Asia's emphasis on social welfare, with the state beginning to purchase social services in recent years. According to Hsu, national economic growth and industrialization were the original definition of 'development' in East Asia during the 1970s and 1980s. However, rapid economic growth has resulted in several social challenges, such as environmental pollution, health problems, and aging populations. East Asian countries must find solutions to these new development challenges in this 'post-development' stage. Also, the UN's 2030 Sustainable Development Goals have formally expanded the notion of development. Currently, developmental states in East Asia are seeking to cultivate a social service market under a strong state to meet the challenges of the 21st century by considering social organizations as another kind of market actor and once again including them in the developmental state system.

The dynamic process seen in the foreign aid programmes of Chinese social organizations can be explained in part by the state–society relationship based on the Developmental State Framework. In other words, the strong state has gradually accepted social organizations' functionality, which is why it is now trying to establish a 'market for social organizations' to address the issues facing East Asia in this new phase of development. In this framework, however, China's foreign aid issues are not explicitly addressed. First, the 'international development market' developed by the Chinese government is less predictable than those other social service markets due to its tentative nature at the state level. Second, in the immature international development market, hardship at the society level is the natural law that determines the survival and growth of social organizations.

## Analytical framework

Based on previous studies and interviews conducted with 12 social organization practitioners in China, which will be described in detail below, this chapter uncovers an interesting pattern: despite the fact that government support is a significant factor, this support, with substantial official background and access to more significant government resources, does not always translate into Chinese social organizations making more progress in foreign aid affairs. Instead, the types of Chinese social organizations along the government-run and grassroots spectrum are more likely to play a more constructive role in China's foreign aid.

What causes this phenomenon? In this chapter, it is argued that it is a result of both static structures and dynamic processes. Developmental states essentially consist of the static structure of strong government with a weak civil society. Thus, official support is crucial for the survival and growth of social organizations. Furthermore, China is also a country in transition, as it is still moving from a socialist planned economy to a Westernized market economy. In fact, the current strong state status results from the Chinese government gradually making room for the market and society to develop out of the previous situation where there was only the government and no market or society. Considering the functionality of the market, the Chinese government has been striving to cultivate a competitive market system to some extent since 1979, which is the characteristic manifestation of a country in transition.

With respect to foreign aid, Chinese social organizations, on the one hand, are underdeveloped because of a strong state and are dependent on government support to operate overseas. On the other hand, the Chinese government is attempting to cultivate a new market for international development with mixed attributes, such as functionality, exploration, and managing hardship. In the first place, the 'functionality' here is consistent with the 'State–Society Relationship based on the Developmental State Framework' (Hsu, 2018). That is, Chinese officials have recognized the importance of social organizations' internationalization and participation in foreign aid affairs for promoting national strategies such as public diplomacy, soft power, and the Belt and Road Initiative, hoping to integrate social organizations into the development state system through public service purchasing, for example. Second, the 'exploration' here refers to the fact that the Chinese government is still in the process of learning the conceptual expansion from 'foreign aid' to 'international development'. The Chinese government is still creating political room for social organizations to participate in foreign aid affairs; the new international development market is still under cultivation; and Chinese social organizations are still emerging and diversifying. Third, 'hardship' here refers to social organizations carrying out foreign aid projects and programmes always working in the most difficult LDC environments. This chapter argues that it is precisely because of these hardships that the two key factors for Chinese social organizations' internationalization and participation in foreign aid are trust and being self-motivated. To put it bluntly, official trust means the ability to secure resources and support from the government, which definitely facilitates social organizations overseas. In the meantime, for Chinese social organizations to survive and develop in the new and challenging international development market, they must be self-motivated to maintain and improve their entrepreneurial spirit and professional abilities.

On a practical level, purely government-run social organizations, such as the Chinese Red Cross and the Chinese Communist Youth League, are often too constrained by bureaucratic rules and lack the internal incentives to carry out long-term projects abroad, especially in the LDCs. When these organizations are asked to participate in foreign aid by the government, they are almost exclusively involved in short-term humanitarian and emergency relief projects rather than medium- and long-term development projects. In addition, purely government-run social organizations are often criticized domestically and abroad for their inefficiency and lack of transparency. Meanwhile, considering social organizations' internationalization and participation in foreign aid as national strategy, the Chinese government might not trust purely grassroots organizations. As a result, Chinese social organizations that are along the spectrum between purely government-run and purely grassroots now play a more active role in foreign aid. For example, the China Foundation for Poverty Alleviation, which used to be part of the bureaucratic system; the Global Environmental Institute, whose leader is part of the so-called 'Second Red Generation' (offspring of former senior leaders of China); and the Amity Foundation, which serves as a bridge between China and global Christian charity organizations. This kind of middle way can gain official trust and support, while being more entrepreneurial because overseas projects and the associated funding are crucial to their survival and growth.

Furthermore, the above phenomenon resembles what happened during China's transition from a socialist planned economy to a market economy between 1979 and the present. That is, those organizations with some official backing but not required to strictly adhere to bureaucratic rules, which need to compete fiercely in the market instead of being fully supported by government funding, tend to be the biggest winners. The middle roaders have benefited most in the transitional China because they can access resources both inside and outside the government and serve as a bridge between the domestic and the overseas market.

## Chinese social organizations and their internationalization

Foreign foundations became more engaged in China after the reform and opening-up policy was adopted in 1979, resulting in the emergence of the first-generation grassroots NGOs. Most of these accepted Western values and viewed the NGO sector as the basis of a civil society and the leading force in promoting democracy in China. The Chinese government once attempted to control the NGO sector by promulgating the 'Management Regulations on Social Organizations Registration' in 1989, establishing a dual management system requiring social organizations in China to register with the Ministry of Civil Affairs (MCA) and apply for affiliation with another official body. Nonetheless, the Chinese government actively hosted the 1995 World Conference on Women to further integrate with the international community. Since then, social organizations in China have become dominated by advocacy-oriented organizations based mainly on Western values.

However, Chinese social organizations have undergone three significant changes in the last 10 years. First, with the enactment of the 'Overseas Nongovernmental Organizations Law' in 2017, the Chinese government has further enhanced its regulation of the NGO sector, barring social organizations in China from receiving funding from foreign foundations. Second, the Chinese government also launched a campaign to eliminate absolute domestic poverty by 2020. The target of this campaign was to ensure the basic annual income in China would be no less than ¥4,000 (equivalent to $580 per year) around the

100th anniversary of the founding of the Chinese Communist Party (State Council Information Office of China, 2021b). The government has encouraged social organizations to be involved in the domestic poverty-relief sector through social mobilization and government purchasing, undermining the primary Western position concerning the value orientation of Chinese social organizations. Third, China's rapid economic growth over the past 40 years has also led to the emergence of numerous local foundations, which serve as an additional source of funding for Chinese social organizations (Lai et al., 2015). As a result of the changing regulations, discourse, and funding sources, China's NGO sector has gradually morphed into a philanthropic sector, with service-oriented social organizations increasingly replacing advocacy-oriented NGOs in the mainstream.

### Chinese social organizations' internationalization

Referring to Huang (2019), there were 816,000 social organizations in China at the end of 2018, nearly double the number a decade ago. However, except for conventional NGOs, the generalized statistical specification adopted by MCA covers not only 200 plus 'public institutions'[3] like the Chinese Communist Youth League, which are quasi-governmental organs, but also various kinds of industry associations and academic and cultural groups, such as writers' associations, international studies institutes, and alien enthusiasts' organizations. In addition, in its 2015 statistical bulletin on social service development, the MCA categorized participating in foreign aid affairs as part of the internationalization of Chinese social organizations. In 2014, there were only 526 internationalized Chinese social organizations or 0.087 per cent of the total. Here, 'internationalization' referred to four types of behaviour: receiving overseas funding, participating in international conferences, cooperating with international organizations, and implementing projects overseas. In addition, the *Report on Social Organizations in China* (Huang, 2019) projected that a total of 700 Chinese social organizations would be internationalized by 2018.

Since the government launched the 'Going Global' strategy in 2001, Chinese overseas investment has increased dramatically, which has fundamentally driven social organizations' internationalization processes. Chinese enterprises in general do not interact well with local communities in their host countries due to a lack of experience and capability. According to some of the social organization practitioners interviewed, Chinese enterprises have been approaching them directly since 2004, offering, for example, to finance these social organizations to conduct social surveys in host countries, make donations to education and water projects, and improve public relations between enterprises and local communities. This differs from the traditional view that Chinese social organizations working abroad are top-down GONGOs pushed by the Chinese government to enter the transnational advocacy network with the aim of enhancing its soft power.

In addition to enterprises involved in overseas investment spontaneously interacting with social organizations, the Chinese government is becoming increasingly aware of the functionality of social organizations' internationalization. Terms related to social organizations' internationalization, such as corporate overseas social responsibility (overseas CSR), public diplomacy, and the BRI, have been appearing on the official agenda since 2004. For instance, the government amended the Company Law to include a CSR provision in 2005; the State-owned Assets Supervision and Administration Commission adopted the CSR Guidelines for State-owned Enterprises in 2008 (Maurin and Yeophantong, 2013). Moreover, due to multilateral diplomatic events such as the Copenhagen Climate Conference in 2009 and the Busan High-Level Meeting on Aid Effectiveness in 2011, the Chinese government has increasingly recognized the importance of social organizations in diplomatic strategy and hopes to encourage them to expand internationally and become more involved in foreign aid affairs. An example of this is the Myitsone Dam project in Myanmar, being built by a Chinese company, which triggered social protests organized by local NGOs in 2011 (Chan, 2017). As a result of the rapidly changing politics in Myanmar at the time, a socio-economic incident developed into a major diplomatic issue, which led to China making public diplomacy a part of its political agenda (Yang, 2011; Mogensen, 2017). Furthermore, the BRI, launched in 2013, has accelerated the Chinese social movement's globalization efforts. 'Connectivity' is the primary connotation of the BRI, consisting of five key areas: policy, infrastructure, trade, finance, and people-to-people connectivity. The internationalization of social organizations and their involvement in foreign aid matters are considered crucial for people-to-people connections.

### Case 1: Advocacy-oriented NGOs withering in China

Interviewee A is a typical example of an advocacy-oriented NGO practitioner in China. She got her bachelor's degree in sociology from China Agricultural University, which received lots of Western aid after China adopted its reform and opening up policy and was regarded as China's academic centre for international development studies. Upon graduation, she worked as a volunteer in ActionAid's China programme for a year and then became a regular employee. She was then awarded a scholarship from the Ford Foundation for a master's degree in non-profit management at Beijing Normal University, another sociology and international development academic centre in China. With her experience and education, interviewee A has developed a deep understanding of the Western NGO knowledge system, and she hoped to promote rights-based, decentralized, social organization values and more scientific project design and implementation in China.

Her next two jobs, promoting the monitoring and evaluation system in the NGO sector and offering consulting services on project design for grassroots social organizations in China, were related to this belief. However, when the 'Law on Administration of Activities of Overseas Nongovernmental Organizations' came into effect in 2017, the social organizations she worked for experienced severe financial difficulties. She resigned voluntarily in order to reduce the organization's personnel costs. The Moderate Management Consultancy Ltd she joined next was directly registered as a social enterprise to avoid excessive restrictions on access to international funding.[4] A growing number of Chinese social organizations now rely on grants from local foundations and government purchasing to engage in poverty alleviation in rural areas and provide social services in urban areas, thus also reducing the market share of the Western value system. Due to this situation and her own feelings of disappointment, she quit this job too and now works as a freelancer.

It is worth mentioning that the second social organization that Interviewee A worked for, the Social Resources Institute, has participated in an overseas project. A Chinese enterprise investing in a gold mine in Cambodia contacted the Social Resources Institute to carry out social surveys and improve interactions with the local community. Meanwhile, Western NGOs also played a constructive role in the project. Oxfam, for example, supported the Social Resources Institute's preliminary field investigation in Southeast Asia for a number of years to promote Chinese enterprises making responsible overseas investment. That prepared the Social Resources Institute to help meet the mining company's overseas CSR service needs.[5]

### Case 2: Service-oriented organizations and philanthropy sector in China

Interviewee B is an example of a service-oriented social organization practitioner in China. Despite growing up in an impoverished area of the country, he was able to complete high school and attend university in Beijing thanks to charitable donations. After graduation, he was hired as a project officer by the China Social Entrepreneur Foundation, one of China's most important local philanthropic foundations. At the same time, he founded a small social organization, the Zhixin Youth Social Innovation Organization, whose main objective was to support children's education in deprived areas. He also ran an online social network platform with about 2 million followers to promote his philanthropic values and public service practices in China.

In the interview, he did not fully support Chinese social organizations running overseas projects. He felt that educational aid projects run by Chinese social organizations in Africa usually had high costs and low sustainability, while there were also great needs domestically, with many children in China dropping out of school because of poverty or often unable to access high-quality education resources. The international travel costs alone for one such overseas education project equalled the amount of money needed to establish one school or upgrade 10 in China. He believed the money would be better spent in China. Despite not having a background in sociology or international development, he believed that his colleagues with development majors from top Western universities spent too much time talking about theory and had only limited capacities to actually implement projects in China.[6]

### Case 3: Social organizations' internationalization and China's soft power

Interviewee C formerly worked at AIECO but now works for the social organization CARECIA that promotes clean energy overseas, with the support of a retired Chinese minister. In addition to acting as a bridge between domestic clean energy enterprises and overseas markets, CARECIA also actively participates in international conferences on environmental protection and speaks on behalf of Chinese social organizations.[7] That is more in line with conventional conclusions about the internationalization of GONGOs in authoritarian contexts. GONGOs enjoy access to specific government resources and aspire to being admitted to various diplomatic circles, such as attaining consultative status on the Committee on NGOs of the Economic and Social Council of the United Nations. Such GONGO activities are an integral part of China's public diplomacy.

Regarding the Chinese government encouraging social organization practitioners like interviewee C to participate in global governance activities, a Chinese scholar who has long studied the Sustainable Development Goals remarked that NGOs from or funded by the West tend to monopolize discussions related to, for example, climate change and aid effectiveness. He could only watch what he felt were China's positive contributions to international society mostly being misunderstood or stigmatized. Consequently, the scholar thought it was appropriate for the Chinese government to promote social organizations' internationalization and encourage them to seek consultative status with the UN.

## Chinese social organizations in foreign aid: motivation and trust

As part of their internationalization efforts, Chinese social organizations participate in foreign aid matters. This section examines three categories of Chinese social organizations that have been involved in or wanted to participate in foreign aid in order to offer a comparison to previous studies on GONGOs. The findings show that the 'Developmental State' by itself cannot reveal the full range of Chinese social organizations' involvement in foreign aid affairs. Official backing and resources are not necessarily associated with a higher internationalization level or more significant involvement in foreign aid matters.

### Case 4: Overseas volunteer programmes and their incentive mechanism

Dr Huang Lizhi, now a lecturer at Beijing Foreign Studies University, carried out a long-term observation of the Overseas Volunteer Programme initiated by the Chinese Communist Youth League (CCYL) and completed her doctoral dissertation based on this data (L.Z. Huang, 2015). According to Huang's dissertation, the CCYL received ¥300,000 in funding from a private enterprise in 2002. The Guangdong Provincial Communist League initially used the funds to recruit and send five volunteers to Laos to work as teachers and doctors. A high point of the overseas volunteer programme came in 2006 when the President of China at the time, Hu Jintao, announced at the Beijing Summit of the Forum on China–Africa Cooperation (CACF) that 300 volunteers would be sent to Africa over the next three years.

The overseas volunteer programme was based on the idea of 'one province for one country', with the CCYL Central Committee assigning the local CCYLs with a target country. For example, Chongqing Province sent all its volunteers to Mauritius, while Guizhou Province sent all its volunteers to Tunisia. However, MOFCOM's motivation for overseas volunteer aid waned after it reached the 300-person volunteer target. The CCYL also did not pursue additional funding, and the provincial CCYL lacked the incentive to manage the complex interviewing, training, and dispatching processes. As a result, the number of volunteers has plummeted since 2009, and the number of overseas volunteers dropped to a single country in each of the years after March 2010. There were a total of 623 volunteers in the programme, with 142 of these going to five Asian countries, 441 to five African countries, and 40 to one Latin American country.

In her dissertation, Dr Huang also compared China's dispatch system with the volunteer programme of the US Peace Corps, Japan Overseas Cooperation Volunteers, and South Korea's World Friends volunteers. She pointed out that China's overseas volunteer programme had two significant problems: poor coordination between the aid agencies and the central committees of the CCYL; and overly ambitious volunteer dispatch targets for the provincial CCYLs, based on an executive order, without adequate local incentives. To sustain the overseas volunteer aid programme in the strong state–weak society structure would have required a reasonable central-local incentive system.

Another example of an organization lacking an adequate incentive system is the Red Cross Society of China which is officially designated to handle overseas humanitarian assistance. However, the agency is primarily a bureaucratic organization due to its being completely government funded and staffed. The organization has no incentive to innovate in overseas projects and expand to the LDCs. The organization is also struggling with corruption and inefficiency domestically and has incurred heavy criticism caused by the 'Guo Meimei Scandal'[8] and the terrible allocation of resources to combat Covid-19. A Chinese businessperson who had been based in Gwadar, Pakistan, complained to me about the inefficiency of the Red Cross Society of China's overseas humanitarian assistance and its reluctance to implement international development projects. He considered it difficult for the Red Cross Society of China to bridge the gap between Chinese overseas investment and the grassroots community in the host country.

In contrast, China's Foreign Aid Medical Team is an example of a successful overseas volunteer programme. The Foreign Aid Agency coordinated by the Ministry of Health has been sending Chinese medical teams overseas since the 1960s when Algeria requested medical help. The crucial difference in this volunteer system is that an incentive mechanism is built into the bureaucratic promotion system in China. That is, most Chinese hospitals are public hospitals, meaning doctors are also part of the bureaucracy system. Participating in foreign aid medical teams is an administrative promotion threshold. In order to be considered for a promotion to a leadership position in a public hospital, the local health administration may require a doctor to join an overseas aid medical team working in one of the LDCs for a year.

## Case 5: China Foundation for Poverty Alleviation: de-administration and entrepreneurship

The China Foundation for Poverty Alleviation (CFPA) was established in 1989 and launched its first overseas humanitarian project in 2005 to provide medicine to the Indian Ocean tsunami victims in cooperation with the International Mercy Corps. The organization has begun long-term international development projects in Sudan and set up permanent overseas offices in Nepal, Myanmar, and Ethiopia. The CFPA is one of the few social organizations that do use the Chinese government's foreign aid budget. Interviewee D described to me how the CFPA used Chinese foreign aid funding to send a volunteer to Nepal. Furthermore, after China launched the South–South Cooperation Assistance Fund, the CFPA was more eager to participate in Chinese foreign aid and submitted an application. Nonetheless, as China's foreign aid system undergoes bureaucratic restructuring, namely, the newly formed CIDCA taking over the foreign aid administration authority from MOFCOM, the CFPA's application process has been delayed, and the planned projects have not yet been implemented.

The CFPA is the star of Chinese social organizations' internationalization and participation in foreign aid. Both domestic and foreign scholars regard it as the representation of China's GONGOs going global (Li and Dong, 2018; Liu, 2019; Hsu et al., 2016). However, how can the CFPA stand out among so many GONGOs, especially when its official backing is in fact limited? It is difficult to fully explain this phenomenon from the established GONGO perspective. In this section, I argue that CFPA has been excluded from the bureaucratic system and now needs to survive in the fundraising market for social organizations, which has become the incentive to expand its capacity and innovate on its overseas projects.

The CFPA was established in 1989 as a subsidiary bureaucracy of the State Poverty Reduction Office to receive international aid to China. As part of China's continuous transitional process, certain bureaucracies are removed from the 'Big Government' to create space for the market and society. As a result of being de-administrated by the government since 1996, the CFPA has become irrelevant to government staffing and financial allocations, even with Western funding and training resources being funnelled into the reform process (Fulda, 2017).

Interviewee D, an employee of CFPA's international department, has participated in several of its overseas projects. In the 1990s, he came to Beijing to find a job after graduating from university in Liaoning Province. A translator team in Beijing was established at that time by the World Bank and the Chinese government to support the World Bank's consulting and assistance programme in China. Having majored in English at university, he was recruited into this translation team as a contract worker. Afterwards, he joined the de-administrated CFPA and pursued a career in implementing and innovating overseas projects. He was never a bureaucrat, even though his institution was once part of the bureaucracy.

Furthermore, the critically historical timing of CFPA's engagement with international development projects underscores the limitations of the conventional GONGOs literature perspective. I asked interviewee D whether the Chinese government had asked CFPA to launch its first international development project in Sudan, and the answer was no. The historic event took place with structural inevitability and individual contingency. Around 2004, one of CFPA's senior executives attended a middle school reunion and met a senior manager at the China National Petroleum Corporation (CNPC). When the CNPC manager learned that he worked for a Chinese NGO, he mentioned that CNPC's business in Sudan had encountered local opposition mobilized by transnational and local NGOs, and that CNPC had very limited experience of overseas investment, let alone interacting well with foreign NGOs. And the CNPC manager believed that their company did not understand what NGOs wanted and how to work with them, and perhaps a Chinese NGO like the CFPA could communicate better with its foreign counterparts. The CNPC manager offered CFPA some funding for projects in Sudan that would help to improve the local environment for the CNPC.[9]

### Case 6: The third type of local social organization emerging in China

In recent years, a new kind of local NGO has emerged in China, distinct from the two other kinds: advocacy-oriented NGOs influenced mainly by Western values, and service-oriented social organizations mainly focused on local poverty reduction and social service agendas. The founders and most of the staff in such social organizations usually have a postgraduate or graduate degree from prestigious universities in the West. Despite this, they have a high level of trust in China's development experience and are open to discussing their values and practices on an equal footing with the West. They are more like 'Global Citizens' in their identifiability and less binary between China and the West.

An example of this emerging third type of local NGO is the China House. The organization was established in 2014 with the goal of promoting Chinese companies' responsible overseas practices. The organization had hoped to remain financially sustainable by persuading Chinese companies to purchase their CSR consulting services, but few companies were willing to pay for this. China House has since started offering educational consulting services to Chinese students hoping to study abroad to maintain its financial stability. It helps students to improve their résumés (and easily gain admittance to top overseas universities) by offering them the opportunity to participate in remote and field research related to international development, for example, by conducting surveys and writing reports to promote African handicrafts in the Chinese market. Such projects combining overseas education application services with international development factors have enabled China House to maintain financial sustainability and fulfil its original dream at the same time.

China House has not yet participated in China's foreign aid programme, but Interviewee E took a very inclusive stance on this. She said that no matter whether it was a domestic or international project, an overseas CSR project, or foreign aid project, China House was willing to try it as long as the project adhered to its original intention of making China and the world a better place.[10]

However, Chinese officials have some concerns about social organizations without official backgrounds, like the China House, being involved in foreign aid affairs. My research partner interviewed staff at the China NGO Network for International Exchange, which is the official body responsible for facilitating the internationalization of Chinese social organizations. The official then believed that social organizations should participate in national strategies like the BRI. However, the political intentions and overseas operational capability of local social organizations, such as the China House, were difficult to verify in the short term. Therefore, partnering with grassroots social groups in foreign aid may be considered a risky endeavour.[11]

There is more than one case related to trust issues like the one above. For example, the South–South Cooperation Assistance Fund uses a similar approach when it screens partners. When the Chinese government launched the Fund in 2015, scholars viewed it as a Western-style development aid fund. Essentially, it was designed with a new implementation system that enabled social organizations to apply for funding under the foreign aid budget with their project design and implementation style. However, when the approval process occurs later, the lead applicant must be a mainstream international organization or a Chinese government ministry. As a result, if a grassroots social organization wishes to receive funding from the Fund to carry out development projects overseas, it can only succeed if it can find a mainstream or official institution as 'principal applicant' to cooperate with. Upon consulting Chinese officials responsible for foreign aid, I learned that lack of trust is the main reason for such a ban on principal applicants. On the one hand, the official body in charge of China's foreign aid has no confidence in grassroots social organizations' ability to carry out projects overseas; on the other hand, most bureaucrats are also worried about whether grassroots social organizations will always act consistently according to BRI or other national strategies.

## Conclusion

The dual logic of 'Developmental State' and 'Country in Transition' provides a comprehensive understanding of the role of social organizations in Chinese foreign aid. Conventional interpretations of GONGOs are somewhat flawed since those with the most robust government backgrounds and extensive official resources do not necessarily have the highest levels of internationalization or participation in foreign aid in China. In terms of static structure, Chinese social organizations born and raised in a 'strong state–weak society' environment currently have relatively little economic and political room, and their internationalization and involvement in foreign aid are still in their infancy. Most of their overseas projects are short-term humanitarian projects rather than long-term international development projects. And only a few Chinese social organizations have been able to use the official foreign aid budget up to now. Taking a dynamic process perspective, China is also a transitional country, and even the current structure of a strong state–weak society is a result of the Chinese government making room for the market and society. In terms of foreign aid, the Chinese government is attempting to create a new international development market for social organizations.

The emerging market for Chinese social organizations' participation in foreign aid has mixed characteristics, such as functionality, exploration, and managing hardship, determining official trust and being self-driven. In terms of functionality, Chinese enterprises started large-scale overseas investments in 2001 and are trying to improve public relations with local communities in host countries. Initially, these enterprises were the primary source of funding for Chinese social organizations implementing projects overseas. Later, through more interactions with international society, the Chinese government has gradually recognized the role of transnational social networks in the global agenda, for example in terms of climate change, potential social risks associated with overseas investments, and the vital role of CSOs in aid effectiveness and meeting the Sustainable Development Goals. As a result, the Chinese government has adopted concepts like public diplomacy and CSR, which originated in the West. It hopes that Chinese social organizations will accelerate their internationalization and actively engage in foreign aid to implement national strategies like the BRI. In term of exploration, the political room for Chinese social organizations to participate in foreign aid affairs is still being released by the government; the international development market is still being cultivated; and Chinese social organizations are still emerging and diversifying. Hardship refers to the fact that social organizations conducting foreign aid projects always need to do the most challenging work. GONGOs are full of bureaucratic shortcomings, such as corruption, inefficiency, and the unwillingness to take risks, while grassroots social organizations without any government backing have difficulty gaining the trust to become official partners promoting national strategies. As a result, the social organizations located on the spectrum between these two types of organizations, which have a certain connection to the government and are motivated and capable of exploring the international arena, have become the emerging actors in China's foreign aid.

The above phenomenon resembles what has occurred during China's transition from a socialist planned economy to a market economy from 1979 to the present. Neither state-owned enterprises that rely on government subsidies too much nor private enterprises without any government resources are the most successful. Instead, enterprises with some government background that do not have to adhere strictly to bureaucratic rules and need to compete fiercely in the market instead of being fully funded by government revenues are the biggest winners. The middle roaders have benefited most in transitional China because they can access resources inside and outside the government and serve as a bridge between the domestic and the overseas market. That is, 'those who butter both sides of the bread take all'.

## Appendix: Interview outline

1. What is the name of the NGO you work for? What is your main role there? When you decided to work for NGOs, what was the primary reason for your decision? What is your NGO's position in the Chinese social network? Do you think your work is in line with your original goal?
2. Do you think there is a difference between local Chinese NGOs and Western NGOs? What are the similarities and differences between local Chinese NGOs and multinational NGOs in terms of values and behaviours?
3. What is the role of government-run NGOs in the Chinese social organization network, and what is their relationship with Chinese local NGOs and multinational NGOs?

4. What is your opinion about the relationship between the Chinese government and NGOs? Have you noticed any stage divisions and key time points? What are the similarities and differences between the relationship between the Chinese government and government-run NGOs, local NGOs, and multinational NGOs?
5. Have you participated in Western aid projects in China, Chinese aid projects abroad, or any other type of NGO international cooperation? What did the projects entail? What role did you play? And what impressed you?
6. Do you have any information regarding other NGOs involved with China's foreign aid and the Belt and Road Initiative? Are you optimistic about NGOs participating in China's foreign aid?
7. Are NGOs more involved in humanitarian aid or development aid projects? Which types of aid programmes and international cooperation programmes are easier or more attractive for NGOs to participate in?
8. Which countries are the most common destinations for NGOs involved in international cooperation projects? Southeast Asia? South Asia? Or Africa? In what region of the world do Chinese NGOs work better, are more popular, or more influential?
9. Is there any case of cooperation between government-run NGOs, local Chinese NGOs, multinational NGOs, and local NGOs in recipient/host countries? If so, how is labour divided?
10. Are the government's policies, such as the 'Mass Entrepreneurship and Innovation' and the 'Belt and Road Initiative' affecting the development of NGOs and social enterprises in China?
11. Have you interacted with NGOs from Japan, South Korea or Southeast Asian countries? What is your understanding of the NGO sector in East Asia?

## Notes

* The research for this chapter was sponsored by the 'Chenguang Program' (Grant 19CG65) supported by Shanghai Education Development Foundation and Shanghai Municipal Education Commission.
** Assistant Professor at Shanghai University of International Business and Economics, China. zw435@suibe.edu.cn
1. The 'Grand Economic and Trade Strategy' (大经贸战略), proposed by the Ministry of Commerce of China in 1994, refers to the integration of China's trade, overseas investment, and foreign aid to promote economic growth and the establishment of a socialist

market economy in China. Under this strategy, Western aid received by China and Chinese foreign aid are collectively referred to as 'international economic cooperation'.

2. The chapter employs the concept of 'social organization' instead of NGOs or CSOs for two reasons. First and foremost, the term is used in official Chinese discourse and statistics to refer to non-governmental and non-market actors. It is also because in China, the term 'social organization' has a more neutral connotation. Conversely, more commonly used concepts, such as CSOs and NGOs, are associated with an anti-establishment sentiment. That is, NGOs and CSOs are organizations in China that are more or less committed to promoting Western liberal and democratic ideology and a decentralized and empowering social structure (Howell, 2012).

3. 'Public institutions', known as 事业单位 in Chinese, are organizations coordinated by state agencies or other organizations that use state-owned assets for social welfare purposes and are involved in education, science and technology, culture, health, and other activities. Public institutions' operational costs are allocated by government revenue in whole or in a particular proportion depending on state revenue. Public institution employees are similar to state civil servants in terms of their employment conditions and wages.

4. The Chinese government promulgated the 'Law on Administration of Activities of Overseas Nongovernmental Organizations' in 2017, which strictly restricts Chinese social organizations from receiving funding from foreign NGOs or foundations. It has caused some Chinese social organizations to reregister themselves as social enterprises to circumvent foreign funding restrictions.

5. Personal communication with Interviewee A (phone), August 2019, Shanghai.

6. Personal communication with Interviewee B (phone), September 2019, Shanghai.

7. Personal communication with Interviewee C (phone), October 2019, Shanghai.

8. Guo Meimei, a young Internet celebrity in China, claimed online in 2011 that she was the general manager of a company called Red Cross Commerce. She boasted about her luxurious lifestyle, showing off her Maserati and Lamborghini cars, expensive handbags, and a palatial villa. Furious netizens began to question whether Guo had financed her lifestyle using money donations intended to reduce poverty, and then heatedly discussed and criticized her true identity and relationship with the Red Cross Society of China. This led to an unprecedented crisis of trust at the Red Cross Society of China.

9. Personal communication with Interviewee D at the headquarters of the China Foundation for Poverty Alleviation, November 2019, Beijing.

10. Personal communication with Interviewee E (phone), September 2019, Shanghai.
11. Personal communication, the China NGO Network for International Exchange, November 2019, Beijing.

## References

Amsden, H.A. (1989) *Asia's Next Giant: South Korea and Late Industrialization*, Oxford University Press, Oxford.

Brautigam, D. (2009). *The Dragon's Gift: The Real Story of China in Africa*, Oxford University Press, Oxford.

Chan, W. (2017) 'Asymmetric bargaining between Myanmar and China in the Myitsone Dam controversy: social opposition akin to David's Stone against Goliath', *Pacific Review* 30: 674–691 <https://doi.org/1 0.1080/09512748.2017.1293714>.

Fulda, A. (2017) 'The contested role of foreign and domestic foundations in the PRC: policies, positions, paradigms, power', *Journal of the British Association for Chinese Studies* 7: 63–99.

Hasmath, R., Hildebrandt, T. and Hsu, J. (2019) 'Conceptualising government-organized nongovernmental organizations', *Journal of Civil Society* 15: 267–284 <https://doi.org/10.1080/17448689. 2019.1632549>.

Howell, J. (2012) 'Civil society, corporatism and capitalism in China', *Journal of Comparative Asian Development* 11: 271–97 <https://doi. org/10.1080/15339114.2012.711550>.

Hsu, J. (2018) 'The developmental state of the twenty-first century: accounting for state and society', *Third World Quarterly*, 39:1098–114 <https://doi.org/10.1080/01436597.2017.1357115>.

Hsu, J., Hildebrant, T. and Hasmath, R. (2016) 'Going out or staying in? The expansion of Chinese NGOs in Africa', *Development Policy Review* 34: 423–39 <https://doi.org/10.1111/dpr.12157>.

Huang, L.Z. (2015) 'Guo ji shi yu xia de zhong guo hai wai zhi yuan zhe fen xi' [A study on Chinese youth volunteers overseas from an international perspective], PhD dissertation, Peking University.

Huang, X.Y. (ed.) (2019) *She hui zu zhi lan pi shu: Zhong guo she hui zu zhi bao gao [Blue book of social organizations: Report on social organizations in China]*, Social Sciences Academic Press, Beijing.

Johnson, C. (1982) *MITI and the Japanese Miracle: The Growth of Industrial Policy, 1925-1975*, Stanford University Press, Stanford, CA.

Lai, W.J., Zhu, J.G., Tao, L. and Spires, A.J. (2015) 'Bounded by the state: government priorities and the development of private philanthropic foundations in China', *The China Quarterly* 224: 1083–92 <https://doi:10.1017/S030574101500123X>.

Li, X.Y. and Dong, Q. (2018) 'Chinese NGOs are "going out": history, scale, characteristics, outcomes, and barriers', *Nonprofit Policy Forum* 9: 1–9 <https://doi.org/10.1515/npf-2017-0038>.

Liu, X.W. (2019) 'Zhong guo zheng fu xing fei zheng fu zu zhi de guo ji hua jin cheng zhong de guan xi wang luo yan jiu' [Research on the relationship in the process of internationalisation of Chinese GONGOs], PhD dissertation, Peking University PhD.

Maurin, C. and Yeophantong, P. (2013) 'Going global responsibly? China' s strategies towards investments', *Pacific Affairs* 86: 281–303 <http://dx.doi.org/10.5509/2013862281>.

Mogensen, K. (2017) 'From public relations to corporate public diplomacy', *Public Relations Review* 43: 605–14 <https://doi.org/10.1016/j.pubrev.2017.03.011>.

Organisation for Economic Co-operation and Development (OECD) (2018) 'Framework for dialogue between the DAC and civil society organisations'. Available from: https://www.oecd.org/officialdocuments/publicdisplaydocumentpdf/?cote=DCD/DAC(2018)28/FINAL&docLanguage=En [accessed 1 March 2022].

Punyaratabandhu, P. and Swaspitchayaskun, J. (2018) 'The political economy of China–Thailand development under the One Belt One Road Initiative: challenges and opportunities', *The Chinese Economy* 51: 333–41 <https://doi.org/10.1080/10971475.2018.1457326>.

Schmitter, P.C. (1979) 'Still the century of corporatism?', in P.C. Schmitter and G. Lehmbruch (eds), *Trends towards Corporatist Intermediation*, pp. 8–13, SAGE Publications, London.

State Council Information Office of China (2021a) *China's International Development Cooperation in the New Era*. Available from: https://english.www.gov.cn/archive/whitepaper/202101/10/content_WS5ffa6bbbc6d0f72576943922.html [accessed 1 March 2022].

State Council Information Office of China (2021b) *Poverty Alleviation: China's Experience and Contribution*. Available from: http://english.www.gov.cn/archive/whitepaper/202104/06/content_WS606bc77ec6d0719374afc1b9.html [accessed 11 November 2022].

Suárez, D. and Gugerty, M.K. (2016) 'Funding civil society? Bilateral government support for development NGOs', *International Journal of Voluntary and Nonprofit Organizations* 27: 2617–40 <https://doi.org/10.1007/s11266-016-9706-3>.

Wade, R. (1990) *Governing the Market: Economic Theory and the Role of Government in East Asian Industrialization*, Princeton University Press, Princeton, NJ.

Westad, O.A. (2005) *The Global Cold War: Third World Interventions and the Making of Our Time*, Cambridge University Press, Cambridge.

Yang, J.C. (2011). 'Nu li kai tuo zhong guo te se gong gong wai jiao xin ju mian' [Striving to open up a new horizon of public diplomacy with Chinese characteristics], *Qiu Shi* 4: 43–46.

# CHAPTER 10
# Conclusion

*Sanae Ito*


While we were writing this book, the global community began discussing the return of 'the bossy state', and with it, of 'industrial policy' ('Welcome to the era of the bossy state', *The Economist*, 15 January 2022). State intervention is making a comeback, and 'industrial policy', which went out of fashion in the West in the 1980s in favour of laissez-faire policy, is recovering lost ground (Aiginger and Rodrik, 2019). The reason for this comeback is attributed to heightened fears about the Covid-19 pandemic, climate change, national security, and China's protectionist policies, among other things. Democratic countries' responses to these fears have included 'soft' government interventions which, according to the *Economist* article (2022), are generally well-intentioned but may eventually lead to market distortion, inefficiency, and cronyism. This book has argued that, in the context of international development, the changing relationship between governments and businesses is bringing back the old foreign aid practices that are blended with trade and investment in donors' national interests. East Asia's developmentalist cooperation may be viewed in this light as one facet of the broader interventionist trend gathering force on a global scale.

As mentioned in the introduction, the popular notion of East Asia's developmental state, after flourishing for about a decade starting in the mid-1980s, saw a decline amid the growing pace of globalization and a shifting balance of power between the state and non-state actors within the domestic context. The Asian financial crisis of 1997–1998 has also been often cited as evidence for the failure of East Asia's developmental states. Some would argue that the rise of the post-Washington Consensus in the 1990s obliterated the need to pay special attention to the developmental state and its industrial policy (Fine and Mohamed, 2022). The post-Washington Consensus, a more state-friendly version of the Washington Consensus, a set of neoliberal economic policy prescriptions for developing countries promoted by Washington-based institutions, is believed to have integrated the Japanese perspectives on its own state-led development (Engel, 2007).

Against this background, this book explored the possibility that the post-2015 global discourse revolving around the Sustainable Development Goals (SDGs) has revived East Asian donors' impetus to use development cooperation as industrial policy instruments. These developmentalist cooperation policies are characterized by their reliance on the strategic use of official development assistance (ODA) in close alignment with countries' industrial policies. Its partner countries are simultaneously encouraged to deploy their own interventionist policies, with the goal of harmonizing both countries' policies. As Haggard (2018) points out, state interventions on both sides of such partnerships are arguably intended to strengthen international production networks stretching across East Asia. This book did not directly address the political economy of developing countries' engagement in donor-driven international production networks, but the question is an important one in understanding the full impact of East Asia's developmentalist cooperation.

The type of 'development' pursued through such partnerships inevitably departs from the conventional notion of development which is more closely associated with poverty reduction approaches promoted through vertical donor–recipient relationships. The process of reframing 'development' as state-led public goods provision for regional prosperity started alongside the post-2015 discussions on the development agenda, culminating in the formulation of the SDGs. The process triggered a 'paradigm shift' in international development, which occurred parallel to East Asia reinforcing its developmentalist cooperation. This book has argued that East Asia's approaches to international development can be characterized by the state's interventionist role in coordinating the strategic use of ODA for economic development of the region. If the interventionist state is regaining its influence elsewhere, and is coordinating the increased involvement of the private sector in providing public goods in developing countries, then the East Asian approaches may arguably be viewed as setting in motion the Easternization of development globally.

While keeping in sight the broader picture unfolding in East Asia, the different chapters of this book have discussed South Korea, China, and Japan separately. Their relative positioning vis-à-vis developmentalist cooperation differs, reflecting the varied histories of their engagement with the international development community. South Korea is a relatively new member of the Organisation for Economic Co-operation and Development's Development Assistance Committee (DAC), with its ODA embedded in the historical trajectories of the country's developmental politics. Japan, on the other hand, is a long-term DAC member which, having once struggled to overcome its developmentalist use of ODA, has recently appeared to be reverting to its old practices. For China, a South–South Cooperation provider, the state clearly is interventionist, whether or not it recognizes itself as such, and its developmentalist cooperation is synonymous with regional economic cooperation through its Belt and Road Initiative.

Despite these differences, each of the three countries individually attaches great importance to communicating its own unique development experience as distinct from the dominant Western form. Their experiences taken together represent a configuration of the state, business, and society that is based on relatively more conciliatory, rather than conflictual, relationships, at least on the surface. The degrees to which citizens of each country endorse such relationships differ within the region. It is also uncertain to what extent the 'Easternization' of development can spread beyond the region where no such relationships can be found. The current revival of state interventionism globally seems to be associated with rising fears about a pandemic, climate change, and war that exacerbate social divisions and the marginalization of the poor and disadvantaged. The question we must then ask is how we should determine our priorities when rich countries' national interests, served through providing public goods in developing countries, happen to conflict with the interests of poor and marginalized people in those countries.

### References

Aiginger, K. and Rodrik, D. (2020) 'Rebirth of industrial policy and an agenda for the twenty-first century', *Journal of Industry, Competition and Trade* 20: 189–207 <https://doi.org/10.1007/s10842-019-00322-3>.

*The Economist* (2022) 'Welcome to the era of the bossy state', *The Economist*, Leaders, 15 January [online] <https://www.economist.com/leaders/2022/01/15/welcome-to-the-era-of-the-bossy-state> [accessed 15 February 2022].

Engel, S. (2007) 'The World Bank and the post-Washington Consensus in Vietnam and Indonesia', PhD thesis, School of History and Politics, University of Wollongong. Available from: http://ro.uow.edu.au/theses/707 [accessed 25 February 2022].

Fine, B. and Mohamed, S. (2022) *Locating Industrial Policy in Developmental Transformation: Lessons from the Past, Prospects for the Future*, SOAS Department of Economics, Working Paper No. 247. Available from: https://www.soas.ac.uk/sites/default/files/2022-10/economics-wp247.pdf [accessed 15 November 2022].

Haggard, S. (2018) *Developmental States*, Cambridge University Press, Cambridge.

# Index

Page numbers in *italics* refer to tables.

Milton Keynes UK
Ingram Content Group UK Ltd.
UKHW020353040823
426284UK00001B/4